Sven Hedin (1865–1952) was one of the world's greatest explorers. His travels through Russia, Iran, Iraq, Turkey, Central Asia, China and Tibet led to some of the most important discoveries and achievements of their kind. He produced the first detailed maps of vast parts of the Pamir Mountains, the Taklamakan Desert, Tibet, the Silk Road and the Transhimalaya (Gangdise today). He was the first to unearth the ruins of ancient Buddhist cities in Chinese Central Asia and in 1901 he discovered the ancient Chinese garrison town of Lou-Lan in the Taklamakan. The many manuscripts he found there are of huge historical importance. His great goal – never realised – was to reach the forbidden city of Lhasa. His books, which include *Through Asia*, *Central Asia and Tibet*, *Overland to India*, *Transhimalaya*, and *My Life as an Explorer* have been excerpted, translated and published in dozens of languages throughout the world.

'There is breathless excitement in this story. Suspense, action, all the elements of a good adventure story, only this is not fiction.'   *New York Herald Tribune*

'Hedin's lively account of his travails is related with the immediacy and urgency of a war correspondent.'   John Hare

D0772133

Tauris Parke Paperbacks is an imprint of I.B.Tauris. It is dedicated to publishing books in accessible paperback editions for the serious general reader within a wide range of categories, including biography, history, travel and the ancient world. The list includes select, critically acclaimed works of top quality writing by distinguished authors that continue to challenge, to inform and to inspire. These are books that possess those subtle but intrinsic elements that mark them out as something exceptional.

The Colophon of Tauris Parke Paperbacks is a representation of the ancient Egyptian ibis, sacred to the god Thoth, who was himself often depicted in the form of this most elegant of birds. Thoth was credited in antiquity as the scribe of the ancient Egyptian gods and as the inventor of writing and was associated with many aspects of wisdom and learning.

THE TRAIL OF WAR

On the Track of 'Big Horse' in Central Asia

Sven Hedin

Foreword by John Hare

TPP

TAURIS PARKE
PAPERBACKS

Published in 2009 by Tauris Parke Paperbacks
an imprint of I.B.Tauris & Co Ltd
6 Salem Road, London W2 4BU
175 Fifth Avenue, New York NY 10010
www.ibtauris.com

First published by Macmillan and Co. Ltd. in 1936
Copyright © 1936, 2009, The Sven Hedin Foundation, Stockholm

Cover image: 'Northwestern Xinjiang' © Li Gang/Xinhua Press/Corbis

ISBN: 978 1 84511 702 3

A full CIP record for this book is available from the British Library
A full CIP record is available from the Library of Congress

Library of Congress Catalog Card Number: available

Printed and bound in India by Thomson Press India Ltd

CONTENTS

LIST OF ILLUSTRATIONS

FOREWORD

In the spring of 1934, China's far-flung north-west province, Xinjiang, had descended into chaos. The Chinese Xinjiang governor, Chin Shu-jen was notoriously intolerant of the Chinese Muslims and Turkic (Uighur) peoples who inhabited the province. For a number of years he had been openly antagonizing them by making discriminatory government appointments in favour of Chinese immigrants, restricting travel, increasing taxation, illegally seizing property and executing those suspected of espionage or disloyalty. As a consequence, Xinjiang's finances were systematically destroyed, gold and silver disappeared and the currency became worthless. In addition, letters, newspapers and telegrams were subjected to a monstrously tight censorship. Chin attempted to seal off Xinjiang, to prevent any complaint and account of conditions there from reaching the outside world.

In 1930, when Chin annexed the Kumul (Hami) Khanate, a small semi-autonomous state lying within the borders of Xinjiang, which for centuries had been ruled by its own Khan – the King of the Gobi – matters came to a head. The newly-subjected ex-Khanate citizens had their land expropriated by Chin Shu-jen in order that it could be given to Chinese settlers. After being subjected to months of iniquities the already tense situation ignited when a Chinese tax-collector assaulted a young Muslim girl.

Rebellion broke out in Kumul and the Turkics appealed to a charismatic, 23-year-old, Muslim Chinese war-lord, Ma Chung-ying (Big Horse or Baby General), based in neighbouring Gansu Province, to come to their assistance. This mercurial figure, who had been promoted to colonel at the age of seventeen by the Chinese government, exercised an extraordinary power over his soldiers who followed him with a level of devotion verging on cult worship. There was nothing of which Big Horse was not thought capable and his phenomenally swift forced-marches through the desert meant that no one knew exactly where he was.

After some initial reluctance, Ma responded to the appeal when it was promised that he would be proclaimed Governor of a newly-named province called Turkestan, and over the next few months he became engaged in a serious of spectacularly bloody sieges and assaults on Kumul.

By 1934, anarchy reigned throughout the area. Various different leaders attempted to seize power; bloodshed was widespread, and rival groups, some abetted by White Russians and Cossacks, fought each other, captured and executed opponents and ambushed and massacred each other's troops.

At the very peak of this situation, the redoubtable Swedish explorer Sven Hedin entered Xinjiang from the east in a convoy of Ford sedans and lorries (nicknamed, 'the grey sows'). His mission, which had been sanctioned by the Kuomintang Chinese authorities in Nanjing and financed by the German government, was to demarcate two motor roads between Nanjing and Xinjiang.

In a province where motor vehicles of any kind were extremely rare, Hedin's motorized caravan, laden with 44-gallon drums of petrol, spare parts, tyres and vast quantities of food, presented a significant prize for the warring factions.

Governor Chin Shu-jen hated foreigners. He took a perverse pleasure in hindering them at every opportunity and although he could not halt Hedin's expedition due to Nanjing's sanctioning of it, Chin continually tried to thwart his plans. In doing so, he caused Hedin huge expense and great hardship as he drove steadily forward into the heartland of Xinjiang.

When Hedin reached Turpan, to the north of the Desert of Lop, Ma Chung Ying was poised to lay siege to the capital

Urumqi. Turpan had fallen under Ma's control and, not unnaturally, he commandeered the four 'grey sows'. Hedin was outraged, protested vehemently and narrowly escaped being shot when at first he refused to part with them. Following the loss of his vehicles Hedin was twice imprisoned in the city of Korla and managed to avoid being blown up by bombs dropped by enemies of Ma Chung-ying. By the time of Hedin's second imprisonment Ma was on the run and the tattered remnants of his army were holed up in Kucha to the west of Korla.

Hedin's lively account of his travails and imprisonment in Korla is related with the immediacy and urgency of a war correspondent. Normally cast as a man of action and master of his own fate, Hedin flutters frustratingly within his cage, but intriguingly by the end of the book he had developed a grudging respect for the extraordinary character of Ma Chung-ying. It is fascinating to see how Hedin, in his late sixties, is reluctantly driven to admire the leadership qualities of this inspirational soldier youth, who was in his early twenties.

Hedin never met Ma but his two Swedish lorry drivers, George and Effe, did and they were totally captivated by Big Horse and his courage, unquenchable optimism, personal bravery and iron will. Speaking to the starving ragamuffins who comprised his remnant army, George, Effe and the Mongolian driver, Jomcha, watched as Ma addressed them with a self-confidence worthy of Tamerlane. He spoke, they said, with as much certainty and conviction as if 'his brow were already crowned with a victor's wreath' and 'as though he was about to conquer the last remaining corner of Xinjiang' and not sneak out through the backdoor in ignominious defeat.

Ma despised Russians of all political persuasions, detesting the fact that they had been brought in to defeat him with superior weaponry. But his plight when he reached the border city of Kashgar must have been desperate because the Soviet Consul-

General stationed there persuaded him to escape to Russia. He crossed the Chinese–Russian border on 5 July 1934 together with adjutants and secretaries, some 30 men and 40 camels, loaded with booty and gifts for Stalin. He was believed to have been taken to Moscow as 'a respectful guest of the Soviet Union,' where most accounts hold that Stalin had him killed in 1936 or 1937.

As for Hedin, the hated Chin Shu-jen had been deposed and a General Bekteieff, having satisfied himself that Hedin and his party had not been too overtly sympathetic to Ma Chung-ying, allowed them to continue with their expedition. They headed for the wandering lake of Lop Nur, and the ancient city of Lou Lan, both of which had been discovered by Sven Hedin and his Uighur guide, Ordek, thirty-four years earlier. The end of Hedin's turbulent tale sees him head off for 'another world, aloof and serene, through which the desert breezes murmur … whose greatest charm is that no cruelties and no sufferings disturb its peace, and that no men tread its classic soil.'

John Hare

PREFACE

IN August, 1933, I was commissioned by the Central Government in Nanking to conduct an expedition to Sinkiang in order to mark out two motor roads between China proper and that remote province. I wish to thank the Chinese Government most warmly and sincerely for the confidence which was shown me before, during and after the journey.

When, on my return to Stockholm, I began to write down our experiences in the form of a book for the general public, I found the material much too ample to be contained in one volume. The subjects I had to deal with belonged to quite different fields—war and politics, the technical communications problems of Central Asia, and certain geographical and hydrographical changes which are taking place in the interior of that great continent. I resolved to devote a separate book to each of these three topics. My account of the journey through the Gobi desert was already complete in manuscript when I began to reflect on the swiftness with which political groupings in Asia nowadays change shape, and realised how important it was to describe the position as it was in 1934, before it was rendered out of date by new political storms and revolutions.

So there lay to my hand, quite unsought, a travel trilogy: the War, the Road, the Lake.

In the present volume, the first of the three, I tell the story of the bloody war which made a desert of Sinkiang from 1931 to 1934, and in the last stage of which our expedition, against our will, became entangled. The chief character is the young Tungan general Ma Chung-yin. The Tungans are Chinese who have embraced Islam and are probably also separated from the Chinese by certain racial differences. Ma is the Chinese version of the name of the prophet Mohammed. But *ma* also means "horse", and so we always called Ma Chung-yin "Big Horse".

The second book, to be entitled *The Silk Road*, will deal with the 10,000-mile journey by motor-car through Eastern and Inner Asia. It will be a historical account of the classical Silk Road which two thousand years ago joined China, the land of the Seres, to the Roman Empire, and finally of our captivity at Urumchi, the capital of Sinkiang, which lasted for four months and, while certainly lenient, was nevertheless a trial to our patience and our nerves.

The third book, which I shall call *The Wandering Lake*, will describe a journey by canoe on the new branch of the Tarim to Lake Lop-nor, and our experiences on a most interesting trip with only two cars westward from Tun-hwang to the Lop basin, through completely unknown country.

As the composition, equipment and personnel of the expedition really form part of the book on the Silk Road, I will here say only a few words about its organisation.

Our medical man was Dr. David Hummel, our topographer Mr. Folke Bergman. We had two road and railway engineers from Nanking, Mr. Irving C. Yew and Mr. C. C. Kung, and also a surveyor and astronomer, Mr. Parker C. Chen; he had previously accompanied Dr. Nils Hörner on his travels, which lasted four years. Both our mechanics, Georg Söderbom and Karl Efraim Hill, were Swedish missionaries' sons from Northern China. These two and Hummel each drove a car, and besides them we had two Mongol drivers, Serat and Jomcha. The cook's name was Chia Kwei. The other servants were Chinese called Li, Liu Chia and San Wa-tse, and the Mongol Chokdung. So we were fifteen strong.

I thank every one of these my comrades most heartily for the loyalty, zeal and efficiency they showed and for the courage with which they faced the most perilous situations.

The convoy consisted of a Tudor Sedan and four lorries, all Fords. Three of the lorries were 1932 four-cylinder vehicles; the

fourth, a 1933 eight-cylinder lorry, was a present to me from
Edsel Ford—a kindness for which I here express my gratitude.

Finally, I would thank all those with whose photographs the
book is illustrated.

SVEN HEDIN

STOCKHOLM,
September 20, 1935

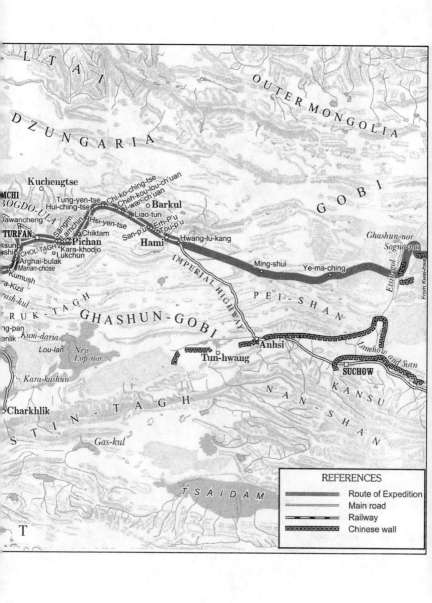

REFERENCES

Route of Expedition
Main road
Railway
Chinese wall

GENERAL MA CHUNG-YIN, "BIG HORSE"

INTRODUCTION

THE WAR IN SINKIANG

FROM time immemorial Central Asia has been a theatre of war; various peoples have fought with one another for lordship over the immense areas which later became known by the names of Dzungaria and Eastern Turkestan and under the common name of Sinkiang.

In 1759 the Emperor Chien Lung brought practically the whole of Central Asia under his sceptre. A century later, in 1867, the conqueror Yakub Beg pushed forward to Kashgar and held Sinkiang in subjection for a few years. His fame still endures.

After twelve years of autocratic rule his part was played to a finish.

In Yakub Beg's time the capable and energetic Marquis Tso Tsung-tang was governor-general of Shensi and Kansu. In 1876, at the age of sixty-five, he put forward a plan for the reconquest of Sinkiang. The Emperor granted his request, and in April, 1876, Tso Tsung-tang's army was led along the Imperial Highway to Hami and Kuchengtse. Urumchi was taken; Manas fell. In a memorial to the Son of Heaven Tso Tsung-tang pointed out that Turfan was the gateway to Tien-shan-nan-lu, or the country south of the Celestial Mountains. He urged that Great Britain was afraid of a Russian invasion of India and would therefore like to have Yakub Beg's domain as a buffer state. Tso maintained that Yakub Beg must restore the towns and territories he had taken, which had belonged to China since 1759.

Kara-shahr fell in March; a month later Toksun and Turfan were captured. The loss of life was great, and prisoners were taken by thousands. When Yakub Beg, who was at Korla, received the news of the fall of Turfan, he committed suicide.

In a fresh memorial Tso wrote: "A strong defence in Sinkiang means safety for Mongolia and protection for Peking. If England needs a buffer to protect India against Russia, one can cut off a bit of India to be the buffer. . . . Kashgar became Chinese in the days of the Han dynasty. . . . Now England is sending ambassadors to Peking. Let them come to me; I know how they should be treated."

In the autumn the army advanced via Korla and Kucha. Aksu and Yarkand were taken, and in January, 1878, Kashgar too. There 1166 of Yakub Beg's faithful adherents were executed. His son Beg Kuli Beg fled to Pskent, in Russian territory, where I visited him in 1890. Sinkiang was Chinese again. Tso Tsung-tang's achievement was a great one; he had won by conquest over a million square miles, and his lines of communication were two thousand miles long.

Directly after the establishment of the republic in China in 1911, a man of unusual stature, Yang Tseng-sin from Yunnan, was appointed governor-general of Sinkiang. He put down a number of rebellions in the province with energy and vigour. Immediately after the Russian revolution between thirty and forty thousand Russian soldiers were in Chinese territory. As Yang had only ten thousand men at his disposal, the Russians could easily have conquered the whole province. By shrewdness, vigilance and tact Yang saved Sinkiang for China.

When he fell by a murderer's hand on July 7, 1928, our scientific expedition lost a powerful protector and friend, and Sinkiang the clear-sighted statesman who for seventeen years had been a guarantee that it would remain a part of China.

His successor, Chin Shu-jen, a man of humble origin from Kansu, showed himself from the very start totally unfit to hold so responsible a post. By misgovernment, greed and oppression he provoked rebellion and civil war; at the end of five years he had desolated and crippled the province and broken all links between China proper and Sinkiang. He appointed his two brothers to the highest military posts and placed his valet in command of a regiment.

Only a few months after Yang's murder Chin began to rule the country arbitrarily and despotically. The taxation screw was tightened; freedom to trade and ply a craft came to an end. Chin's newly enlisted troops were a horde of ruffians without an atom of discipline and order, a scourge and torment to the people. Customs duties were raised; the collectors stole ruthlessly; trade with China was cut off, and internal commerce was dominated by Soviet Russia. The country's finances were destroyed; gold and silver disappeared; notes with no backing were used as currency. The value of money fell swiftly. The chief source of revenue, the trade in furs and wool, was turned into a monopoly. No complaints were answered. Spies were placed everywhere. A thoughtless word meant imprisonment. Letters, newspapers and telegrams were subjected to a monstrously strict censorship. A man might not even travel within the province without a passport signed by Chin himself. To leave the province was a matter of the greatest difficulty. He tried hermetically to seal Sinkiang so as to prevent any complaints and accounts of the real conditions there from getting out.

Chin hated foreigners. He took a cynical pleasure in tripping them up, in hindering or frustrating their endeavours. Thanks to our patience he could not suppress our expedition altogether, but all our requests met with mean, shabby answers, he held up our plans and thereby caused us heavy expense. Marshal Yang had decided that a house should be placed at the disposal of the expedition so long as it remained in Sinkiang, arguing that our work was of benefit to the development of the province. For this house Chin demanded an unreasonable rent, which he made retrospective. For that matter, the narrow-minded despot treated everyone with the same meanness.

Discontent increased; the people clenched their teeth and bided their time; the atmosphere was tense and gloomy. Inflammable matter accumulated, and only a spark was needed to fire the powder magazine.

Hami was the scene of the outbreak of the rebellion. A powerless Turki king had reigned there for centuries. Chin abolished the monarchy and so angered the Turkis.

At the same time a hundred starving peasants from Kansu fled to Hami. Chin ordered that the Turkis' tilled fields should be allotted to his countrymen and that the legal owners should receive complete wilderness to cultivate in exchange. This roused the Mohammedans to fury. They saw that he meant to oppress the native population through an unjust agrarian policy. Chin in his blindness sharpened the dangerous antagonism between Mohammedans and heathens, between subjugated vassals and foreign invaders, between peaceful farmers bound to the soil and arrogant parasites from without.

The drop which made the cup run over was supplied by a Chinese tax-collector who compelled a Turki woman to become his property. This insult set the torches of rebellion ablaze. In March, 1931, the Turkis killed the tax-collectors and all the refugees from Kansu, and persuaded the Kirghiz in the Tienshan to join the insurrection.

Chin sent troops to suppress the revolt. They behaved with barbarous cruelty and killed all their prisoners. The Turkis fled to the mountains, boiling with rage and lust for revenge.

The counsellors of the King of Hami, Hodja Nias Hadji and Yollbars Khan, the leaders of the Turki population in this part of Sinkiang, applied in their sore straits to the young Tungan general Ma Chung-yin in Kansu, and begged for help.

While they were negotiating with him, I will interpolate a parenthesis to introduce this remarkable man.

He was born at Hochow in southern Kansu, and at the age of seventeen became a colonel in Ma Pu-fang's army at Sining. When the "Christian general", Feng Yu-hsiang, was waging his war in Kansu, Ma Chung-yin raised the banner of revolt, marched to Hochow with several thousand men, and besieged the town for eight months. He failed in his object, for the town was relieved by Feng's men.

After this defeat he roamed about as a robber chief, plundering, devastating and murdering. Then he fled with his adherents to Yung-cheng on the Imperial Highway, where he sought vainly to stir up the people to insurrection. In his wrath he killed three thousand people, and an equal number at Chen-fan.

In the winter of 1929–30, after a fresh defeat, he was wandering about as a robber in the Ninghsia district. At this time the governor-general of Kansu, Liu Yu-feng, had Ma Chung-yin's father executed as an act of vengeance for his son's rebellion. This action embittered Ma and intensified his hatred of the Chinese.

In the spring of 1930 he paid a visit to Nanking, where Chiang Kai-shek admitted him to the military academy. Three months later he went to Chung-wei on the Yellow River and reassembled his old soldiers. He appointed himself general commanding a division and moved off to Kansu. The governor-general promoted him to be commander-in-chief at Kanchow. All western Kansu was under his rule. Everyone had to serve in his army, which was ten thousand strong. A Turk from Stambul, Kemal Kaya Effendi, was his adviser in military matters.

When Ma began to rule western Kansu with the airs of an autocrat, and refused to obey orders, Ma Pu-fang was sent to chastise him. Ma Chung-yin suffered a fresh defeat.

Nothing, therefore, could have been more welcome to him than Yollbars Khan's appeal to him to come to Sinkiang and help the Turkis against Chin. He collected about five hundred men and, with an audacity that rouses admiration, marched the great distance of 215 miles from Anhsi to Hami in the middle of the hot summer (1931) through a waterless desert and with inadequate supplies.

He marched first to Barkul. Everywhere he was received as a liberator. The commandant of Barkul went over to Ma, who took two thousand rifles and a quantity of ammunition. Then he besieged Hami for six months, but was beaten by the Chinese generals and returned to Anhsi to rearm his troops—and to pacify Kansu, as he himself said. At Anhsi he plundered the Citroën expedition's big store of petrol, spare parts for cars, wireless equipment and food supplies.

In February, 1932, Ma made his entry into Suchow. He was appointed by Nanking to command the 36th Division and in that capacity was able to enlist fresh recruits. Then he remained quietly at Suchow for a whole year.

Meanwhile the war went on in the Turfan basin. Chin sent several generals to punish the Turkis, foremost among them General Sheng Shih-tsai, whose name will often occur in my story. He moved from place to place, inflicting chastisement and vengeance for the Turki rebellion and reducing towns and villages to ashes. Even the castle of the King of Hami was laid in ruins and his well of gold, in which treasure had accumulated for centuries, was emptied. There was hard fighting between Sheng Shih-tsai and Big Horse's adjutant Ma Shih-ming. Chin's cruelties to the people continually brought grist to the revolutionaries' mill.

In the winter of 1932–33 Ma Shih-ming marched north-west in the direction of Urumchi. Chin sent an army to the Dawancheng Pass to check the Mohammedan forces. These troops were drinking and making merry when Ma Shih-ming took them by surprise. A hundred escaped, the rest were killed. The Mohammedans were beaten in a later engagement and had to retire southward towards the mountains.

In the first half of January, 1933, when the cold was at its worst, the Turkis dashed upon Urumchi like wild beasts, slaughtering every Chinese they met on their way. Chin ordered the Russian *émigrés* and Chinese living in the neighbourhood to move inside the fortified walls of the Chinese town. The atmosphere in the capital was one of gloomy resignation. The Chinese heard the beating of the wings of an inexorable fate, but did nothing to organise their defences. The streets were dead; no one dared go out. The missionaries, both the China Inland Mission and the Catholics, Societas Verbi Divini, remained calm, waiting for God to punish the devil in human guise whose greatest pleasure it had been to inflict suffering and torment on his fellow-men, and who had on his conscience the deaths of so many innocent people. Quite lately he had basely and treacherously caused the spiritual

6

and temporal ruler of the Torguts, Sin Chin Gegen, to be shot
down in the courtyard of his (Chin's) own *yamen*. It was Sin Chin
Gegen who presented the King of Sweden with a temple *yurt*[1] and
received so kindly one of our men, Lieutenant Henning Haslund.
Now the storm-clouds were gathering over Chin's head. His days
as executioner, thief and murderer were reckoned.

Those who showed themselves out of doors soon heard bullets
whistling by. The sentries on the wall had orders to shoot anyone
who defied the order not to go out.

Gates and doors were barricaded. A civilian guard was set
up, for the soldiers were flung against the rebels. Thanks to the
Russian *émigrés*, the assailants were repulsed, but by no means
defeated. They gathered for the decisive struggle.

Stealthily they returned. In the dark night of February 21 they
stormed the western suburb of Urumchi. The rebels occupied
houses and made loopholes. The fighting was savage and bestially
cruel. At twilight the firing ceased and the place became as quiet
as in time of peace. Next day fierce fighting developed in the
western suburb. The scenes which were enacted there defy all
description. No one was spared; the victims were not shot, they
were slowly tortured to death.

The government troops did not gain an inch. The Russian
artillery unlimbered and set fire to the houses which had been
occupied by the rebels. The whole suburb was set ablaze. The
missionaries served in the field hospitals, witnessing scenes of
bestial cruelty which simply cannot be reproduced in print. The
two English doctors Fischbacher and Mathers died of typhus,
martyrs to their labour of love. Heaps of carbonised bodies were
carried away on carts. Innumerable people had been executed on
suspicion of being concerned in the insurrection. Six thousand
poor innocent people lay dead among the ruins.

The rebels' position was hopeless, but they held out for twenty-
four hours longer; then they fell back with heavy losses and fled

[1] The complete equipment of a lama temple in a *yurt* (Mongolian felt
tent). Used by Mongol princes on journeys.

towards the mountains. The suburb, lately so flourishing, presented a horrible aspect: a mass of ruins, heaps of bricks, burned furniture, fire-blackened corpses.

Urumchi was only the prelude to continued devastation. All the oases for sixty miles round were plundered; those who would not join the rebel movement were killed.

In the spring of 1933 the Turkis assembled their forces once more and besieged Urumchi. They concentrated outside the northern and western gates. The town was completely blockaded, and all food supplies cut off. If the rebels had not succeeded in taking the town by force, they would succeed by starvation. Chin's brother confiscated all the wheat and sold it to the people at huge prices. The discontent grew; everyone wanted to be rid of Chin.

Without the help of the Russian *émigrés* Urumchi would have been taken and transformed into a shambles.

Thanks to their better organisation and military spirit, and to their courage, they had won victories which excited the astonishment of the Chinese authorities indeed, but did not awaken their gratitude. Chin's judgment was darkened by suspicion and envy. When the leader of the Russians demanded a vigorous attack which would provoke a speedy decision and make an effective pursuit possible, the governor-general turned a deaf ear. No attack was made on the rebel besiegers. The Russians were, with intention, poorly armed. They were given no horses, and when they refused to march out on foot, they received emaciated screws: the best horses were given to the Chinese soldiers who were keeping in the background. And when the *émigrés*, who themselves were no Sunday school, had got their horses all right, they were given no saddles.

So Chin treated the only force which, well equipped, could have saved him when he stood on the edge of a volcano. He seemed to grudge the poor *émigrés* from Tsarist Russia a success which would have made them too powerful.

Yet the Russians were sent forward to the most dangerous posts. Their indignation grew. Chin himself never dared put his nose outside his *yamen*. He was cowardly and timorous. But now his obstinacy had gone too far. The Chinese in high places made common cause with the Russians and they decided to overthrow Chin, the more readily since the rebels had sent a message saying that they were willing to cease hostilities altogether if Chin disappeared.

When asked in writing to resign, he begged for three days' grace. His brother, the Minister for War, told him that if he went he himself would take over the leadership and fight to the last man.

When the three days had expired, on April 11, 1933, a deputation of Russians went to Chin's *yamen*. Having waited in vain all day for an audience, they went home. But on the 12th they returned in greater numbers. When they demanded entrance, the reinforced guards slammed the gates, but not quickly enough to prevent some seventy Russians from forcing their way into the courtyard. Firing began and several men fell.

An audience was now no longer needed. They knew where they stood. Horsemen galloped to the only regiment, five hundred men strong, which was held in readiness in the town. Without delay they stormed the *yamen* in face of Chin's bodyguard, which was twice as strong.

It was Wednesday in Easter week. The first thing to do was to disarm the guards at the town gates and on the wall. But the Russians were too few. Only two of the seven gates could be occupied; all the rest and the greater part of the wall remained in Chin's power. The fight went on with varying fortunes. The Russians wavered. The Chinese were reinforced in the middle of the night.

Chin Shu-jen, protected by the darkness and his disguise as a common soldier, succeeded in escaping by a back gate and getting away with a few horsemen. His brother and a few other senior officers were captured and executed.

The Russians were in a tight corner. An officer shouted that Russian women and children should be conveyed out of the town, as the situation was hopeless. Another cried: "If we don't win now, we're all dead men. Better go down fighting than be tortured to death."

The exhortation kindled every man's courage. They mustered up all their energies and rushed straight at the enemy like raging wild beasts. When Thursday's sun set Chin's bodyguard had been forced into a corner by the western gate of the town. This was opened, and they fled in defeat. The Russians had gained their object; Chin was overthrown and his government had fallen.

Hardly was the battle decided when a meeting elected the old Minister for Education, Liu Ting-shan (Liu Wen-lung), provisional governor-general. On April 14 General Sheng Shih-tsai was provisionally appointed tupan or military governor of Sinkiang.

Even on his flight with three hundred faithful followers Chin managed to stain his road with blood. A smaller force from Altai which he met was cut down to the last man.

While the Russians in Urumchi on the 16th were greeting one another with the words "Khristos voskres, Sinkiang voskres!" ("Christ is risen, Sinkiang is risen"), Altai and Chuguchak were being warned that Chin was approaching, and that he himself had declared that he would organise his troops in the latter town and retake Urumchi.

On April 19 he reached Manas, and despite warnings from his own men had five Russian members of the garrison there shot. Just as he was about to turn back with five hundred soldiers and surprise Urumchi, he learned that he himself was being pursued by Kirghizes and Turkis and resolved to continue his flight to Chuguchak. A few days later it was heard that he was conspiring with the military chiefs at Chuguchak and Kulja with a view to recapturing Urumchi. According to the plan all the White Russians in Sinkiang were to be executed. But he was tricked by those whom he sought to draw into the conspiracy.

At the end of May he telegraphed to Nanking that he had been driven out by the Russians and that Sinkiang was lost to China for ever. At last he himself appeared at Nanking, where he was arrested.

Marshal Yang had already, in 1920, concluded a treaty with Russia concerning trade between Soviet Russia and Ili. By the terms of a general treaty between Russia and China Chuguchak, Urumchi and Kashgar were also opened to Russian trade. Other places, too, were opened to trade without special authority. The Chinese, on the contrary, did not receive the right of trading in Russian territory.

Chin imported arms from Russia for the war against his subjects, the Turkis. This was done without the knowledge of his own commissary for foreign affairs. On October 1, 1931, a commercial treaty with the Soviet was signed—without a report being made to the government at Nanking. Not till June, 1933, was the secret treaty discovered by the Nanking government's commissary for pacification, General Hwang Mu-sung, who had been sent to Urumchi. It was drafted in such a way as to give Russia complete control over the business life of Sinkiang.

Chin was accordingly put on trial at Nanking for secret negotiations with foreign powers and sentenced to four years' imprisonment.

After Chin had been expelled a period of quiet followed. The new government sent messengers out into the countryside promising peace and freedom, and urging the people to hand over their arms and go back to their fields. But the Turkis were not satisfied with promises. They demanded one of the two highest posts in the government. The Chinese could not agree to this. Manchuria and Jehol had been lost; China owed it to her prestige not to lose the Far West in the same way. The Mohammedans, disappointed, began to arm again.

Worse than all else was the menacing spectre on the white horse which was rising above the eastern horizon. In May, 1933, the emissary of the Turkis had gone to Kansu again and called upon Ma Chung-yin ("Big Horse") for help. Ma had obeyed the summons at once and handed over to Ma Pu-fang all that part of Kansu which was under his administration. Then he had got his army into marching order and himself followed in a lorry.

He was the most dangerous and the strongest of all Urumchi's enemies. He marched unhindered to Kuchengtse and became the absolute autocrat of that part of the country.

The government at Urumchi tried negotiation. Ma was ready to talk. They offered him the whole of Eastern Turkestan and Hami, the eastern gateway into the province. Meanwhile his troops, several thousand strong, pushed forward in the direction of Urumchi. Then the government troops, mainly Russians, took the field at the beginning of June, 1933, and met Ma half-way between Kuchengtse and the capital. This time the Russians were beaten.

When the Japanese took Manchuria, a Chinese army fled across the frontier on to Soviet Russian territory, where it was disarmed and sent to Sinkiang. Seven thousand strong, it made its way to Urumchi via Chuguchak in the spring of 1933.

It was this army, or part of it, which the Urumchi government, in its sore straits, sent to help the Russians against Big Horse. And now their combined forces succeeded in inflicting a decisive defeat on Ma. A thousand rebels were killed, the rest fled in disorder.

The Chinese did not know how to make use of their victory. Instead of pursuing Ma Chung-yin they gave him time to collect his scattered troops and reform his battalions. He took Turfan and thence commanded the two roads to Eastern Turkestan and to Urumchi. Hodja Nias Hadji at Kara-shahr was beaten, and Big Horse was master of the whole country from Hami to Korla and Kucha and thence to Kashgar.

The government tried further negotiations. But as Ma demanded Turfan, Hami and Altai, there could be no peace. In Altai, the Kirghizes and Tungans rose in a fresh revolt. The goldmine of Sinkiang was lost to the Chinese, and the spirit of Big Horse already hovered over Dzungaria.

The governor of Ili, General Chang Pei-yuan, who considered that he had been neglected in the allocation of high posts, approached Ma Chung-yin.

In July there was a feeling of general insecurity in the province. The fields were not sown, as the peasants were being enlisted in the army. All produce was confiscated, and there was a shortage of food everywhere. All carts were requisitioned for the army, so that food could not be transported from one district to another. Urumchi was cut off on all sides. There was only one connection with China proper—by air in the aeroplanes of the German-Chinese Eurasia Company. But when we arrived at Hami, at the beginning of February, 1934, that way, too, had been barred.

At the time of the battle between Kuchengtse and Urumchi the newly appointed general Hwang Mu-sung arrived at the last-named town by aeroplane. He insisted on a complete cessation of hostilities. Negotiations began, but the war was continued.

A conspiracy against Sheng Shih-tsai was detected at Urumchi. Three high officials were executed, and Hwang Mu-sung, who saw that his mission had failed, returned to Nanking by aeroplane.

In September the Foreign Minister himself, Lo Wen-kan, came from Nanking to Urumchi and tried to arrange a peace between the two rival generals Sheng and Ma. With this object he went to Turfan also. But when Sheng demanded that Ma should make Hami his headquarters and put himself under Sheng's orders, Ma refused, well knowing that he had a much stronger strategic position at Turfan, which dominated Urumchi and Eastern Turkestan. Ma took good care not to accept Sheng's invitation that he should go to Urumchi for a conference.

Big Horse's position was strong. He had the whole country south of the Tien-shan in his power, and an army of ten thousand men. The provincial government possessed only the region from Kuchengtse to Chuguchak. The governor of Ili, Chang Pei-yuan, was not to be depended upon. Sheng Shih-tsai was thus surrounded by enemies and his prospects were not bright. He had supplies for two months, whilst Ma commanded the routes to the fertile oases in Eastern Turkestan. The White Russians counselled war.

And the war blazed up again. There was fighting at several places in Dzungaria. The Ili general allied himself openly with

Ma, who was also in touch with a faction in Urumchi. They were to keep the town gates open while the combined army poured in.

The detachment from Ili marched towards the town. On November 26 it captured a convoy of lorries with war material from Russia. A courier from Chang to Ma was intercepted, and so Sheng obtained proofs of an extensive network of conspiracy against the government. On December 10 a number of generals of the Manchu army were arrested, and several Russians. General Bektieieff, who a few months later was to play an important part in determining our fate, was appointed commander of the Russian émigré contingent. General Antonoff, a friend of ours from 1928, became one of Sheng Tupan's right-hand men.

On December 31 the town of Si-hu was taken by the government troops. Chang Pei-yuan went southwards from Kulja in order to reach Aksu over the Tien-shan. He had gone thirty miles from the town when a violent snowstorm burst. Frozen and starved, his troops deserted in masses and returned to Kulja. At last Chang was left almost alone, and when he saw that his position was hopeless, he put a bullet through his head.

So this scoundrel, too, was visited by Heaven's just chastisement. Well-informed Chinese at Urumchi, whom I met in the summer of 1934, were fully aware that the foreign commissary Fan Yao-nan, who had been accused of the murder of Marshal Yang in 1928, was innocent, and that the real perpetrator of the crime was Chin Shu-jen, supported by Chang Pei-yuan. These men put an end to the wise and loyal rule of the capable Yang Tseng-sin and flung Sinkiang into an era of disaster, misery and devastation which will endure for years to come.

After the Altai troops, too, had been driven back, Urumchi took life too easily.

Suddenly, on January 12, Ma Chung-yin pushed forward and was only six miles from the town without anyone knowing it. The generals were sitting at dinner with Sheng Tupan when the bomb burst. So the second siege began. Troops which had been sent to Chuguchak were recalled by telegraph. All Dzungaria lay under deep snow, and they marched slowly. They did not reach the capital till February 11.

Ma Chung-yin, who had been besieging Urumchi for barely a month, retired with the main body of his troops on the night of February 16 to Dawancheng, where he took up a position. On the same day our expedition reached Turfan, close by, without a suspicion of the terrible clouds that were gathering over our convoy.

For many days on end violent winter storms raged over the mountains, and the government aeroplanes had to stop their reconnaissances. Meanwhile Ma's Tungans dug their trenches and established their base camp at the Dawancheng pass itself. At the end of February the weather cleared up, and the aeroplane bombs rained so thick that the positions could not be held. The Tungans fled towards Toksun, while the government troops stormed Turfan, which our convoy had left a few days before. If we had fallen into their hands and been supposed to belong to Big Horse's invading army, I do not know how we should have fared.

General Antonoff was sent across the mountains to Kara-shahr on February 20 to meet the government troops from Ili. The plan was to occupy Kara-shahr and bar the way to Ma. Then Big Horse's life would not have been worth much! Our convoy remained at Kara-shahr from February 28 to March 4, so that we only just escaped being caught between hammer and anvil. We had hardly left the town before it was taken by the government troops.

As a rule we got out of the way a few hours before the situation quite unexpectedly changed to our disadvantage, and when we should have been lost if we had tarried another hour. It was as though the drama in whose plot we had become involved had been planned and directed by a very skilful and kindly stage-manager, and the actors had to follow his guidance whether they would or not.

I have given here a hasty sketch of the main features of Big Horse's war down to the early spring of 1934. Then follows the last act, which we witnessed with our own eyes, so that I have only to relate what we saw and experienced.

I myself never met General Ma Chung-yin. But both our mechanics, Söderbom and Hill, were forced to come into close contact with him. Birger Bohlin met him at Suchow in 1932. He described him as good-looking, tall and slim, with a good figure, intelligent, capable and alert, cheerful and humorous; but said that he made the impression of being casual and bad-mannered. He was a moderate eater and drinker; when entertained by Bohlin he ate only dry bread and prunes for fear of accidentally consuming pig's fat. For he strictly observed the behests of Islam.

His personal courage was remarkable. He was afraid of nothing, and no military task seemed to him too difficult. When a town was stormed he was usually the first man on the wall. But he was also extremely cruel, and could mow down the whole population of a town which refused to capitulate.

His younger brother, who fell at Kuchengtse, was both pleasant and well-bred.

General Ma carried a rifle like a common soldier and used to play football with the troops. He was exacting and severe in his dealings with his men. He was capable of shooting down with his rifle, before the lined-up troops, soldiers who had committed any offence or ill-treated the inhabitants. He could disarm a whole squadron and degrade its officers. Despite his severity he cannot have been able to maintain any discipline in the higher sense of the word. It was a dozen of his soldiers who in June, 1931, not far from Suchow, attacked our comrades on the earlier expedition, Gerhard Bexell and Friis-Johansen, in their tent, fired on them with rifles and pistols and robbed them of everything of value they had.

A conspicuous feature of Ma's character was his boundless ambition. In conversation with his advisers he calmly worked out a plan for the conquest of the whole world in alliance with Germany, Russia and Turkey. In that dance, of course, the Great Powers were to follow his piping.

If he had had strength of mind and patience enough to wait

16

till he had acquired a thorough training in the modern art of war, he could, with his talent and determination, have risen to supreme power in China. But as he lacked this self-control, he could not even swallow Sinkiang. He was not so shrewd and clever as Tso Tsung-tang. But he was very near winning the game at the New Year of 1934, and would have won it if Sheng Shih-tsai had not bought aeroplanes, armoured cars, machine-guns, ammunition and motor-lorries from Russia, and even hired troops from that country. His miserable arsenal could not compete with the Russian equipment, and Russian training was too much for his nondescript force.

I once said to Father Moritz, a German missionary who had known him well at Suchow: "What a romantic autobiography Ma could write if he had the time and inclination!"

"He cannot write his autobiography," the Father replied, "if he is to stick to the truth. It would be a description of the most horrible cruelties and brutality, which would draw down upon him the condemnation of all mankind."

He was like the rider on the pale horse, which appeared when the fourth seal was broken: "And I looked, and behold a pale horse; and his name that sat on him was Death, and Hell followed with him. And power was given unto them over the fourth part of the earth, to kill with sword, and with hunger and with death, and with the beasts of the earth."

Suspecting no evil, we were about to put ourselves into this strange man's power.

"THE DIE IS CAST! WE CROSS THE RUBICON!"

WHEN at the beginning of February, 1934, we advanced through uninhabited country towards Hami, the first large oasis in Sinkiang, we knew practically nothing about the military and political situation in the province.

On January 5, on the Etsin-gol, we had learned by chance through a broadcast from Nanking that three or four thousand Turkis had taken the town of Hami, which was under General Ma Chung-yin's rule, and that the latter had retreated to Turfan.

Next day the wireless announced: "The fighting in Sinkiang has stopped; no further details are known. It is said that the central government has decided to send a commission of inquiry to Sinkiang."

On January 29, in our camp at Yeh-ma-ching ("Wild Horse's Well"), we picked up the laconic message, "No news of events in Sinkiang". And finally, on January 30, we heard at Ming-shui ("Clear Water"): "The first secretary of the executive council (in Nanking) has informed the press that General Sheng Shih-tsai denies the report that southern Sinkiang has declared its independence".

Perhaps it would have been wise to patrol and reconnoitre before risking the safety of the whole convoy. We could possibly have got from marauders, refugees or peasants who had remained in their homes information which would have warned us not to take the fatal step. From our last camp east of Hami we could already see the row of telegraph poles along the road to Anhsi, down which we had imagined a retreat on the Imperial Highway, if such a thing should prove necessary. But as yet no obstacles had checked our progress, the war-scarred province of Sinkiang lay open before us, and not one of us hesitated to take the fatal step through its eastern gateway.

And yet I understood more than well that whatever happened the next day, February 6, 1934, would be a great day in my life.

My responsibility was fearfully heavy. I was in the service of a foreign government, with orders to make motor roads across the greatest desert in the world. But what was more, I was also responsible for the lives of those who were under my orders, and no one knew better than I that it was a wild, almost crazy adventure I had undertaken, a gamble in which I was risking not only other men's lives but also my own honour. For if the undertaking failed, and we were compelled to return the way we had come, we should, even if we preserved our lives, have suffered a defeat, a fiasco, which would have made me impossible in China. As the shadows grew dark over our road, I seemed to hear the mocking laughter which awaited me on my return to the coast if I lost the game.

The night passed quietly. Not a sound disturbed our peace. The same grave-like silence as in the desert surrounded us on all sides. Not the bark of a dog was heard, and our own sheepdog Pao did not even growl. If there were frontier guards, they had not yet discovered us. On the morning of February 6 we did not hurry ourselves. We were not precisely longing to throw ourselves straight into the lions' den, or rather into a nest full of vipers. Breakfast, striking tents, loading, all went as quietly as usual, perhaps more quietly. None of us knew if this was our last day of freedom, or whether, before the sun set, others would be controlling our movements—or our sojourn in a dark, dank Tungan prison.

It was nearly ten before our cars began to hum along the road westward. The track was extremely dusty, and deep ruts had been cut in the clay by the high wheels of the *arbas*, or Turki carts. Out of a sea of tall yellow reeds the ruins of a watch-tower rose like a lonely rock. The bearings of our map-makers became shorter than usual amid the dry winter vegetation which hid the ground.

Serat was leading the column. He stuck in a shallow sand-dune, backed, got up speed and surmounted the obstacle. Jomcha and Georg followed close on his heels and performed the same man-œuvre. Jomcha came running back and made signs to us that the road was clear. We rushed hissing through whirling clouds of dust. Only Effe was not there. Bergman was his passenger, and was taking compass bearings with the small car as a mark.

On both sides were to be seen the ruins of farms, but not a glimpse of men or animals. The three elephants, or grey sows, as Georg's, Serat's and Jomcha's lorries were called, disappeared in impenetrable clouds of whirling dust. We followed half suffo-cated, and the heavily creaking convoy went slowly on. Every-thing was grey. The back of Jomcha's lorry loomed out of the fog, and the convoy stopped. Serat had got stuck again. Spades were produced. The clouds of fog were scattered by the light breeze. Bluish-white glaciers shimmered on the Tien-shan mountain-chain to the northward. To the south was a large ruined farm, consisting of clay buildings and walls.

When we had been travelling for an hour and a quarter the reeds grew thinner and lower, and at length almost came to an end. The country became more open, the view was no longer hidden. Several farms came into sight, isolated trees and orchards. Everything was devastated. All the roofs were burned and had fallen in. The trees nearest the houses were black and carbonised. Only the trunks were left, like the crosses in churchyards. Count-less trees and avenues had been cut down. The stumps stuck up out of the ground, silent witnesses to Chin Shu-jen's cruelty to the peaceful, industrious Turki people, who, in this oasis, so flourish-ing three years before, had cultivated their land and fought for their own existence and the lives of those who were dear to them. . . . Eagles and hawks hovered over the scene of desolation, watching for the rats and mice which now ventured out.

Half an hour farther on and to the left of the road, quite near the ruins of a farm, we perceived something which brought the whole column to a halt. Eleven camels and a few horses were grazing there, watched by two men. Kung, Serat and Jomcha hurried to the spot. The two watchmen were terrified and seemed to be on the point of flight. What were they to think? Five motorcars from the east! Of course they must be the advance troops of the army which the Nanking government, according to continually recurring rumours, was to send to Sinkiang to restore peace and order in the province. But Kung, who was ahead, shouted reassuring words to the two men and made them stop. When he had talked to them a little while, he approached my car accompanied by one of the pair, who proved to be a Chinese boy of twelve named Ma. In a moment he was with me. The whole of our force assembled round the poor boy. He told us in a trembling voice that his family was one of the six last which had remained in that village, Hwang-lu-kang ("Yellow Reeds"), and that he was watching over its last animals. In addition to them General Ma Chung-yin had several soldiers in the village. The boy got a bright silver dollar and we went on—certainly to his indescribable relief.

A little further on we saw eight men and women in rags by the ruins of a house, and right in front of us were four little children standing and staring. They could not but believe that we were new tormentors who had come to take from them their last possession—life.

Hummel, Chen, Kung and I were in the small car. Yew was a little ahead of us in Serat's driver's cabin. They were first in the procession, Effe and Bergman last. We had no choice but to follow the cart track. At one place the ruts became so deep that the frame of the car was caught up by the ground between them. Effe came running up with spades, pick-axes, a jack and a plank. The car was raised, the hole filled up, and we went on.

Meanwhile Chen was talking to some Chinese. They had fled to Anhsi in 1931 and returned to their devastated homes in May, 1933. They thought Ma Chung-yin was at Urumchi, negotiating with Sheng Shih-tsai about the partition and administration of Sinkiang.

Straight in front of us we saw a tent to the left of the road, and to the right one fairly large and five smaller *paotais* or signposts of clay. The three "elephants" had stopped. Soldiers were running to and fro, and fresh soldiers were coming from a farm behind the tent. We hurried on and drove up to the head of the column.

A dozen soldiers, clad in furs and with rifles in their hands, had surrounded a few of our men and were closely examining their passports. When Serat's lorry, with Yew in the driver's cabin, was about a hundred yards from the tent, the soldiers had rushed out and lain down under cover of the earth wall on each side of the road with their rifles pointed at the drivers, ready to open fire if the cars came on. Thereupon Serat had stopped dead and Yew had jumped out with his hands up to show that he carried no weapons. Then the soldiers had lowered their rifles, and some of them had got up and waited till Yew arrived. When they heard who we were, they had been reassured. They were Tungans and Turkis belonging to General Ma Chung-yin's army. A most arrogant young puppy was in command of the post, and stamped our passports. He announced domineeringly that we must wait where we were till the commandant at Hami had been informed by telephone, when the latter would probably come in person and find out more precisely what kind of people we were.

One of the Turki soldiers asked me to come to the commanding officer's house and have some tea. One or two of us drove there in the small car and were conducted into a miserable hovel, where a fire was burning in the middle of the floor and a *chugun*, or can containing cups of water for tea-drinking, was placed upon the embers.

A Tungan hooked a telephone wire on to the telegraph wire and rang up the commandant at Hami. A bombardment of questions about us was answered. The final orders were that all our weapons should be taken out and put in one place in one of the cars, and that two soldiers were to be responsible for the arsenal on our way into Hami, whither we might proceed at once.

While our rifles and pistols were being taken out of the cars, the Turki told us that the inhabitants of the village had fled to

22

Anhsi, Tun-hwang and the mountains to the northward, but that many people still remained in Hami. Yollbars Khan, our host in January, 1928, was at Turfan, but his son Nias Beg was in his father's house in Hami. The King of Hami and his son were dead and no new king had been placed on the throne. Ma Chung-yin himself was either at Turfan or at Urumchi, the road to which was certainly barred to us.

After we had returned to the convoy all our fire-arms were placed on one of the lorries, on which two soldiers took their seats. We got in and off we went. We soon left behind the outskirts of the oasis, which are reached by irrigation water, and a hard gravel soil began, covered with tufts of vegetation. But even these tufts became scanty, and there followed a belt of absolute *gobi*.

The road led over two *kares*, or underground canals. These curious irrigation channels are as characteristic of the Turfan basin as of Iran (Persia). A perpendicular shaft, six feet or more deep, is dug in the earth, and from the bottom of this shaft horizontal passages uphill and downhill, almost parallel to the slope of the surface. Twenty yards farther down the slope a new shaft is dug, and so on for miles. The bottoms of the shafts are connected by the underground passage, which drops exceedingly slowly till it comes to the region where the soil allows of cultivation. The underground canal starts at a spring or a hollow where melted snow and rain collect. From this point the water runs the whole way to its destination underground, protected against sun and evaporation. In this way grain is conjured out of the soil even in the driest regions. But the canals must always be clean. Now the peasants had either been enrolled in the contesting armies, had been shot or had fled. The result was that the canals were silted up, their streams had run dry and the ploughed fields had been turned into desert.

It was three o'clock when we crossed the eastern border of the irrigated vegetation-clad area of the Hami oasis. More ruined farms and devastated gardens appeared. Even in Marco Polo's time the Hami oasis was renowned for its luxuriant gardens and its aromatic fruit. A current proverb runs: "Hami is famous for its melons, Turfan for its grapes, Ili for its horses and Kucha for its girls". But for three years past no melons or any other fruit had ripened under Hami's sun. Where in 1928 we had walked through orchards only isolated trees now remained. Even the charming poplar and willow avenues which, within the boundaries of the oasis, cast their shade over the great caravan road, had been levelled to the ground. Only stumps bearing the marks of axes bore witness to the splendour that had been. Here Chin's avenging hordes had passed by to chastise Hami for its rebellion in 1931. The oasis was to be wiped off the face of the earth and the Gobi desert invited to extend the frontiers of its empire. We saw everywhere with astonishment traces of the curse this one man had brought upon the country which he had got into his power by murder and treachery.

The slightest signs of life attracted our attention. A man came along leading a horse laden with reeds. At one farm a solitary individual stood staring at us. There were five donkeys in an enclosure, and twenty camels grazing outside. Grey monuments of clay indicated a burial-place. We congratulated the dead on having escaped murder, fire and atrocities.

Slowly and cautiously the heavy lorries rolled along the winding dusty track between desolate ruins and avenues of stumps. Close to the road on the right were the ruins of a Chinese temple. An officer and three soldiers sprang up by one wall, as though from an ambush, and rushed forward towards my car, which was leading the way. They held their rifles at the ready. The officer made a sign with his hand and shouted to us to stop. Next moment he and his men were by the car talking to Chen. The officer poured out a regular torrent of questions, and demanded that our arms and ammunition should be handed over to him. There was a long delay. But we must have impressed him favourably, for at last he said that the cartridges need not be handed over till we reached Hami.

The officer placed himself on the front seat by Hummel's side.

24

He and his men were Tungans. His manners were impeccable, he spoke politely and considerately, and it was quite clear that he knew who we were and had received special orders as to how we were to be treated; for he suddenly informed us that a house was being kept in readiness for us at Hami—the headquarters of the Sui-yuan–Sinkiang omnibus company. The object of his examination had obviously been to make sure that we really were the commission from Nanking, the news of whose approach had been telegraphed to General Ma Chung-yin by General Fu at Kwei-hwa.

When his soldiers had mounted, the officer gave the signal for us to start. We had not got far before ten more soldiers rushed at us from a ruined farm on the left. Each had his rifle at the ready and his first finger on the trigger. They raised their rifles and seemed to have the intention of receiving us with a hail of bullets. But our escorting officer stretched out his hand and shouted an order which stopped and pacified them. He told us that some of the omnibus company's cars, which had not stopped when ordered to do so, had been fired at with live cartridges.

Everywhere misery, débris, devastation! It would be twenty years or more before the Hami oasis regained its former prosperity.

Now we were in the town, going along its empty main street. One or two Turkis were loafing about, homeless and aimless. The shops in the bazaar were shut with massive wooden shutters. All trade was dead. At one or two street corners a few ragged boys were playing.

No women were to be seen.

We stopped at the gate of Commandant Chang Feng-ming's *yamen* in the Chinese town. He received me in the same room as General Liu six years before. Now the Chinese were driven out, and Ma Chung-yin ("Big Horse") ruled over what little was left of Hami. Chang, a short, stout man, was polite and friendly. He read our big passport made out for the expedition; the others—personal passports and arms and ammunition permits —did not require examination. He would inform General Ma of our arrival and get orders as to how we were to be treated and what roads were open to us. A reply might be expected in two days. The general's headquarters were now somewhere north of Turfan.

An hour later we drove to the omnibus company's premises, where the manager, Mr. Yu, received us. He had only learned by wireless a week before that we had reached the Etsin-gol, and we must therefore excuse the place not yet being in proper order. The yard was so small that the cars could only just turn round when parking. Two rooms were placed at our disposal, one quite small and one very large; the latter was used as a warehouse for bales of cotton. These now served as mattresses for some of our sleeping-bags. A stove was lighted in the middle of the room. Along the long wall at the back ran a narrow table, in front of which Mr. Yu's camp-bed was set up for my use. Dinner, consisting of preserves, bread and eggs from some resurrected bazaar shop, was served on another table. Lights were put out earlier than usual, and we went to bed for our first night in the land which General Ma had conquered.

Our first day at Hami was devoted to official visits. We called on the commandant again and received the pleasant news that the telegraph line to Nanking was open via Lanchow. We therefore telegraphed to the Minister for Railways, Dr. Kuo Meng-yu, telling him that we had arrived safely in Sinkiang, had been well received by the commandant, and intended to call upon General Ma Chung-yin. We also sent a message to the latter asking for permission to continue our journey to Turfan and thence to his headquarters. A third telegram was addressed to the postmaster at Suchow, with the request that our letters might be sent on to Hami.

We paid a visit to the mayor, Ma—an elderly man, whom we had known in 1928. At the offices of the Eurasia, the German-Chinese aircraft company, we met its head, Mr. Yang, and his two assistants; all three spoke German.

In the afternoon we had a series of return visits according to ancient Chinese etiquette, with tea, tobacco and small talk. When all the gossip we had heard in the course of the day was summed up and analysed, we extracted from it the following military-political probabilities. Ma Chung-yin was besieging Urumchi, the fall of which might be expected at any moment. When the town had fallen Ma would be absolute ruler over the whole of Sinkiang, and his goodwill would therefore be an advantage to our expedition, which, by the way, had been ordered to remain entirely neutral. But Ma was short of troops, and was therefore getting hold of all the men he could; he was continually making fresh calls on Hami and sucking dry the already impoverished and depopulated oasis.

All communications with Urumchi were cut, and it was impossible to go there without passing through the fighting lines, where we should have been suspect to both sides—and should probably have been shot. On the other hand, we could drive to Turfan, Korla and Kucha—if we were not afraid of robbers. All Tien-shan-nan-lu, or "the road south of the Tien-shan", was said to be in Ma Chung-yin's power. What the situation was at Kashgar, Yarkand and Khotan no one knew. In general we found news of the military position as unreliable as a few months before in Peking.

A Tartar from the Kazan region called Karimoff, who dealt in foxes' skins between Kucha and Tientsin, believed that the whole of Eastern Turkestan was quiet, because trade had been resumed.

Spring was approaching. On the night of the 7th the thermometers showed 11·7 degrees.[1] We were far from being alone in our quarters. A numerous rabble from east and west inhabited the place, and to keep the inquisitive at a distance we roped off the part of the yard which was nearest to our dwelling.

A white-bearded old Turki merchant, Ahun Bai, whom also I knew from 1928, paid us a visit; he had an inexhaustible flow of stories about conditions and events in the province. He said, among other things, that General Chang Pei-yuan at Kulja had

[1] Fahrenheit (and in subsequent passages).

entered into an alliance with General Ma, and that these two intended to rule Sinkiang jointly when they had defeated Sheng Shih-tsai. Shah Maksud, the old king, whom we had met in his palace six years before, was dead, and his son, the new king, had also died. The latter's son, a youth of about twenty, was at Hami, but had neither power nor influence.

Ahun Bai had formerly lived at Alma Ata (Vernij), but had been for twenty-two years a "Komuluk"—an inhabitant of Komul, as the Turkis call Hami. The war had destroyed his house and farms and all his property. He now lived in a rented house and was waiting for better times. He estimated the population of Hami before the war at ten thousand. Most of these had now fled to neighbouring towns, even to Kucha and Suchow— "for fear of the war, and then there was war everywhere".

We had at Hami a foretaste of the countless rumours which flashed through the air like dragonflies. The Turkis were cautious in their utterances. They cherished an inextinguishable hatred both for the Chinese and for the Tungans. The Chinese were infidels and ate pork; the Tungans were at least Mohammedans like the Turkis, but hankered after absolute power over the province. So long as Ma Chung-yin was lord over Hami, the Turkis must stand by him; if anyone expressed any opinion at all it must be to Ma's advantage, and he was generally declared to be sure of victory. The result was that we got from the beginning a false idea of the real situation, which was not corrected till we reached Turfan.

We had already heard that General Chang Pei-yuan, military governor of Ili, with Kulja as his capital, was in league with Ma Chung-yin. Now Yew picked up a rumour that Chang had gone over to the military governor-general at Urumchi, Sheng Shih-tsai, which had made General Ma's position more difficult. But it was still declared that Ma had surrounded and was besieging Urumchi.

We were invited to a dinner of welcome at Commandant Chang's. We arrived punctually, and had to wait a very long time before he himself crossed the threshold of the little room. He had a temperature, and could not, therefore, be present at dinner. The real reason for his not wishing to eat with us was religious; he was a follower of Islam, we were pork-eaters. But we had chicken rissoles (swimming in soup among pigeons' eggs), shark-fins, fishes' roes, seaweed, lotus buds, bamboo shoots, white bread and other delicacies—things which could not be bought for money in Hami and had presumably been stolen from tradesmen in the bazaar of the Chinese town. Hot rice brandy was handed round too, though it was forbidden in the army and might only be served out to wounded soldiers.

A couple of Chang's understrappers did the honours, and the tone was gay and cheerful. At the beginning of dinner one of our party had spoken of a hot bath as a solace after the journey through the desert and all the dust from the roads we had collected on us and swallowed during the last few days. Hardly had we risen from the table before one of our deputy hosts announced that the bath-house was heated and ready.

Escorted by the officer who had driven in the small car from the temple, and, guided by the light of lanterns, we went in procession across small yards and along narrow passages, where dark forms crept about like ghosts, to a hovel which we were told was the bath-house dressing-room. A light was burning on the table, and tea, sweets and cigarettes were set out. One after another we crept into a bath full of piping hot water and then let the douche play upon our bodies, all in a pitch-dark room. Here too the highest spirits prevailed. The Chinese were as mad as the Swedes. There was singing and shouting; Indian dances were danced and warfare waged with ice-cold jets of water, while one witticism followed another. The young officer who was looking after us must have thought he had got among a party of escaped lunatics. But he smiled approvingly at the strange circus performance he witnessed.

The most probable and most important news which reached us came through Yew, who was always keen-witted and critical and reported everything to me. In some Chinese quarters we had been advised not to go to Turfan with the whole convoy—assuming we got permission to go there—but only to risk two of the lorries and send the rest to Anhsi or some other place where they would be in safety. We resolved, however, not to divide the expedition into two parties, but to keep together at all costs.

We now received fresh details of the rebellion west of Hami, of which the wireless had told us. A few hundred Turki robbers from Kucha had advanced by stealth against Hami with the intention of capturing and plundering the town. General Ma had sent fifteen hundred soldiers to surround them. They had been defeated and scattered. Some seventy prisoners had been beheaded on the spot, but the leader and the rest escaped. This had happened a week before we arrived at Hami, and that was why we had been advised to look out for robbers on the road to Turfan.

Five hundred men of Ma's force had been recalled to Turfan; the rest had left Hami that very day, February 8, taking with them seven hundred Turki youths who had been called up for military service. The engineer Kung had seen them start. They had been kept like cattle in a closed yard, while their mothers, wives and sisters stood outside the gate weeping and lamenting. Commandant Chang, in his report to General Ma, had begged that he might keep a few hundred of them, as otherwise the little cultivated soil that remained would disappear and the remnants of trade and the crafts would be paralysed. Nor did he himself wish to be commandant of a heap of ruins in a desert.

Another day, February 9, dawned upon our wandering band at Hami. That night the thermometer was no lower than 12·4 degrees. We were approaching warmer regions and a milder season. There would be no more cold now. The winter had been kind to us. The gods were on our side. The days were lengthening and life becoming easier; we need not be continually worried by lack of fuel and water.

The Tartar Karimoff reappeared. Wheresoever the carcase is, there will the eagles be gathered together. He wanted to tell us

30

that he had a good friend, a Turki, who lived a few days' journey this side of Turfan and knew a mountain in the Turfan region which was full of huge beds of fossilised dragons. There were whole dragons—head, spine, tail, legs and all. The place was kept a dead secret, but Karimoff meant to find out where it was and sell "dragons' bones" to China. The thing might be worth millions! The fossilised remains of animals are called "dragon's bones" in China; such fossils are highly valued and are sold for medicinal purposes in the Chinese chemists' shops. Behind Karimoff's vague information there might be a fossil "find" of immense value.

We had a visit from our deputy hosts at the previous day's festivity. One of them was the head of the commandant's tele-graph office. Yew asked him if any answer had come yet from General Ma. No information on this point was given, which Yew interpreted to mean that Chang had had an answer, but that it was so unfavourable that he was unwilling to convey it to us. In the evening Chen went to the Eurasia company to take the time. One of the commandant's men was there too, who told him that General Ma's reply had arrived; but Chen could not get him to say what the reply was. This seemed to us more suspicious than ever. If the answer had been "yes"—that is, if we had been free to travel to Turfan and farther westward—Chang would prob-ably have told us at once. We were left in a state of disagreeable uncertainty.

Had anything happened in the theatre of war which made the presence of emissaries of Nanking and foreigners in the province as witnesses less desirable? Was Hami to be our first and last halting-place in Sinkiang?

Our one room being at once dining-room, reception-room and bedroom, it did not suit me very well as a study, because it was filled all day with visitors, who were offered tea, cakes and cigarettes. I worked, therefore, in the small car, as if I was in the desert, and there I received a young man with the sonorous name of Yakub Beg, second son of Yollbars Khan, the mighty Turki chieftain in Hami. Yakub Beg for his part was convinced that we should not be expelled but welcomed, and advised me to telephone to his father, who was at Turfan, and ask him to prepare comfortable quarters for us.

On our former visit in 1928, Norin, Ambolt and Bergman had on different occasions stayed in the house of a rich merchant, Mosul Bai, at Turfan. It was now said that he had had to flee for political reasons and had become a robber chief on the road between Korla and Kashgar. Perhaps we should now see him again in other circumstances than before. We were also told that Ma Tao-tai, the governor of Kashgar, had sent Ma Chung-yin a message saying that if he succeeded in taking Urumchi the whole of Eastern Turkestan would declare for him, but if Sheng Shih-tsai won the game, the southern half of the province intended to go over to his side.

Early next morning two soldiers appeared and reported that they, with two comrades, had been detailed by the commandant to escort us to Turfan. Splendid! The road westward lay open to us! We were expected and welcome at Ma Chung-yin's headquarters.

An hour later we had this news confirmed by the officer who had been told off to command our escort. He proved to be the same rogue who, when the Foreign Minister, Lo Wen-kan, landed at Hami, had searched the whole of his luggage. The proud warrior tried to show his teeth at us too, and said to Yew that as we had so much luggage on our lorries, it was obvious that we had brought with us goods for some merchant in Sinkiang. Yew answered quietly that the government at Nanking, in whose service we were, did not carry on trade with Sinkiang merchants.

Chin, an adjutant of Commandant Chang, brought us fresh confirmation of Ma's friendly answer. The general had replied in his telegram that the sooner we started the better. This Chin brought at the same time a less agreeable message from his chief —namely, that the latter wished to "borrow" from us 150 gallons of petrol which he needed for his wireless station. I replied that this was impossible, as we ourselves needed all the petrol we had, and we had long journeys before us. We could let him have sixty gallons against a receipt, and that with difficulty—and Chin was satisfied with this. He guaranteed on Chang's honour that the same quantity of petrol should be handed over to us at Turfan, and later gave us a receipt signed by Chang.

When we left Kwei-hwa we had 3260 gallons, at the Etsin-gol, 2320, and at Hami, 1900; we were now relieved of sixty, so that 1840 gallons were left. From Kwei-hwa to Hami we had done 885 miles. One gallon lasted 4·89 miles. If Chang meant what he said, the transaction would be to our advantage and would save transport. But he was lying; his receipt was worthless at Turfan, and we had been cheated out of sixty gallons. We had not really believed in him, but at Hami of all places it would have been dangerous to incur the commanding officer's displeasure. He could have smashed us by so wording his telegram to General Ma that we should have been hurled back into the desert. So we had to swallow the bitter pill. If only we got into the province and played our cards diplomatically, we should always be able to manage without the sixty gallons we had lost. In the worst event there were camels, horses and carts to fall back upon. We should not for ever have our habitation among the tents of Kedar.

We spent the evening as the guests of Yakub Beg and his younger brother Ahmed Beg. There we were regaled with mutton chopped small and swathed in a cloak of thin dough, and steamed; also *ash* or *pillau*, ordinary rice pudding mixed with small pieces of mutton, carrots and raisins, and tea. They told us that two hundred Turkis at the most had been killed at Hami, but eleven thousand at Pichan. At Turfan all was quiet and the bazaars open again.

On February 11 there was a minimum temperature of 19·4 degrees. Some of us went for a drive in Hami, accompanied by Yakub Beg and Ahun Bai, to witness with our own eyes the devastation which the governor-general Chin Shu-jen had left to the province as a memento of his stewardship. The levelling to the ground of the brave and capable general Tso Tsung-tang's temple, with his portrait by the high altar, was probably done by Turkis. Their fathers had been ruled by the great Yakub Beg, Bedaulet (the "Happy One"), and in the dark days through which the country was now passing they could not forget that Tso Tsung-tang had recaptured Sinkiang from the vanquished Yakub Beg, and so set flowing all those streams of blood and tears which now had poured, and would continue to pour, over the province's dusty streets and roads.

How well we remembered our visit to the old King of Hami, Shah Maksud, with his white silk turban and chalk-white beard, who had received us in his stately palace! Everywhere were carpets and luxurious divans, and on the wall a letter written by the famous Empress Dowager of China with her own hand. The palace was partly built on the wall round the Mohammedan town, and looked out proudly over the streets and houses of Hami.

Two years had passed since Chin Shu-jen's avenging hordes had plundered the king's palace of all its valuables at their master's orders; then they had burned its pillars, balconies and roofs and broken down its walls of sun-baked brick.

We ascended into the higher storeys, where Shah Maksud had lived and, after his death, his son Nasir had had his royal apartments. Nasir's son, a young man of twenty, had lived as a private citizen since the abolition of the monarchy. We did not meet him. He was said to be a distinguished, intelligent and kindly man; it was his intention, we were told, when peace was once more established in his former kingdom, to rebuild the palace of his ancestors in its former splendour.

What a fearful sight! All the walls had been pulled down, everything which would burn set on fire. One had to walk carefully and keep one's footing among the broken fragments of wall if one would reach the edge and see far below the little wilderness which had been the king's garden. There Shah Maksud's harem and summer pavilion had stood amid odorous fruit trees, grapes and melons, but nothing was left of them now but a few scorched timbers, and the trees were cut down to the roots.

And beyond the garden spread the unhappy Mohammedan town, a greyish chessboard of demolished houses. Only the streets remained, but most often blocked by débris and rubbish. Between them nothing was to be seen but heaps of ruins and a few isolated houses, probably built up again by their homeless owners.

On the summit of the palace was a well, many feet deep and two feet in width. There for centuries past the kings of Hami had accumulated all the silver and gold they had squeezed out of their subjects, and it was rumoured that at Shah Maksud's death the well had been brimful. But the place was ingeniously and cunningly hidden, and only one or two of the king's sworn confidants knew where it was. Chin's robber bands had orders to find the well at all costs and carry its piles of treasure to his *yamen* at Urumchi. A traitor, for a liberal reward, showed them the way to the spot, which was in one of Nasir's private apartments. The well was emptied and the treasure taken to Chin. He had it loaded on to a caravan, which was to go via Barkul to Kwei-hwa and Tientsin. But before the caravan with the royal booty had crossed the frontier of Sinkiang, it had been attacked by robbers and thoroughly looted.

We stood at the edge of the well and looked down into its empty black depths. A pair of crows sat on the top of the wall which the soldiers had been unable to pull down. "The spider has spun his web in the king's palace, and the owl calls from Afrosiab's castle."

We entered, not far from the palace, the king's rather imposing mosque, Hardga Meschid, with its pretty hall of prayer. The roof is supported by solid wooden columns, and the pillared hall yields effective alternations of light and shade. Here the faithful used to assemble for the great religious ceremonies of the year according to the commands of the prophet, and no doubt still do, though their ranks have been thinned.

Outside we found Altunluk-mazar (the "Golden Saint's Tomb"), a quite simple rectangular building with a low cupola, under which the former kings of Hami and their relations rest in their tombs. In the chamber itself, above ground, we found the sarcophagus-like oblong monuments which mark the situation of the actual tombs in the crypt underground. If the tablets commemorating the dead spoke the truth, they certainly recorded no epics for posterity. Shah Maksud was an avaricious old rogue, who enriched himself at the Turki peasants' expense, and his forefathers were probably little better than he. But the glory was departed, the monarchy had been abolished, and all that remained of the vanished splendour was the mausoleum and the mosque, all gone to ruin, where the followers of the prophet pray for the souls of their slumbering tormentors. There Shah Maksud sleeps his last sleep, his palace a heap of ashes and his gold scattered to the four winds.

THROUGH RUINED VILLAGES TO TURFAN

At last all obstacles to our starting were removed, and on the morning of February 12 we turned out before the sun had risen above the horizon. Lights burned and the fire in the stove crackled. The yard was full of people. There were sick people seeking help from the doctor, and he patched them up one after another. There were soldiers belonging to the escort, clattering their rifles, and merchants selling bread and eggs to Chia Kwei, our Chinese cook. Yu, our kind host, would accept no money for our rent; he said that our work on the desert road would benefit the omnibus company at Kwei-hwa.

There was endless running about and shouting. In the midst of the confusion Yakub Beg came to say that his wife was ill and her hands paralysed. The doctor promised to go in and see her as we passed by.

Then arrived the noble commandant Chang Feng-ming and gave his last orders to our escort. He produced six men, but we explained that we had no room for more than four. He gave us five, one of whom (we decided) was to get out at the first village.

The colonel whom Chang now presented to us as commander of our escort was a Tungan named Ma Ying-piao. His glorious career may be briefly summarised. He had been under the command of the young general Ma Chung-yin in Kansu and was there called Ka Chun-chang (the "Little General")—Ma Chung-yin himself is best known in Kansu by the name Ka Sse-ling (the "Little Commandant"). About 1931–32 he raged like a fiend over all the country from Ninghsia by Lianchow, Kanchow and Su-chow to Anhsi, sacking, murdering and devastating in country-side, town and village along the old Imperial Highway. He was said to have thousands of lives on his conscience, all Chinese and mostly women and children. Where he had passed by, villages and farms lay in ruins and ashes.

When General Ma invaded Sinkiang, Ma Ying-piao was a member of his staff and was ordered to Hami. After his examination of the Foreign Minister's luggage, mentioned in the preceding chapter, the Minister complained to General Ma. The general thereupon removed Ma Ying-piao from his post at Hami and made him instead commandant at Barkul—a change which was hardly a punishment. He made himself so hated at Barkul by both Chinese and Turkis through injustice, caprice and cruelty of all kinds that it was decided to get rid of him. He only saved his life by speedy flight. He fled to the western gate of the town with half a dozen followers; but there the party were seized by the soldiers on guard and all beheaded—except Ma, who managed to escape in disguise. He fled all alone through the mountain passes of the Tien-shan and, half dead from starvation, arrived at Pichan, whence he had reached Hami three weeks before our party.

It was this hero whom Commandant Chang had now placed in charge of the escort for our convoy. We could be pretty sure that no robber band on the road to Turfan could be more dangerous than Colonel Ma Ying-piao. But he was not dangerous to us. Chinese we had met in Hami had told us that he had accepted the command of our escort in the hope that we should speak well of him to General Ma, and that on our recommendation he would be taken into the general's good graces again. It was predicted, therefore, that his conduct on the journey would be peaceable. Commandant Chang was without doubt glad to have found, thanks to us, an excuse for getting rid of a worse rogue than himself.

It was half-past nine before everything was ready and the motor-lorries were carefully working their way out of the small yard and through the narrow gate into the main street, which itself is no wider than a corridor. We stopped a while outside Yollbars Khan's aristocratic house, which, strange to say, had been

38

spared by Chin's looters, and went into the rooms of his son Yakub Beg. Her grace was sitting with her back to the light and thickly veiled. The doctor examined her hands, took out his medicine-chest and treated her according to all the rules of his science. Meanwhile Ahun Bai appeared with his young daughter, who was suffering from the same complaint and was treated in the same way.

Fresh patients assembled round the philanthropic doctor, and we who waited had to arm ourselves with patience. Among those seeking help was a fat Turki, with the figure of a *pavan* or wrestler, who entertained us with stories of Chin Shu-jen. He assured us that Chin's troops had behaved like devils from hell, and had killed fifty thousand Turkis, men, women and children, in towns, villages and farms. He trembled with unquenchable hate when he spoke of it. When we sometimes (and later very often) met opponents of General Ma, these used to remind us of the ruined villages and felled orchards and avenues as proofs of his atrocities. But it was really Chin Shu-jen who turned this part of the province into a wilderness.

Meanwhile the doctor was ready and we were able to make a start in earnest. We followed the track of the lorries past Altunluk-mazar, swaying and lurching through regular pillows and mattresses of fine yellow dust, loosened by the wheels of carts and the hooves of donkeys and oxen. Now we met only a few carts and a small camel caravan. Otherwise the road lay desolate and silent. Through clouds of dust we now and then caught a glimpse of the Tien-shan to the north in majestic grandeur with its snow-crowned peaks, in curiously soft and subdued colouring.

Later on, rather more traffic appeared on the road. We met one or two countrymen riding horses or donkeys, a few ox-carts, a small camel caravan, or overtook other travellers. Several times we passed small parties of soldiers, and once a train of sixteen mounted Turkis with bundles and boxes on pack animals. They were probably refugees who had now ventured forth from their hiding-places and were making their way home to their devastated farms. Once or twice we drove across or through ice-covered watercourses.

Some eighteen miles out we came to the village of T'ou-p'u (the "First Fortress"), which the Turkis call Sumkagho. We had rested there in 1928 in a Mongol officer's quarters. The village was now nothing but heaps of clay. The orders for its destruction had been thoroughly and conscientiously executed. A number of trees were still standing, but bore deep scars made by axes a foot above the ground, and were condemned to wither. There had formerly been sixty families in the village. Thirteen of them had been killed, the others had fled; twelve had returned and were sowing wheat and maize.

We waited at T'ou-p'u for an eternity. Hours passed, and the lorries did not arrive. It was not map-making that delayed them, for within the war zone we were obliged, for our own safety's sake, to abstain from everything that could arouse suspicion. No; something had happened to them! One rider after another whom we had passed on the road arrived. One of them told us that a lorry had gone through the ice of a frozen watercourse, another that a plank had been laid down to get it out, a third that it had started again.

But why did they not come? Ah, there was a row of yellow dust-clouds along the road! Alas, they were only whirlwinds of dust chasing one another like yellowish-grey spectres.

At last Serat came in sight with his lorry. He reported that Effe had stuck in a hole in the ice and that the whole of his cargo had been unloaded. But the whole outfit had at last been salved. We turned back to see how things were going. He had stuck fast in the sand at another spot. Poor Effe, he had bad luck. Matting had been spread out on the sand dunes. Soon after he stuck in the mud on the edge of an irrigation canal. Some passing horsemen were stopped and induced to help for an ample reward. The whole supply of wood which we had bought at Hami was used to build a bridge through the mud. When they got Effe out again he had several punctures. It was quicker to ride a beast at a walk than to motor at a snail's pace like this. But it is often so on Asiatic roads. Patience, patience!

Erh-p'u (the "Second Fortress") is the Chinese name for the next village, which the Turkis call Astana. A few houses were left, but otherwise the whole of the lower part of the village was razed to the ground. Not a human being was to be seen; not even a dog. Some trees also were undamaged. Water from springs or melted snow was pouring down from the mountains; the canals were full and covered with ice. The village street—which is always along the main road—was under water, and the road was flooded for some distance outside the village as well. The surface often held, but just as often it gave way.

At the entrance to Erh-p'u Serat's right back wheel sank in up to the axle, and after a time the left followed, so that the car was resting on the frame. One could see that it would be a long business. But we drove on in the small car and encamped in a field beyond the western edge of the village, where at long last the lorries assembled. It is always easier and more comfortable to drive through sheer *gobi* than within the boundaries of the oases, where one has to cross canals with no bridges or small bridges, high and ramshackle, and go through deep beds of fine dust.

Next morning, while the lorries were being loaded and cleaned after all the recent casualties, I drove up the hill which rises north of the village proper, now devastated, and on which the *guristan*, or burial-place, of Astana lies. Countless graves with horizontal stones of dressed sun-baked brick lie on the summit of the hill, in a regular grove of tall white-stemmed poplars. All the grave-stones are parallel to one another, for the dead must face towards Mecca. Among them are several *mazars*, or saints' tombs, and a good-sized monument of a sultan, adorned with a cupola. The rays of the morning sun fell almost horizontally through the clear air and gilded the eastern faces of the tree-trunks and gravestones, while the western sides threw long black shadows on the ground. Through the tree-trunks in this natural cloister shone the many-coloured rocky heights of the Tien-shan, crowned with blinding white snow-fields. Seldom have I seen a more singular grove, a more impressive burial-place. The dead in Astana were incomparably more finely housed than the living. It would have been tempting to stay there a day to enjoy that romantically beautiful view. But when the cars were ready and loaded, the signal for departure was given. We took leave of the handful of survivors who lived in a few huts near the graves, and of whom one *hadji*, or pilgrim to Mecca, had twice been in India and Istanbul.

Outside the village we crossed a few frozen canals and a stream fifty yards wide, where one or two carts had to try the ford first. The passage was successful; none of our five cars stuck. West of the stream hard *gobi* began, alternating with soft yellow loess in blocks, terraces and furrows. One of these was so deep-cut and so narrow that our lorries had difficulty in worming their way through.

Pei-yang-k'ou is a village with gardens and canals. The southern desert road to Turfan, which was more level than that which we were following, but too sandy and soft for loaded lorries, breaks off here to south-west and west.

At San-p'u (the "Third Fortress"), called by the Turkis Toghochi, were living fifteen families, who had started ploughing and sowing. The village consisted mainly of heaps of ruins, but a three-storeyed pagoda still towered over the scene of desolation. At the village of Liu-shu-ch'uan, or "Willow Spring", our wheels cut through the too thin frozen surface on the edge of a canal, and it took an hour to get out again. While waiting we shared out a couple of melons which we had got from the people at Astana.

A few light-grey wolves were roaming about off the road. War-time is good for wolves. Jomcha cut right through a rotten bridge with his back wheel, and caused delay. Now the country was scrub-covered steppe, now *gobi*. From time to time we saw a few antelopes. A caravanserai had been levelled to the ground, and the site of a few small villages was marked only by heaps of clay. A watch-tower stood there as a memorial of past ages.

42

We drove into the village of Liao-tun, where we had slept a night in February, 1928. Its clay houses were in ruins, but the caravanserai was still standing, though in a tumble-down state. We went into its untidy yard. Three dogs, one horse, one goat, one cock and two sheep seemed to be the entire population of Liao-tun. We entered the wretched dark hovels which flanked the yard. In one of them was a rifle and a telephone wire hooked on to the telegraph wire. The place must be a military post. But the village was empty and abandoned.

We waited in the yard for an age. The sun set; it grew dark, and the shades of night began to play their silent tricks. The door-openings into the hovels in the yard gaped black—the doors had been used for firewood. The darker it grew the more ghostly the place became. While it was still light we had looked into one or two of the hovels and found them empty, dusty and dirty. But there were a number of them, and a robber band might have made them its lair.

After a time a solitary soldier came into the yard. He had on a shabby grey uniform and shoes which had once been white, but no cap. He took our arrival calmly and thanked us politely for a cigarette. He told us that the Liao-tun post usually consisted of four men, but that three had been detached for duty elsewhere. The solitary soldier had his home in Anhuei, had served in Honan under Feng Yu-hsiang, the "Christian general", and had then gone to Kanchow and been enrolled in Ma Chung-yin's army in July, 1933.

According to his own story he was designated *fu-kuan*, or adjutant. He had been promised 390 liang a month pay, but had not got a cent so far, only his rations.

He also told us that the two hundred Turki bandits, previously mentioned, had carried out a raid on Erh-p'u about ten days before. Then Ma Chung-yin's troops had come, and some of the cavalry had been quartered in the Liao-tun caravanserai. The inhabitants fled, leaving some of their domestic animals, which the soldier was taking care of. But now he must go to his hovel and be ready

43

to answer the telephone. The poor solitary fellow made a mournful impression.

The stoves and two lamps were burning in the tent which Hummel, Bergman and I shared when San Wa-tse woke us at six on the morning of February 14. It was absolutely pitch-dark outside. But before the porridge and coffee were ready the eastern horizon began to brighten, and at 7.30 it was light. The whole sky was clouded over except just above the horizon, where a warm rose-red tinted the lower edges of the clouds and higher up gradually changed to opal and violet. The ruddy glow became fiercer and more splendid just before the sun rose in an iridescent sky—a marvellous, mighty, awe-inspiring spectacle.

The temperature had only fallen to 27 degrees, despite the fact that since leaving Hami we had climbed to a height of 3600 ft.

Little Colonel Ma Ying-piao came to my tent, saluted, and clicked his heels in military fashion. He told me that he had been with General Ma Chung-yin two years before when Liao-tun was captured, and his view was that Chin Shu-jen had devastated the whole country to make its invasion more difficult for General Ma. The trees had been cut down by the fugitives themselves because they needed fuel. Speaking of our escort, he told me that an elderly man, who was always pleasant and cheery, had been a commissioner of taxes, another foreman in an ammunition factory, and a third in charge of the provision of furs for winter uniforms for Ma's army.

The convoy started at eight o'clock. To southward the desert kept its watch, a long basin in various shades of red, with stripes which were undulations or terraces. The road led up into a valley between red hills. A narrow gateway in the mountains led to an equally narrow corridor with belts of ice along the bottom. Here we passed a covered cart, in which a merchant's family was driving to Turfan.

On both sides rose low mountains, some snow-clad. Then we drove out from among the mountains on to a gravel plain of no great extent. Close to I-wan-ch'uan, or "One Cup Spring", stood

44

TSO TSUNG-TANG, GOVERNOR-GENERAL OF SHENSI AND KANSU, WHO
RECONQUERED SINKIANG IN 1876–78

MARSHAL YANG TSENG-SIN AT THE AGE OF SIXTY-ONE, A FEW
MONTHS BEFORE HE WAS MURDERED

TUNGAN SOLDIERS IN WINTER UNIFORM

Photo by Yew

Photo by Norin

CHIN SHU-JEN, GOVERNOR-GENERAL OF SINKIANG (1928–33), WHOSE MISGOVERNMENT CAUSED THE REBELLIONS AND CIVIL WAR (1931–1934). IN THE LOWER LEFT-HAND CORNER MAY BE SEEN TWO LARGE BLOCKS OF JADE STONE FROM KHOTAN—A SYMBOL OF HIS AVARICE

SIN CHIN GEGEN KHAN, PRINCE AND "LIVING BUDDHA" OF THE
TORGUTS. HE PRESENTED A TEMPLE *YURT* TO KING GUSTAF
OF SWEDEN IN 1928. MURDERED AT URUMCHI IN 1932 BY THE
GOVERNOR-GENERAL CHIN

DEVASTATED HAMI, SEEN FROM THE TOP OF THE PALACE

Photo by Bergman

OUTSIDE THE COMMANDANT'S *YAMEN* AT HAMI. FROM LEFT TO RIGHT: EFFE, CHEN, HUMMEL, YEW, KUNG, THE AUTHOR, COMMANDANT CHANG FENG-MING; FARTHEST TO THE RIGHT GEORG AND BERGMAN

RUINED PALACE OF THE LAST KING OF HAMI

ALTUNLUK–MAZAR AT HAMI

Photo by Bergman

AT HAMI. IN THE CENTRE YAKUB BEG, YOLLBARS KHAN'S SECOND SON

Photo by Bergman

TOMBS OF SHAH MAKSUD AND HIS KINSMEN AT HAMI

HALL OF PRAYER IN THE GREAT MOSQUE NEAR THE ROYAL TOMBS
AT HAMI

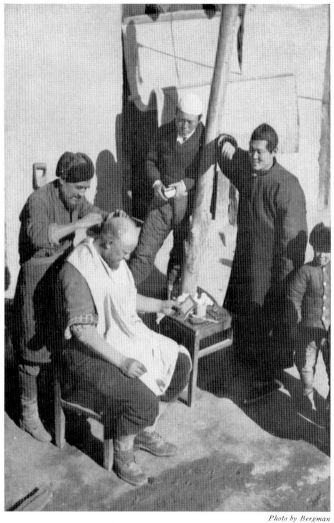

Photo by Bergman

GEORG IN THE BARBER'S SHOP AT HAMI. IN THE DOORWAY IS SAN
WA-TSE, IN FRONT OF HIM MR. YU

Photo by Hummel

BURIAL-GROUND NEAR THE VILLAGE OF ERH-P'U (ASTANA)

Photo by Hummel

OUR CARS PASSING A RESTING CARAVAN NEAR CHEH-KOU-LOU-CH'UAN, IN THE TIEN-SHAN MOUNTAINS

Photo by Hummel

WE PASSED ON THE ROAD, IN CLOUDS OF DUST, HUNDREDS OF YOUNG TURKIS CALLED UP FOR SERVICE
IN MA CHUNG-YIN'S ARMY

five *paotais*, small truncated pyramid-shaped signs—"milestones" we called them. Here there were a large number of caves excavated in a conglomerate terrace. No one was visible, but smoke was still rising from several fires both in and outside the caves. The remains of meals showed that three sheep had lately been slaughtered and eaten by these fires. It seemed likely that a party of soldiers had spent the previous night there. It was probably part of the force Ma had sent out to scatter the robber band from Kucha.

After an hour's wait the four lorries came snorting up, and the convoy proceeded. To the south the horizon seemed to be at an enormous distance; it was impossible to say where the earth ended and the misty cloud-banks began.

Again we drove in between mountains. The telegraph wires lay on the ground across the road. We went up hill and down dale, pretty steep at times. A chaos of black, red and brown ridges. A board marked the boundary between the administrative areas of Hami and Shan-shan or Pichan. Camels' skeletons were a fairly common sight.

At Cheh-kou-lou ("Cart-wheel") we passed a caravan of twenty-five Turkis driving 230 donkeys. They were bound for Turfan; they reckoned it would take them another seven days, and they had been walking from Hami for five days.

The few houses of the place were in ruins, among which a Chinese cotton caravan was resting. Here the altimeter showed 4160 ft. The road descended again, and the valley widened into a plain in the heart of the Tien-shan.

Here we drove right into a party of young Turkis on foot, the same who had left Hami a few days before. They, like the donkeys I have just spoken of, were on their way to General Ma's army to be slaughtered in the war. They carried red and blue Kuomintang flags and had donkeys, horses, camels and carts for the transport of their kit and provisions. Their leader, Nias Beg, Yollbars Khan's eldest son, came up to my car and asked for a lift. He was given a seat on Jomcha's lorry.

45

It was sad and touching to see the young men who were to be sacrificed to Big Horse's ambition with a *morituri te salutant*. They desired only peace, but the country's peace had been disturbed by the heartless opium-smoker Chin Shu-jen. No wonder their women had wept when they left Hami. Later on we heard a rumour that the northern army from Urumchi, pursuing the fleeing Ma, had come upon the party from Hami and killed every man of it; but according to other accounts this rumour was not true.

We stopped for a while to look at these youths as they marched singing Mohammedan songs under the Chinese banners. They stirred up clouds of dust, through which we had glimpses of their ragged, gaily coloured costumes. They carried no arms; these they would receive from Ma's arsenal at Turfan.

We were now 3190 ft. up. At one o'clock we reached Chi-ko-ching-tse (the "Heptagonal Well"). The few houses were surrounded by a high, newly built wall and had two gates in good repair. There was quite a strong military post there, for at this point the road forks and branches run off to Kuchengtse and Pichan.

A sad memory is attached to Chi-ko-ching-tse and its parting of the ways. We had heard already in Peking of the able young German Hanneken, son of the general who served on the Chinese side in the Sino-Japanese war of 1894. He had travelled to Hami along the Imperial Highway with the object of going to Urumchi to investigate trading prospects. His caravan was quite small. He had reached Chi-ko-ching-tse in September, 1933, and continued his journey along the high road towards Pichan. But the caravan had not got far along this road when Hanneken's servants from Lanchow advised him not to go on that way, but rather to take the road from Chi-ko-ching-tse through the mountains to Kuchengtse. Hanneken followed their advice and started off through the valley along the road to the last-named town. But he never arrived, and not a word about his fate has ever been heard.

When I describe our stay at Urumchi I shall return to this deeply moving tragedy.

A Chinese temple and a pagoda stand outside the village. Dead horses and rags marked the scene of recent fighting. The commander of our escort, Ma, told us that the Kirghizes in the neighbouring mountains had not long ago attacked the village, murdered people and looted houses. He warned us, and advised that the escort should be reinforced. Commandant Chang at Hami, when we started, had spoken of the insecurity in this region and assured us that he would telephone to the commander of the garrison about our arrival and the measures of precaution which ought to be taken. The escort commander considered it necessary to place two extra soldiers on each lorry, who were to accompany us for ten miles, or to the end of the danger zone. As the commander of the escort, according to all we had heard, was a notorious scoundrel, we wondered if he needed eight more men to stage an attack on us and get possession of the convoy. We took with us only one extra man on each lorry.

When we had reached Tung-yen-tse, or "Eastern Salt Lake", we stopped for a short rest and dropped the superfluous Tungan soldiers. We were driving right into the mountains, with a high mass of rock on our left. From time to time we passed riders and ox-carts. The road in the narrow valley, where the Hui-ching-tse spring lies, was not bad. The sun was hidden by the higher peaks, but lit up the eastern side-valleys gloriously.

It was five o'clock when we reached the head of the pass, at a height of 5300 ft. On the western side of the pass the road ran straight down towards the sun. The slope was fairly steep. The valley grew wider. At the western end of the lake Hsi-yen-tse ("Western Salt Lake") lies a village; Ma had ordered four fresh soldiers to meet us there and help us on our way to Turfan. They had been waiting for us there for three days.

The sun was setting and twilight was gathering. We emerged from the Tien-shan mountains, and drove in pitch darkness over plains of grass and reeds with a soft dusty soil. Here we met a few carts drawn by oxen and horses, twenty donkeys and a camel caravan, four strings of beasts, carrying bales of cotton to Hami;

thence they were to be taken on across the desert to Kwei-hwa.

We had covered ninety-five miles, pretty good going for Asiatic roads, when at a quarter past ten we reached the village of Chiktam, our camp No. 37, 1300 ft. above the sea.

Only 31 degrees of frost on the night of February 14. We were getting near spring in the Turfan basin. As soon as we were awakened the camp was surrounded by a crowd of spectators— and no wonder they were curious! A whole convoy of motors with five Europeans and a dozen Chinese and Mongols! There, in that country over which in recent years only troops, recruits and fugitives had roamed! In Chiktam abnormal conditions prevailed, in that the village, which formerly was inhabited by only twelve families, now had a hundred. But most of them were refugees from Kuchengtse. Among them we saw Turkis with a square white patch of cloth sewn to the left side of the breast. This was said to mean that they were called up for military service.

Just outside the village we had to cross a canal by a doubtful bridge. Serat was ahead. The right plank lengthways cracked with a horrible rending noise, and the heavily loaded lorry heeled far over. We waited with our hearts in our mouths to see the clumsy hulking thing overturn and finish up in the canal, wheels uppermost. But Serat stepped on the gas and got across safe and sound. Then the bridge was repaired. It took time, but the convoy was saved.

The village of Bir-bulak ("One Spring")—in Chinese Ying-tsui-shu ("Eaglebeak Tree")—still had a few groves of trees standing and alive, was inhabited by four families, and lies among low bare hills. Here too we were checked by a dangerous bridge, but got over safely.

The next village was called Tatze. It was uninhabited. All along the road the convoy was invisible amid impenetrable clouds of dust. The small car went ahead, so that its passengers did not get so much dust into their lungs as those behind. Close to the village of Tokuz-kares ("Nine Canals") a watch-tower called Kargha-tura ("Crows' Tower") rises from a terrace. To the south-west a belt of sand dunes stood out in the landscape. We met creaking ox-carts, mounted soldiers, and now and then a refugee coming home to see how much was left of his farm.

We nearly stuck in a horrible deep canal. The next bridge was altogether too dangerous, and we thought it better to make a long detour north of Pichan.

We made our entry into the little town with incredible windings and convolutions like figures of eight, between ancient, still intact trees. We came into a fearful street with so deep a gutter in the middle that the cars all but overturned. We drove into the bazaar just after two and stopped outside a good-sized house, where we were received by Commandant Ho, senior adjutant in Ma's service. He was young, tall and good-looking, and was polite and attentive. He told me that he had read the Chinese translation of my book *Back to Asia*.[1] He was, in fact, not an understrapper of the usual illiterate type.

The commandant invited us into a fair-sized room, where tea, pea-nuts and sweets were served on two round tables. One was for the leaders, the other for our drivers and servants. Dinner followed, large pieces of boiled mutton and rice pudding.

At Pichan five of our soldiers were to be left behind. We wanted to tip them, but Ho explained that Ma had forbidden them to accept presents. We were his guests, and our visit to the country he occupied must not cost us anything. Ho, and the dignitaries of Pichan who surrounded him, begged us to stay the night. His hospitality was quite touching; he tried, indeed, an original method of persuasion, saying, "If you stay I will let you tip my servants".

But we were immovable, and after an hour and a half of feasting, Chinese brandy, jokes and merriment, we said good-bye and went out to the cars. The bazaar outside was packed with people, the great majority Tungans. They stood row upon row, and their gaily clad women and children had assembled in every door and

[1] Dr. Hedin's book, *Åter till Asien* (*Back to Asia*), has not been published in English. It has appeared in German under the title *Auf grosser Fahrt*.

alley. For long stretches the streets were under water from canals in flood.

Outside the little town we drove up a steep terrace some sixty feet high. We rested on its summit for a moment to look out over the oasis, which lay in a pronounced hollow, and the wide spaces of yellowish-grey desert round it. To southward the jagged out-line of a high belt of dunes called Kum-tagh, or "the Sand Mountain", stood out sharply. On its lee side it fell steeply to the east. A watch-tower was visible in the middle of the belt of sand.

The others had been left behind again; only Serat was ahead of us. We stopped with him outside a cave in a terrace and waited. After a flaming red sunset the moon's shining silvery crescent rose and watched roofless, homeless wanderers coming and going. At last Jomcha appeared with his lorry and reported that Georg had no water in his radiator. We therefore sought for a brook, filled an empty petrol tin, and returned to Georg, to rejoin the others later at the cave.

We drove in the dark through villages and groves of trees, over dangerous bridges and treacherous watercourses, and finally pitched our camp outside the large village of Lamjin, 550 ft. high and inhabited by three hundred families, four Chinese, twenty-five Tungan and the rest Turki.

On the morning of the 16th we had a charming view from the village burial-ground, situated on a hill, towards a ravine to the south-west and all the country round about. On a terrace stood a time-worn old watch-tower. The day was brilliant, the sky turquoise-blue. Our road led west-north-west. A ramshackle bridge was repaired before we entrusted ourselves to its rotten timbers.

On the road to Turfan lay three inns, right on the caravan route, with open doors and poplar groves which had been spared by the pillaging hordes. To the left were the hills through which runs the road to the ruined city of Kara Khodjo. The lower parts of the hills are curiously eroded, which gives them a markedly sculptured appearance.

Long rows of earth-rings marked the course of the great underground canals, or *kares*. One of them has given its name to the village of Emir-kares. In the village of Su-bashi barley, maize, wheat, melons and cotton were being grown.

Fifty families lived in Su-bashi. Young girls in blue and red followed us with wondering looks, and poor, but very pretty young mothers carried their little children in their arms. A few Lombardy poplars grew along the roadside.

One of the lorries, in trying to avoid the water-softened gutter in the middle of the road, listed so heavily that some of the luggage slipped off, including Chen's instrument-case. A thermometer and the glass of two chronometers were smashed. The wheels sank into the mud above their axles, and the lorry had to be unloaded. Spades, planks, matting and jacks were at work once more, and the wind whispered its well-worn counsel: "Patience, patience!"

Carts and mounted men grew more and more numerous—we could see that we were approaching a town of some size. We left the village of Sängim to our right and descended through the valley of the same name. There a brook flowed between white strips of ice. Lower down it ran between perpendicular walls of loose scree, like a cañon. According to the altimeters we were now on sea-level and were crossing the boundary of the deepest dry basin in the world—the deepest place, south-west of the village of Lukchun, is about 650 ft. below sea-level.

In the village we overtook and passed twelve carts laden with wheat for General Ma's soldiers. It was never paid for, only requisitioned.

The road grew narrower on the left summit of the cañon, and we had the steep drop with the stream at the bottom on our right. Horrible wheel-tracks, an unpleasantly swaying bridge over a side-valley! The right wheel-track often went disquietingly near the sharp-cut edge, and we wondered whether the crumbling loess cliff would collapse under the three tons weight of a motor-lorry.

We rested and waited again far down the valley, near the village of Sängim-aghis. Two of the lorries came rolling along that break-neck road, like a shelf over the abyss. But the two others could be seen high up the valley. It appeared that they had been held up by three Turki boys, who had started from a village close to Kara Khodjo, tried to take a short cut over the mountains, and wriggled their way down steep descents till they got to a ledge with a perpendicular drop down to the left-hand side of the Sän-gim valley. One of the boys had been careless, lost his foothold and fallen, a hundred feet it must have been; and now he lay moaning at the bottom of the mountain. Hummel, who luckily was on one of the two lorries, attended to the boy, bandaged his fractured lower jaw and other injuries, and took him to a house where he could be kept quiet and looked after. The other two held on like grim death to the narrow ledge they had reached. They had the precipice before them, and behind them the steep mountain-face which seemed to offer no possibility of retreat.

While we were waiting for Hummel and the two lorries, a young officer came up to us and asked us to have tea with him. His name was Ma Teng-yuan, and he was commandant of the military post at Sängim-aghis. He took us to his quarters, a pitch-dark subterranean hole down to which a precipitous flight of steps led. In Turfan and the surrounding country people have holes, or rooms below the surface of the ground, as a protection against the stifling heat of the summer—and Ma Teng-yuen was quartered in one of these holes.

When Hummel arrived, and we heard of the three boys' mis-adventure, we begged our host to send out men to rescue the shipwrecked ones. He solemnly promised to look after them, but whether he actually did we could never find out.

WITH BIG HORSE'S CHIEF OF STAFF AND THE TIGER PRINCE

WHEN we reascended from the military post's underground lair, approaching night had already plunged the earth in darkness.

Ten li, or two and a half miles, from Turfan we were met by three distinguished persons who stopped and welcomed us. They were our old friend from 1928, Yollbars Khan (the "Tiger Prince"), General Li Hai-jo, chief of staff to General Ma, and Mr. Pai, General Ma's representative in Peking, whose acquaintance we had made in the autumn in the old Imperial city. I invited Yollbars to take a seat in the small car; the two others had to ride back on their own horses.

It was nearly nine when we reached Kona-shahr ("the Old Town"), where the Turkis live. Our entrance into ancient Turfan was "something to write home about". It might have been a scene out of a story of adventure.

Rumbling and rattling, the convoy of heavy "elephants" swayed in the wake of the small car into the main street of the bazaar, pitch-dark and resembling a railway tunnel. Just here and there an oil lamp or Chinese paper lantern was still burning, and at a few still open stalls stood belated Turki loafers, caravan guides, tramps and homeless boys, gazing at our nocturnal procession. Sentries and policemen looked at us questioningly, but Yollbars calmed them. He gave our driver directions where to go; he had already had a house prepared for us. We stopped at its door and entered. A large room was placed at our disposal and furnished with the boxes we required for daily use. We had also a smaller room and a kitchen. A Chinese dinner was laid in the big room.

The conversation was long and animated. Yollbars asked:

"Can I borrow two of your lorries for a few days? General Ma needs them."

"No, not on any account," I answered decidedly.

"At any rate you can lend me fifty gallons of petrol for the only car we have. We have not enough petrol."

"Nor have we," I replied. "We must carry out our task in the service of the Nanking government, and need every drop ourselves."

"I'm only asking for a loan. There are stores of petrol at Kara-shahr and Kucha, and you can get back there what you have lent me."

"Chang Feng-ming borrowed sixty gallons from us at Hami and promised that the same quantity should be handed back to us directly we got to Turfan. Here is the receipt, in his own writing. Chang promised to telephone to you, as well. Has he done so?"

"We had some petrol for you, but as Chang did not telephone again about it, we sent it to General Ma's headquarters at Dawan-cheng."

"As I can't rely on Chang's word or on his receipt, I have no guarantee that you will keep your word. The people at Kara-shahr or Kucha may reply that the quantity we need has just been sent somewhere else."

"If I make a promise I keep it," said Yollbars. "It isn't pleasant to ask such a thing of a guest, but Ma is sending Mr. Pai and fifteen others to Kara-shahr, Kucha, Aksu and Kashgar to-morrow morning in our lorry. They are to urge these towns to take our side. It is a mission of the very greatest importance, and so I *beg* you to help us in this way."

"I'll telegraph to Kara-shahr and Kucha first, and ask if there's any petrol there," I said.

"The telegraph line is out of order. Please let me know if you can lend me a smaller quantity at any rate."

Georg was consulted, and we decided to offer Yollbars twenty gallons. He thanked me, and asked if he might fetch the petrol next morning. We were running the risk of being robbed of our entire store of motor fuel. But we were in their hands, and they could wring our necks if we were quite unyielding. It was clear from the way in which Yollbars talked that Ma's position was weak, and that a great deal hung on his sending this message to the towns on the Tien-shan-nan-lu (the road south of the Tien-shan).

Yollbars told us that enemy aeroplanes had dropped small bombs and masses of proclamations on Turfan that day and the day before. The latter, which were signed by the military governor at Urum-chi, Sheng Shih-tsai, contained a threat that if the inhabitants of the town continued their resistance he would soon send ten large aeroplanes to Turfan.

As bombing planes might be expected on the following day as well, Yollbars thought it inadvisable to let our cars stand out in the open and attract bombs. He proposed a house with a covered passage, where they would be in safety. The airmen from Urum-chi had come at twelve o'clock on the two first days, and would probably appear the following noon as well.

On the morning of February 17 the four lorries were taken to the house which Yollbars had suggested. A sheltered spot in our yard was found for the small car. In the afternoon Hummel and I went to Georg's house and found the cars in a passage with a vaulted roof, which might have been made for them.

Two mysterious Russian-speaking Poles had been living in that house for four months—a so-called doctor of medicine called Leszczynski and his assistant, Plavski by name. According to their own story they had taken part a year earlier in a scientific expedition which had started from Tonkin and set its course through Yunnan for Tibet. For some unknown reason they had left the expedition and journeyed on foot, with their baggage on horses, to Kumbum, Sining, Lanchow, Suchow, Anhsi and Hami, and so to Turfan.

Leszczynski said he was acting as a kind of medical officer under General Ma. He expressed his views on the military position without the least reserve. He had quite lately been at headquarters at Dawancheng, and had seen with his own eyes how things were. Guns with no ammunition, soldiers like rag-bags, insufficient food. Aeroplanes from Urumchi had flown low over the general's camp at the Dawancheng pass and had caused great confusion among the troops, which had scattered and some of them fled in all directions. He maintained that the Tungan general's invading army was scarcely more than a thousand strong and was already in flight to Toksun and Kara-shahr. He advised us most strongly not to travel in that direction. We should find ourselves among wild, undisciplined soldiers, who were nothing but robbers, and would without hesitation take our lorries and our belongings and probably shoot us. War was raging in the Korla district too.

"Don't go to Kara-shahr or along the road to Kashgar," he cried. "There is war everywhere, the roads are hellish, you'll never come back alive."

And yet he begged Hummel to persuade me to let him come with us to Kara-shahr and Kashgar! I suppose he had nothing to lose.

When we visited the Poles three young Soviet Russians were with them. They and some thirty other Russians had driven to Manas with war material in ten lorries, and continued along the road to Urumchi. But about seven miles from the capital the convoy had been attacked by a Tungan cavalry squadron; a few of the Russians had fled, several had been beheaded. Four Russian heads were at the moment hung up in small wooden cages at the gates of Turfan. These three men had been taken prisoners and brought to Turfan.

The three young Bolsheviks had been drivers in the captured convoy. They were fair-haired, healthy and sunburned, courteous and pleasant, and described their adventures quietly and coolly. But they were in the greatest anxiety as to their fate, and asked what in my opinion awaited them. I tried to calm them, arguing that if Ma had intended to do them any injury he would have carried out his intention long before.

As soon as I met the chief of staff, General Li, I expressed the hope that the three youths' lives would be spared, as they had done no harm, but only obeyed their officers' orders. Li replied:

"General Ma's principle is to have all Russians who fall into his hands shot at once. The fact that these three drivers have been brought from Urumchi to Turfan, and are still alive a month after they were taken prisoners, is the best proof that Ma does not mean to have them shot."

A month later to the day I heard that the three drivers had fallen to Tungan bullets when the garrison of Turfan evacuated the town.

Several of us drove round and called on the important people in Turfan—the chief of staff, General Li Hai-jo; Yollbars Khan; the grandson of the former King of Hami, who was commandant of the town, and his chief of staff, Chang Sin-ming, who also commanded the training corps. Only Yollbars was at home, and at his house we met the mayor of Turfan, a dignified old man with a white beard and turban.

Pai, Ma's representative in Peking, was a Tartar. He had started with Turfan's one and only motor-lorry, our twenty gallons of petrol and fifteen other emissaries to the towns on the Tien-shan-nan-lu. We wondered how far they would get before the car broke down or the petrol ran out.

Then all the potentates came to return our calls, and we spent an eternity drinking tea, smoking cigarettes and talking rubbish. General Li, whom some of our party had known in the days when he was governor at Chuguchak, was cheery and lively, but did not hesitate to admit that the position was serious. He doubtless understood that we ourselves had not failed to notice this. He had been on Sheng Shih-tsai's side at the beginning of the war, but had been taken prisoner by Ma Chung-yin, who had appointed him his chief of staff. He had neither power nor influence.

Li assured us that we might start off westward whenever we liked, but that he, who as Ma's representative was responsible for our security, must get news of the situation on the road to Kara-shahr before he could let us go. This road had been anything but safe till now.

Chang Sin-ming declared that we could not and need not go to Dawancheng and wait upon General Ma, "because the road is so bad and the pass is dangerous". General Ma would probably not come to Turfan while we were there, although he wished to meet us. But his time was so very fully occupied, and he had been in Turfan for the Chinese New Year a few days before.

The prospects for our journey into the interior of Sinkiang seemed more than dark. The curious thing was that Ma's representatives at Turfan not only put no obstacles in the way of our journey to Kara-shahr, but actually encouraged it, and obviously intended to take the necessary measures to safeguard our journey.

Hummel was summoned to the commander of Ma's cavalry, who was a particularly close friend of the commander-in-chief. The cavalry general had been wounded in the leg by a splinter of bomb and barbarously tended by the Polish "doctor" and a Chinese medical man. Now he came into expert hands.

Turfan made a sinister impression. With a few exceptions the bazaar shops were shut, barred and bolted. Trade was paralysed, the springs of life had run dry. There was practically no movement in the streets. There was a feeling in the air that something was going to happen. The unhappy citizens of Turfan, who like all Mohammedans had wanted to get rid of Chin Shu-jen, had got a permanent war instead of the peace they longed for.

We took everyone's advice about our position. Of course it was serious, though Yollbars cheered us up with melons, apples and raisins. We took events as they came—with philosophic calm; and it was cheering to see the unruffled coolness of our Chinese, Chen, Yew and Kung. I am convinced that they never dreamed, any more than we Swedes, of a retreat to the Sabbath peace of the Gobi desert. In any case, this would have been absolutely impossible in our present position, and if we had asked permission it would have been politely but firmly refused. We were in reality prisoners, with a certain strictly controlled freedom of movement.

The only thing we could do was to play our cards as well as possible.

We were told that when the Tungan general first captured Turfan, the mayor of the place had taken seventy-five Chinese families and fled along the road to Urumchi. The band of fugitives had not got far when it was overtaken by Tungan patrols. The commander had reproached the mayor, and asked him if he did not see what harm he was doing to the invading army by running away just when it was entering the town. Then he had shot the unfortunate man and had the seventy-five families killed, men, women and children. Not one of them escaped.

February 18. 30 degrees the night before. We had visitors all day. General Li was unwearying in his attentions, and said that he had orders from the commander-in-chief to place himself entirely at our disposal and fulfil all our wishes. The commander of the training corps, Colonel Chang Sin-ming, was a particularly amiable and pleasant man, and most attractive to look at. He was our officer in attendance or adjutant.

The town was full of rumours. It was said that General Ma meant to stay at Dawancheng for another three weeks and scatter his army among the mountains to protect it against aeroplane bombs. He was anxious to get into touch with the Soviet Consul at Chuguchak, and it was believed that he intended to send Kemal Kaya Effendi to Moscow with one of the two aeroplanes captured outside Urumchi. But Kemal did not like air travel, so the plan came to nothing. This Kemal was a Turkish officer from Istanbul who had for several years been Ma Chung-yin's military adviser in Kansu. Some of the members of our previous expedition had met him there, especially Bohlin, Bexell and Bökenkamp.

It was said that twenty per cent of Ma's army were down with some epidemic, and that the number of wounded was very large. Three of his best generals were said to be incapacitated by wounds.

We heard that Ma Chung-yin himself was recklessly brave and had a boundless contempt for death. He was always in the front line under fire, and exposed himself to aeroplane bombs with contemptuous defiance. His character was complex and puzzling. He could be childlike, naïve, helpful and sympathetic, but he could also display barbarous cruelty and kill the whole population of places he captured. If he was annoyed, he could shoot down with his own pistol an officer or soldier who had committed some error. He was said to have treated his own cook thus when dinner was not ready one day at the appointed time. He was incautiously frank and would tell anyone who cared to listen about his plans. But no one but himself knew what he really meant to do.

The chief of staff Li, General Ma's deputy at Turfan, seemed to have plenty of time to spare, for he would sit with us talking for hours. It was curious that neither Ma nor Li showed any mistrust of us. We had absolute freedom of movement. We were never allowed to pay for anything; everything was placed at our disposal, which was painful to us when the goods were certainly simply requisitioned from the poor, sucked-dry population.

Yollbars Khan told us about Hodja Nias Hadji, a Turki from Hami, who during the first stage of the war had been his adherent, but later had left him, stirred up the Turkis against Ma in the towns between Hami and Uch-Turfan, and gone over to Sheng Shih-tsai at Urumchi.

At 2 P.M. on February 19 the temperature was 54 degrees, real spring weather; 129 degrees had been recorded in Turfan the summer before. At that time of year—as I mentioned above—everyone lives in underground rooms just as in Baghdad and Mosul.

Our large room had been decorated with Chinese and Swedish flags, and the Swedish colours flew on a flagstaff in the courtyard. On one end wall of the room stood the words "Lyckliga år",[1] and a charming message of good wishes in Chinese character. When I came down in the morning, all our fellows—scientists, engineers, drivers and servants—greeted me with hurrahs, speeches, and a march played on our gramophone. The fact that it was my birthday had leaked out, so I was congratulated by Chinese,

[1] In Swedish, "Happy years".

Tungans, Turkis and Poles as well. The military commanders wanted to get up a big dinner, but we had already invited them to a simple meal. The resulting arrangement was a very trying one. Ma's officers, including the head of the commissariat at Turfan, Yollbars Khan, were to entertain us to dinner at four, and we them at seven.

Yollbars' manner of congratulating me was very unusual. He asked Yew to let him examine all our luggage, and remarked that Kashgar was not mentioned on our Nanking passports.

"I am surprised", I told him, "that we, who are emissaries of the central government, are treated by you as suspects. We have been here three days, and just as we are ready to start, you ask us to open all the boxes which are lashed on to our lorries. As for Kashgar, it is called by its Chinese name, Su-lei, on our passports."

"I have had orders once for all from General Ma", replied Yollbars, "to examine all baggage and all goods which pass through Turfan, and I must do my duty. It was not done before because I didn't see your passports till yesterday. As for Kashgar, I apologise for my mistake."

At my suggestion he began with the boxes which were in our rooms. Then he went, accompanied by Chen and Kung, to the house where Georg and Effe were quartered, with the lorries in the vaulted passage. Georg was warned in time, and put the boxes belonging to the wireless apparatus under a tent carelessly dropped in the middle of the passage.

Two hours later Chen and Kung came back and reported that the big heavy boxes had been opened. Those which contained ammunition and instruments specially excited Yollbars' interest. The former were compared with our arms permits and found in perfect order. He did not discover the wireless apparatus, although he nearly tripped over it.

Another of the eccentric, mysterious wanderers we met in Turfan was a little black-bearded professor Li, who had started from Peking with four students in June, 1933, and walked all the way to Hami; they had arrived there in October and come on to Turfan, which they reached in December. Li and his party of young men called on us too, and told us that they intended to stay in Sinkiang for five years at the most, to study the local languages and literature. Literature in Sinkiang! they would not need five years for that.

At four o'clock our hosts arrived. The Poles and Professor Li were invited too. It was a real big dinner, some thirty dishes with hot Chinese brandy in little cups. Various drinking games were played, the object of which is to make people drink. The entertainment was not over till eight; then there was an interval during which the table was laid afresh.

Just then Kemal Kaya Effendi came to see us. He talked excellent French. The conversation turned mainly upon my travels in his native country Turkey, to which he longed to return. He had had enough of Kansu and Sinkiang, and wanted to go home. He was now at Turfan on a special mission for General Ma, and was to return to him next day.

Kemal also was invited to stay for our dinner, which consisted of European dishes. Pretty speeches were made by Hummel, Yew and Professor Li. The last-named having expressed a wish to be accommodated on our lorries with his students on the journey westward, I explained, in returning thanks, that as an official mission from the central government we were not entitled to take any passengers other than the escort which the military authorities thought necessary for our safety.

General Li told Yew that the lorry containing Pai and the fifteen emissaries had been ordered to await our arrival at Toksun, because the road had been rendered unsafe by Kirghiz and Mongol robbers, and it was better for both parties if we kept together. The sooner we started, therefore, the better. We suspected that in reality the emissaries' lorry had broken down or needed petrol from our drums. This suspicion was shown later to be unjustified, for when we reached Toksun they had already left that town, and we did not overtake them before Kucha, to which place their mission was directed.

Kemal expressed the opinion that in two months we should be back at Turfan with General Ma, but this prophecy was not correct.

On the morning of February 20 Yollbars sent us a message that we could not leave Turfan for three days, because the road to Toksun was harassed by Kirghiz robbers, who had killed two merchants and carried away a number of camels, horses and cattle. Orders had been given that military patrols should clear the road for us, and we could not start until this had been done.

The Poles had tried to persuade Yew and me to take them to Kashgar; they were bound for that place, and the British consul-general there was keeping their mail from home. When we turned a deaf ear to their entreaties they applied to Kemal, and he, who was returning to General Ma on the 20th, wrote me a very polite letter in which he assured me that General Ma would be particularly grateful if I would take the two Poles in our cars. I replied "no" equally politely. Our apparently disobliging and hard-hearted behaviour towards people who asked us for lifts was shown later to have been justified and wise. Professor Li was later on arrested at Urumchi and one of his students was shot. When we met Plavski on a later occasion, at the beginning of June, he told me that Leszczynski had been executed. He himself was arrested a few days after his arrival at Urumchi. To have been in any kind of intimate relationship with people who were suspects, justly or unjustly, might have had serious consequences for us too. Happily, the report of Leszczynski's execution proved later to have been considerably exaggerated. I heard quite recently that he was present at General Ma's entry into Kashgar.

We had a telephone message from General Ma asking us for a few rolls of film, and desiring that we should photograph his arsenal at Turfan.

Bergman and I were taken in Shah Maksud's old carriage and drove through Kona-shahr. A few shops and booths were open outside the east gate of the town, and a number of people were going about there among camels, horses and carts. Several streets were under water, for no one was regulating the flooding of the irrigation canals. No demolished houses were to be seen at all. Turfan had been spared; its people had evidently not joined the first rebellion at Hami.

We drove in through the west gate of Yangi-shahr, the Chinese town, and once inside it was not far to the artillery depot. In front of the main building eighteen old field-guns and fourteen machine-guns were drawn up to be photographed. Bergman took half a dozen photographs. In a large hall were two thousand worn rusty rifles set up in bundles and pairs, German, French and American; some dated from 1866, but most would have been in their proper place in an artillery museum. There were no new models. Chang Sin-ming, who was with us, told us that quite as many rifles were distributed among the armourers of the town for repair. Fancy making war with rubbish like that! Chang thought that Ma had twenty-seven thousand rifles and sixty machine-guns along the route from Hami to Kashgar.

General Li insisted that all the negatives we had taken should be handed over to him after they had been developed, and that we must not keep one single copy. Of course we obeyed this order, especially seeing that this absurdly defective arsenal did not interest us in the least.

During the day soldiers roamed about the streets and laid hold of unoccupied men and youths, who were mercilessly enrolled in the tottering army.

In the evening all of us and the Tungan officers were invited to a cheery party at Yollbars'. Hummel was late, as usual. He had been attending to the cavalry general Ma's wound, which went right through the thigh and was full of matter. But our doctor made his bed for him and received as fee five hundred Hatamen cigarettes, ten melons and some Russian caramels.

The first night with no frost was noted on the morning of February 21 (36·7 degrees). A fearful coming and going at our quarters all day! Two officers came down from Dawancheng and asked us to take eight of their comrades to Aksu. We replied that we meant to use only one or two cars from Korla to Aksu on account of shortage of petrol, and therefore had not room for so many. Then we had a talk with General Li, who arranged that only four should accompany us.

Curiously enough Li begged us to start at once. It looked as if Pai's lorry was badly stuck at Toksun. I replied that we should not be ready till next morning.

He gave us special letters of introduction to the military commanders at Kara-shahr, Korla, Kucha, Aksu and Kashgar, with orders to do everything possible for our comfort and safety. I told General Li about Commandant Chang at Hami and the sixty gallons he had promised us at Turfan, and how Yollbars, instead of repaying us the loan, had taken another twenty gallons. He then gave us a special letter about petrol to the commander at Kucha, where he knew there were supplies.

During the day someone had listened to Kemal talking to Ma on the telephone. Kemal had said nice things about us and urged that it was important that we should be well treated, as the outside world would get to know all about our expedition, and how I certainly intended to write a book, in which I should say what I thought about Ma Chung-yin. The general's answer remained a mystery, but all that day we were treated with noticeable politeness, and were even begged to accelerate our departure. Nor had they asked if they might "borrow" petrol, though they certainly needed it, for General Ma had invited the fair Miss Lin to Turfan with two pilots to take charge of the two aeroplanes he had captured. We had already heard of her at Peking, where the papers announced that she intended to travel to Hami by car by the same route as we. Some of the younger members of the expedition scented piquant adventures. But we now heard that she was at Lanchow and was going to fly to Hami. Fate so disposed that neither we nor Ma saw a trace of the flying beauty.

It was rumoured that two of the omnibus company's cars

which had gone to Kashgar had never been heard of again. They had been attacked by Kirghiz bandits and the travellers taken prisoners.

General Li presented to us the four officers who were to travel with us and at the same time serve as escort. They made an unpleasant impression from the first moment.

That evening some of our fellows saw a party of young Turkis being driven to one of the town's two assembling-places for recruits. They looked unhappy and gloomy, and walked with bent heads and dragging feet, now and then urged onward with a rifle butt. There must have been two hundred of them. Weeping women were no unusual sight in the streets.

Hummel inspected the Turfan hospital, a caravanserai, in whose rooms the patients lay on *kangs*[1] and the medical orderlies were boys of fourteen. The place was bare, dirty and evil-smelling. There had been talk of some cases of typhus, but the doctor could not discover any.

We had now 1220 gallons of petrol left. A few merchants had paraffin for sale, but we could get that much more cheaply at Kucha and Aksu, for oil is brought to those places from Alma Ata (Vernij) and Prshevalsk (Karakol).

Blessed day, February 22, on which we succeeded in leaving the hellish hole called Turfan—which we had seen six years before peaceful, pleasant and prosperous. Our packing had been completed and the heavier loading done the day before. But the doctor was at the wounded cavalry general's quarters with Yew as interpreter, so Chen and I waited with the small car. General Li and Yollbars kept us company. The former conveyed to us General Ma Chung-yin's best wishes. The general had got two of my books in Chinese and asked Li to send them up to Dawancheng at once.

Yollbars entertained me with an account of his worries as head of the commissariat. He had to get about between two and three

[1] A dais built of bricks, hollow to allow of a fire being lighted underneath, used as a bed in northern China and Manchuria.

tomans of *gin*[1] (about a ton and a half) of wheat a day for Ma's army and the same quantity of maize for his horses. In addition, he had to keep a thousand civilians and several hundred soldiers in Turfan. But he exaggerated. Of Ma's army only fragments remained. At the close Yollbars uttered a confession: "If Ma doesn't take Urumchi, I shall leave the country and go to Sweden or Germany".

At last, at half-past twelve, the doctor came, accompanied by Yew. After a hurried good-bye we jumped up into the car and rolled off down the bazaar street of Turfan.

[1] A toman = 10,000; a gin = $1\frac{1}{3}$ lbs.

THROUGH GORGES AND BURNING VILLAGES IN
ROBBERLAND

OUR satisfaction at leaving Turfan behind us reconciled us to some extent to the wretched bridges, marshy watercourses and treacherous canals we had to cross. We overtook Professor Li and his four students. They had a horse and two donkeys for their baggage. The two Poles were travelling in their company, in a country cart. We stopped and had a chat with the mysterious party, and did something to reinforce their certainly very modest funds. Half an hour later we drove by the village of Yamchi-bazar. After that most of the road was under water. Another half-hour and we were 290 ft. below the level of the sea. An hour later an aeroplane was droning like an organ over our heads. It can hardly have been 3000 ft. up. We expected to get a bomb through the roof of the car at any moment, and stopped. But the organ music died away in the distance.

Then we came to the village of Yamchi-kares, where there was a rickety bridge over a fairly large and deep canal. The bridge was eight feet long and nearly ten feet wide. The log on the western side of the bridge looked as if it would bear; the eastern bent under even a man's weight. Serat put on speed and drove across diagonally. The two right wheels were supported by the western log, but the two left pressed down the eastern severely. The car took on a heavy list, but it had speed enough to get over.

Now it was Jomcha's turn. He drove slowly and carefully in Serat's tracks. Crash! the left back wheel went through the bridge axle-deep. We all hurried to the rescue. The lorry must be unloaded before the whole outfit tumbled down into the canal. Two villagers passed. They were promised a reward if they would get wood to repair the bridge. In a little while they returned with a few very thin tree-trunks and were sent back to the village.

It took an hour to free the lorry; then beams were obtained and the bridge was repaired with wood, fallen telegraph posts, and sun-baked brick for the two last cars. Effe put on speed. The bridge held, but creaked. Georg was the last to cross with "Edsel". The bridge swayed and bent, but still held. Meanwhile the Polish and Chinese travellers had overtaken us; but now we were ready to go on, and continued our journey.

The road we were following soon led us into a labyrinth of furrows cut deep by wind and water between more or less sharp-edged ridges of clay, as much as three feet high. I had seen this *yardang* formation before in the Lop-nor desert and the country round Lou-lan, and described it in an earlier book.

It was half-past six. Serat was ahead. The sun had sunk in a fiery glow. It was nearly dark already. Serat stopped and reported that these ruts and ridges were becoming more numerous, and that the road we were on was quite impassable for cars.

About turn, back to the bridge at Yamchi-kares! We had wasted a few hours on the most hopeless surface, and pitched camp No. 40 by this bridge the building of which had given us so much trouble. We would look for another road next morning. The only thing necessary to complete our misery was that we might have to go over that wretched bridge again.

We climbed above sea-level again, and the temperature at night was 23·4 degrees. Two of our four Tungan officers had been into the village and fetched a guide, who was placed on Serat's lorry. A brilliantly clear morning! The mountains to northward were magnificent with their shimmering sunlit slopes and shadowy blue valleys, in the quiet, subdued tones of objects seen at a distance. Twenty-eight degrees west of north Bogdo-ula, God's mountain, towered over the rest of the earth and the snow-clad giants of the Tien-shan.

We did not have to test again the bridge we had rebuilt the previous day; our guide indicated a road a little farther north, with the canal on our right. It led north-west, parallel to the patterned ridges. Gravel desert, tussock-dotted steppe. The clear

Tatung brook was easy to cross, for its bottom was hard and gravelly.

The road became splendid, hard and level. Not a single tussock was seen now. We crossed several *kares* or underground canals —then some open canals with broken-down bridges! At the village of Kara-bulak the ground grew swampy. To northward, Bogdo-ula shone like a lighthouse on a sea-coast. The chain of mountains to the south was Chol-tagh.

It was so hot in the middle of the day that we had to stop again and again to cool the engines. Then the cars drew up side by side so that the drivers should be able to have a chat. We took out one of the melons which Hummel had got as a fee and cut it into slices lengthways. It was seven minutes past twelve.

Just then the loud, warning organ music was heard again. Then an aeroplane was seen to southward over Chol-tagh. Five minutes later it was making straight for us. The drivers were ordered to go ahead immediately, with long intervals between them. Serat buzzed off, Jomcha followed; then came Effe and Georg, throwing up surging clouds of yellowish-grey dust, which must have been seen perfectly from the air.

The airman came nearer. Of course it was us he was peering at, for he must be thinking that the enemy, the invader Ma, was in one of the cars, probably the small car, and that the lorries belonged to the Tungan general. That was why he was making straight for the small car. Was he going to drop his bomb just at that moment? Now he was right over our heads. Another second. There was no explosion. He departed northward in the direction of the Tien-shan, the Celestial Mountains, flying at a height of 3000 ft. The organ music grew fainter and died away in the distance, and the aeroplane vanished over the mountains like an eagle.

Next time we stopped it was owing to a flat tyre. But the airman did not come back.

A few Turkis were walking westward. They were refugees who

wished to escape being called up and sent to the front at Dawancheng.

We were moving in a curve towards south-east. The road was
sunk three feet deep in the clay soil. The bridge over the Toksun
river held, and a few minutes later we drove into the bazaar.

The air filter of Serat's motor was broken. We therefore drove
to a caravanserai and sent for a smith. While he was at work the
whole of our party, masters and servants, went to a Tungan
restaurant in the bazaar and had minced mutton with onions and
scrambled eggs. At Toksun we met the Poles and Li with his
students. They were travelling by side-roads because the high road
was unsafe.

Just as we were about to start the Tungan commandant came
to call. He told us that Pai and his fifteen companions had left
Toksun a few days before. So we were not troubled with them.
The desire of the gentlemen at Turfan that we should start without delay was thus not due to the cause we had supposed. We
knew nothing *then*. But perhaps General Li and the others knew
that General Ma had been defeated and was going to retreat via
Kara-shahr and Korla, and that it might be of vital importance
to him to have our car-park close at hand. If one pieces together
the events which happened later, this explanation is the only
probable one. For what interest could General Ma's staff, which
acted on direct orders, otherwise have in doing everything to
accelerate our departure westward along the road the fugitives
would take? We could be quite sure he was not opening this road
for us out of kindness, nor could it help his ambitious plans that
Europeans and Chinese should witness his defeat and flight.

It was half-past five before the smith had finished his work and
we rolled off through the Toksun bazaar. A young soldier jumped
on to one of our cars with his kit and a few melons. He was
thrown off again despite his and the escort's protests. The whole
town was on its legs and staring at us. At every gate and every
corner stood groups of Tungan women and young girls in bright
red and blue dresses.

Our course was now southward. The thick clouds of dust which were stirred up by our wheels hung motionless in the air, without the slightest breath to scatter them. It was like travelling through the "sea of mists" in the moon. The sun was sinking. Bogdo-ula still glowed crimson above the earth's shadows. The road was awful, nothing but ledges, bumps, gutters and deep cart-ruts in yellow layers of loess. Time after time we had to stop to remove with spades and picks hillocks and ridges that hindered our progress.

Twilight was giving place to darkness when we reached the last village, Sarik-dung, or "Yellow Hill". After that the road grew better, with a hard gravel foundation; we steered for the foot of the mountains and drove into a river-bed, which we crossed again and again. It led to the mouth of a valley which grew ever narrower between the terraces and low hills which closed it in. Before us a white porous sheet of ice gleamed in the bottom of the valley, fifty to a hundred yards wide. We drove up over its edge. The porous ice crackled and creaked under the weight of the cars. Soon the sheet of ice broke up and lay in narrow belts along the banks of the stream. Then the ice stopped, but the stream murmured along the bottom of the valley. It was nearly eight when we stopped at Su-bashi ("Water-head"). Here there was a demolished rest-house with a watch-tower. We were 875 ft. above sea-level and had crossed the stream seventeen times, wondering every time if someone would get stuck.

In the morning sunshine we saw spread round us a landscape whose picturesque features had been hidden by the darkness when we encamped. The narrow valley we were in was like a corridor. To northward it dropped towards the plain; to southward it ascended through wild mountains to a pass.

Around the camp lay ten dead horses and fragments of military equipment, pack-saddles and so on. The four officers of the escort lamented that we had not made an earlier start, for we must get to Kara-shahr that evening, before the robber bands gathered to attack us. At Kumush, on the other side of the pass, there had formerly been a military post of two hundred men, but it had been attacked by robbers and had withdrawn to Kara-shahr. The dead horses had been shot in the fighting, to which the fragments of clothing also bore witness.

The whole morning rifle fire crackled round our tents and echoed among the precipices. It was our gallant escort, seeking thus to frighten the robber bands which were sure to be lying in ambush in every crevice.

Now we drove up on to the terrace on the left of the watercourse. It fell steeply to the bed of the stream, and we backed to drive into and across the water. The stream wound along ice-free, between belts of ice; so that we often had to drive down from the ice into the bed of the stream and then up again on the other side. If the edge of the ice was too sharp and threatened to cut our tyres to pieces, it had to be blunted with picks and spades. Blinding white ice-fields, glittering water, precipitous rocks—this road was no sort of a motor road, but indescribably picturesque and exciting.

Our progress was hopelessly slow. Serat's lorry broke through the ice, eight inches thick, and the ice had to be cut away right to the stream. After that the gorge was thirty yards wide, and its bottom was quite full of firm ice beneath which the stream murmured. We drove through a world of wild, sheer rocks with magnificent views. Where the valley was always in shadow the ice was firmer; the places on which the sun shone were brittle.

Our drivers made a reconnaissance up the valley on foot. The road grew worse the higher we got. We were approaching the limits of the possible for cars. But we *must* get on that way, for there was no other road to Eastern Turkestan. The Citroën expedition had gone that way under G. M. Haardt; we must manage it too. Pai's car also had taken that road.

The cars took a sharp bend on the dry gravel of the left bank. And then the convoy stopped again. Next came a few short, sharp bends with little ice, but more swiftly rushing water. The tracks of Pai's wheels were plainly visible. Yellow drift-sand covered the lower slopes of the mountains. We were seldom able to drive for four minutes on end before the next difficult place held up the convoy.

The body of a dead soldier lay on a spot where the bank was dry. Of Kona-oertang (the "Old Inn") only the ruins remained. Here there was an ice-bridge which held. Another six minutes, and we were stopped again. We had done less than four miles in two hours! The sharp edge of a sheet of ice was smoothed out with axes, a perpendicular gravel wall three feet high transformed into a gently sloping bank. We were all walking except the drivers.

The ice ceased, and after another five miles, so did the water. The valley bottom was strewn with gravel. We were 1800 ft. above sea-level.

A few small elms grew on a sandy slope. The telegraph line, which hitherto had gone over hills and peaks, now descended to the valley bottom. We drove unblushingly over the wire. Was it surprising that this line was out of order? Now and again we passed the mouth of a large side-valley, and many small, short ones in between. Now we were going for a quarter of an hour between the interruptions, and we stopped for several minutes to cool the engines. Slate rocks, yellow, brown, grey and red, rose in wild rugged masses on either hand. Sometimes obstructing stones had to be cleared out of the way, or holes filled up; or sharp stones which had stuck between the twin wheels removed.

The telegraph wire lay along the foot of the mountains or in the bottom of the valley, the posts having been cut down for fuel. The ravine grew wilder and wilder, and wound to and fro in the sharpest zigzags. We saw the body of a soldier half covered with sand. On one quite short stretch we counted seventeen dead horses. Snow lay here and there in narrow streaks.

At half-past one we were at Arghai-bulak, where a stream of lovely, ice-cold, crystal-clear water, as thick as a man's fist, runs out of the perpendicular mountain wall on the left side of the valley. A barricade of stones was erected just above the spring. Numbers of dead horses, fragments of clothing and saddlecloths, and several soldiers' bodies imperfectly concealed by stones, showed what hard fighting had taken place there. We perceived at once that we were on a battlefield, where nothing but the murmuring spring and the wind's breath disturbed the sleep of the fallen.

Just above the spring a narrow raised strip of beach lay at the foot of the cliffs on the left-hand side, with ruined stone walls that marked the site of an old rest-house. The valley took a sharp bend here. This rounded, it was only a few minutes' drive to the foot of a cone-shaped mass of rocks which filled up the valley, at its narrowest point only some sixty feet wide. Many of these rocks were as big as houses, some about eight hundred cubic feet in size; there were others, again, a good deal smaller, and at the bottom of the scale, little blocks of stone and sharp-edged splinters, pebbles and gravel. A whole section of cliff, over a thousand feet above the bottom of the ravine, had fallen from the right-hand side and filled up the valley. When this happened it is impossible to say. But to judge from the weather-worn and rounded edges of the giant blocks, many centuries have passed since this mass closed in the valley like a cork put into a bottle. The principal fall of cliff was presumably caused by a severe earthquake, but shocks in more recent times may have contributed to the pile of rocks.

As early as 1928 I had been planning a motor trip from Urumchi to Eastern Turkestan, and asked Mr. Hunter, a British missionary in that town, if he thought it possible to force the Toksun pass. He replied that it was absolutely unthinkable. Country carts could be taken that way, but only empty and with the draught animals taken out of the shafts. They could be coaxed and steered among the rocks with the aid of ropes and a few sturdy fellows, but for cars the track was quite impossible. Yet the Citroën expedition had gone by that route. But it had carried dynamite and blasted away the worst blocks which obstructed the way, and so got its cars through. Since then the Chinese authorities had kept the road in order. It was, therefore, in a pretty good state when we reached the place. A very steep winding track had been made, the gaping holes between the rocks filled up with small blocks and gravel, and the surface made as even as was practicable.

The lowest slope consisted partly of ledges of firm scree and ridges which we improved with slabs of slate. The small car found its task easy and clambered nimbly up to the summit of the cone of rock. On one of the outside curves a memorial tablet was hewn into a rock. Between some of the giant rocks there were gaps like doorways, through which we had splendid views of the fantastically wild valley. Our height was 3750 ft.

Serat followed us, fully loaded, with a noise which echoed through the valley like thunder. All the men except the drivers were on foot and running beside the lorry to put stones behind the double wheels if the engine refused to bear the immense strain put upon it. I sat on a rock by the wayside. Lurching and creaking over the slabs of slate, which were ground to white powder against one another, the grey elephant came snorting past me. I could see the tension with which Serat gripped the steering-wheel. The hill had already recorded the maximum gradient for a loaded car.

But now he had before him a few yards on which the gradient became two or three degrees steeper. Would the engine succeed in overcoming it, or would it strike?

The engine was victorious, and the lorry ascended to a part of the road which was not so steep. Then the others followed, and all went well. We could breathe again. The four officers and their chief, who had been in such a hurry to escape from the robber bands that morning, were too superior to give a helping hand.

A little higher up came the next difficult bit, where the cars had to be coaxed forward zigzag round bends only ten feet long, between giant blocks which in places overhung the road. The lorries banged and bumped against the rocks now to the right, now to the left. At one horribly narrow passage between two huge blocks the lorries could only get on with the help of an inclined plane of flat slabs, which compelled the car to list heavily to the left in order that it might not strike the overhanging rock on the right.

At three o'clock all the cars were through without the slightest misadventure, only scraped here and there. Then we came into a part of the valley as narrow as a corridor, whose bottom was full of snow and ice. At one place its width was only thirteen feet. We swayed and rolled as we drove through what seemed to be a gateway. Savage, picturesque, defiant scenery!

A little higher up we passed the ruins of the Arghai-bulak rest-house. We were now 4100 ft. up. We drove through snow-fields which crunched where deep blue shadows fell on them. Just now and then we saw a solitary tussock of vegetation in a crevice.

At a height of 4550 ft. we halted again to eat melons. The doctor was collecting clematis seeds in a little sheltered corner.

The valley grew broader and the road better. The snow was still lying only on the northern slopes of the mountains. The outlines became softer and the mountains relatively lower. The valley was still growing wider. The telegraph posts were standing now. During one of our halts, just before sunset, one of the four Tungan officers spread out his overcoat on the ground and said *namas*, or evening prayers, turning towards Mecca. We thought he was a pious man, but he showed himself later to be a mean rascal. By the roadside lay a whole coil of rolled-up telegraph wire.

The pass which forms the watershed is called Manan-chose and is 5700 ft. high. A ruined rest-house, and yet another, called Ujme-dung. After some searching in different valleys we found the right road. The telegraph line had deceived us. The road was hard and good. Far away to the south we saw, bluish in the distance, a new mountain chain; this was the Kuruk-tagh. The valley now became very wide between low rounded hills.

It was nearly seven when we reached the village of Kumush and pitched our camp, No. 42. We were 2900 ft. up. Some Turki travellers were encamped outside the village with their camel caravan. One of them told us that Pai's car had been attacked by several hundred robbers and captured. Another reduced the number of the assailants to seven, and these had only fired on the car. Pai and his fifteen companions had returned their fire and killed one robber and one horse. The rest had fled.

On the night of February 24 the temperature fell to 6·4 degrees. In the Turfan basin the winters are milder than in the surrounding country. Early in the morning hymn-singing was heard from the tent of the two missionaries' sons, Georg and Effe. It sounded beautiful and melodious. They did not know it was Sunday. I suppose they had an intuition that we were not worth much without Heaven's help, and so, in the wilderness, they were drawn towards the Everlasting One's throne.

Three mail couriers in General Ma's pay were stationed at Kumush, but they never drew anything. The village has two wells; the Turkis with the caravan were encamped round one of them. A few tall poplars grow close by. At Kumush there is a rectangular earth wall whose sides are nearly a hundred yards long—the last traces of an ancient fortress. On a height north of the village is a *mazar*, or saint's tomb with a cupola.

Hummel was up there taking photographs when a bullet whistled past his head. Our admirable escort was having some firing practice, still to frighten possible robbers. When we reproached them for their carelessness, which might have cost the doctor his life, they replied that they were only shooting at a crow in a poplar. These wretched louts were a double danger to us, not a protecting escort. Their "shooting practice" was dangerous, not least when they fired from the top of a lorry. Besides that, they smoked like chimneys all day. We warned them, explaining that the petrol drums must not be exposed to risk of fire. If they blew up the escort would come off worst. The fellows laughed derisively and went on smoking.

West of the village we had to cross a flooded ice-covered stream. We all got across but Jomcha. It took an hour to free him. Our hopes of reaching Kara-shahr, seventy-seven miles away, were crushed.

A belt of tamarisks on high dunes runs to the foot of the

Kuruk-tagh hills, with their violent sculptured effects, the result of erosion. We were slowly getting away from the northern mountains. The road was good, but rather sandy. Tamarisks and tussocks of herbage occurred but scantily. A solitary antelope fled across the steppe to northward. After an hour's drive we were 3800 ft. high.

The road led into a valley to the left. Here snow was still lying in shady spots. Solitary elms grew in the valley. Wu-shu-kou or Kara-kizil is the name given to a stone wall round a few small houses inhabited by mail couriers. We climbed higher and higher to westward. Then the ground began to fall again. We had steppe to the left of us and a reddish-yellow mountain range, very high, to our right. Sometimes we met merchants with wares on horses or donkeys, but the country seemed dead and forsaken. A quantity of spades and picks carried by donkeys were clearly meant for Ma's army. Three horsemen in white fur coats we put down as robbers.

To the south-west the surface of the Baghrash-kul shone like a sword-blade beyond the tussocks of the plain. The lake was frozen. Near the village of Ushak-tal ("Dwarf Willow") Georg and Serat stuck fast in the ice-covered river. They unloaded their lorries and carried the baggage to a dry place. The whole village had come out to see us. Boys were playing and fighting in the middle of the slush. Five cars at Ushak-tal were no usual sight. The village was inhabited by seventy Tungan families; all the Turkis had fled to Kucha and Kashgar.

On the wall of a house in Ushak-tal was a notice proclaiming that anyone refusing to accept General Ma's notes to their full value would be shot. A silver dollar was worth 30 liang here, at Toksun 40, at Hami 50 and at Turfan 70. It was said that Hodja Nias Hadji had had all the cattle, camels, horses, sheep and goats in this region driven to Kara-shahr and still farther west.

While we were waiting the men of the military post offered us *mien*—long strips of dough boiled in water—in china bowls. They advised us to take reinforcements as a protection against robbers. Some way this side of Kara-shahr, in particular, we could be sure of being attacked.

We drove out through the west gate. The street continued outside the gate. There was a dangerous bridge, which nevertheless held. There followed wide sheets of porous, melting ice. On our right, to northward, we had the ruddy-hued mountains; on our left, steppe.

The lorry on which the man who said his prayers was driving had to stop when prayer-time arrived. Sometimes we passed single trees or belts of tamarisks. From one of these we collected fuel for the coming night's camp.

At a quarter past six we drove into the village of Chukur (the "Deep"). Profound silence reigned in the village, and the place was ghost-like in the twilight. In the middle of the main street, which lies along the high road, stood a chair, on which Jomcha seated himself with a comic air of dignity while we waited for one or two of the lorries which had not kept up with the rest. They came. We got out of our cars at a house which was in flames. The rafters and everything else wooden was burning. The house consisted of three low wings and a wall round a rectangular yard. A gate in the wall led out on to the high road. Two of the wings were on fire. All the furniture was thrown out into the yard—chests, tables, stools, boxes, baskets, shabby carpets and ragged clothing. The things were lying all over the place, some of them smashed. We walked along the village street. Not a soul was to be seen, nor any dead bodies. No dog barked, no cock crew in those desolate purlieus, where only the flames of arson hissed and flared. Farther on a telegraph wire was stretched across the street just high enough to cut a rider's throat, or at any rate unseat him.

What had happened at Chukur? Incendiaries and looters had been there; the fire might have been burning for a few hours. The gang had probably come down from the mountains close by. The village had been inhabited that morning, and the people had most likely fled into the desert or hidden among the tamarisks of the steppe. It is not impossible that the robbers had been surprised at their task by the buzz of our motors and concealed themselves in the houses on the outskirts of the village. Our admirable escort proposed that we should drive on as fast as we could to Kara-shahr. But I gave orders that we should encamp at the next village, Tagarchi ("Sack maker"), where we arrived at half-past seven.

Here we drove into a small yard with low walls. All the houses round about were destroyed. A few elms grew there, among them a fine old tree built into a little temple. As the neighbourhood seemed unsafe, we decided to post sentries from ten to six, an hour's duty for each man. The five Tungans who formed our guard declared that they did not mean to keep watch. If robbers attacked us, we could wake them. So saying, they slunk into a house close at hand which was only half destroyed.

As long as I lay awake I heard the sentry's step as he passed among the tents. Late at night he had observed six Turki men and one woman, some of them armed, riding past on horseback. Possibly they were refugees from Chukur who had waited for darkness to venture from their hiding-places and were now fleeing to Kara-shahr.

Next morning the sky was overcast and gloomy, and nothing was to be seen of our surroundings through the fog-laden air. The convoy left Tagarchi and was soon driving through a pleasant little wood of poplars, a most unusual sight. After that the road was sunk three feet deep in the clay. Then came another patch of wood, set among fairly rich vegetation, tamarisks and tussocks of grass. The dust swirled; trees and bushes were grey and yellow, for the poplars still had their leaves on them, which showed that there had been no storm since the autumn before. We often passed broken chests and empty boxes which had been thrown away by fugitives.

The village of Tauilga was completely devastated. An avenue of Lombardy poplars stood there, some of them blackened by fire. The street was encumbered with heaps of sun-baked bricks from houses which had collapsed. Outside the village the road wound along like a grey band across the yellow plain. A solitary dog was hunting for something. Not far from the road clouds of black smoke were rising. Was it a village on fire? No; a steppe fire, dangerous to our petrol drums.

The vegetation ceased. We crossed a belt of ice which bore us. Here begins the tract of salt marshes which is called Chong-kul, or "Great Lake". All the ground was chalky white with salt, as with newly fallen snow. Curiously enough, someone had taken the trouble to dig ditches on both sides of the road to keep it dry right through the salt marsh. A bridge, which we avoided—it looked as if Pai's lorry had cut right through its planks. The drivers set about repairing it, but Kung discovered another bridge. On the way there we found that we could get across the depression without using bridges, and were soon on an almost decent road again.

There was no wind to blow away the stifling clouds of dust. The lorries sometimes had to stop and wait till it had settled to some extent.

Now we saw ruined houses; here and there a man, woman or child was visible. Several bridges, ice-covered canals and large sheets of ice. We lost our way, and wandered about for a long time before we found the right road. Everywhere ice, mud and water, holes and bumps; the cars rolled like ships in a storm. One bridge after another, some fairly sound. A country cart, a rider; the people were Tungans. Then a whole string of bridges, all with railings. The traffic increased.

At four o'clock we were at the gate of Kara-shahr. No one interfered with us. We drove into the bazaar and stopped outside a *yamen* where a flag was flying. Our appearance was taken remarkably quietly, and when we had found a suitable place on the left bank of the Khaidu-gol, we halted and pitched camp.

We had found Kara-shahr in a fairly good state; there were not so many houses destroyed and no trees cut down; there was more movement in the streets than at Turfan, and we noticed no acute poverty. We had driven through the town unmolested; and even if the numerous bridges had creaked under the lorries, still they had held. And we had scarcely got our tents up on the bank of the mighty river before the mayor, black-bearded old Han Yung-ching, had come to call in person and asked if he could be of service to us.

The river was covered with ice, and we had a temperature of 24·8 degrees at 8 P.M.; we hoped, therefore, that the ice would bear the weight of empty cars. Carts, riders and oxen were still crossing, certainly with caution, but without having recourse to the three ferry-boats which lay drawn up on the right bank.

I had already turned in when Georg came and asked for instructions about guard duty during the night. There was no real danger, but, to judge from the positively criminal types we had seen among the crowds which surrounded the cars and the tents when we were pitching camp, we had to reckon with pilferers. Accordingly orders were given for sentries to watch over the camp during the night. But the stars which shone pale over the "black city" witnessed no evil designs on our airy dwellings.

TO KORLA, THE CITY OF OUR SORROWS

DESPITE a temperature of 9 degrees during the night, Kung reported on the morning of February 27 that it was absolutely impossible to get the cars across the ice, which creaked and rose in ridges even under empty carts. The ice was as a rule four inches, at the most six inches thick. A ferry-boat he had seen was 26 ft. long by 9 ft. 9 in. wide, and the only way to get the cars across the river was to get the mayor to mobilise a party of Turkis to cut a channel through the ice, even at the risk of its being closed again at once by the ice-floes that were drifting down the stream. But we were told that the safest method was to wait till the ice began to break up of its own accord, which usually happened just at this time and ordinarily took two days. After this had happened we could safely transport the whole convoy to the right bank of the Khaidu-gol on the three ferry-boats.

In the morning we had a visit from the commandant at Kara-shahr, Hwang Wen-ching, accompanied by his staff and also by a general of cavalry named Ma Yung-chu. Both were courteous and pleasant Tungans.

Kung began cutting a passage at once, and by evening his thirty sturdy old fellows had cleared away the ice for a distance of forty yards by three yards.

Then Yew and I paid visits to the three gentlemen who had called upon us. General Ma was not at home, but his adjutant received us, and it was amusing to listen to his outspoken but untruthful conversation. The road to Kashgar was quite open, he said; we could travel entirely at our ease, no one would molest us. The whole country in that quarter, Tien-shan-nan-lu, acknow-ledged the rule of General Ma Chung-yin. General Ma Yung-chu had ten thousand cavalry under his orders, and the total strength of the Tungan cavalry was twice that number. The fact that Ma

Chung-yin could do without half his cavalry in the fighting line at Dawancheng proved better than anything how strong his position was. In June, 1933, the Turkis in Kara-shahr had risen in rebellion and killed multitudes of women and children. Peace had been restored by the general of cavalry Ma whom Hummel had attended. But this peace had not lasted long, for the Torguts had swept down from their mountains and murdered women and children in the villages round Kara-shahr, while the town itself had been defended by its population. The male inhabitants of the villages had fled westward.

Ma Chung-yin had thrice sent negotiators to the Torgut prince to win him and his people over to his (Ma's) side, but the emissaries had been killed. An attack on Kara-shahr was, therefore, now awaited, and the adjutant hoped that we should get across the river and down to Korla before the Torguts stormed the town. He expressed keen astonishment at our having succeeded in getting from Toksun to Kara-shahr with whole skins, for it was just between those places that the Torguts had ravaged the country.

The adjutant thought we should not find it easy to get across the river. He had seen himself how much trouble the Citroën expedition had had in mooring the ferries to the landing-stage and getting the cars on board without the boats capsizing. A passage cut at random through the ice would be very chancy, as the ford depended upon sandbanks which shifted every year and whose position had first to be ascertained by soundings. We had, in his view, no other choice than to wait till the ice broke up, which usually happened during a storm. He promised to put his services at our disposal in all things.

We were well received by the commandant also. He lived in the *yamen* which had been the Chinese governor's, which led me to ask whether the building was the same as that in which I had waited upon the *amban* Wen Ta-jen in March, 1896. He replied that in Kara-shahr houses rarely stood for more than twenty years or so on account of the moisture of the earth and the salt it contained. The present *yamen*, he added, was erected only three years ago, but on the same site as the old one.

The promised supply of petrol of course came to nothing here too. There was not a drop to be had in Kara-shahr. We were shown in a yard six fifty-gallon drums which were said to have been full when the Citroën expedition presented them to the town authorities. The last trickle that remained had been given to Pai for his trip to Aksu.

During the days that followed the mayor himself directed the work upon the S-shaped channel across the river, and our fellows helped. It is said that each spring two human beings and three beasts of burden must be sacrificed to the river before it deigns to break up. A couple of horses and some cows which fell through the ice were saved, but two donkeys were drowned. The three ferry-boats lay frozen up in the ice. A number of Torguts, who lived in four *yurts* on the right bank, were busy cutting them out. All the cars were unloaded and taken down to the left bank to be washed. They were covered both outside and inside with a firmly fixed coating of dust, and became considerably lighter after their ablution.

Near the left, or northern, bank of the Khaidu-gol lies a long island, separated from the mainland by two shallow arms of the stream, ice-free at the time of which I write. I rode over to the southern shore of the island to inspect the work. Fifty Turkis, armed with picks and bars and long sticks, were engaged in cutting the channel, half near our bank, the other half on the opposite side. The sticks were used to loosen whole floes of the ice, which were carried along the western bank by a little ice-free arm. The workers were a picturesque sight, and Kung was untiring in directing and encouraging them. And the work went well. By evening one of the ferry-boats had been brought more than half-way across the river towards the bank we were on.

Chen measured the river about three-quarters of a mile below the channel. Its breadth was 238 yards, its maximum depth just over 8 ft., and the volume of water about 1200 cubic ft. a second.

Soundings and speed tests were carried out through fifteen gaps in the ice. I was not easy in my mind until Chen and Kung had come home in the evening without having sacrificed their lives to the deities of the stream.

The camp was always a picture full of movement. Thither came the high dignitaries with their mounted attendants, and there stood continually groups of tethered, whinnying horses. Soldiers loafed about, and tramps, pedlars, peasants, women and children stood staring for hours on end.

February 28 coincided with the 15th of the Chinese first month, which is the Feast of Lanterns. Our drivers and servants had accordingly ordered a complete dinner from a Chinese restaurant, to which we were invited in my tent, and in which masters and men participated in democratic unity. Serat made a speech and rendered thanks for the presents in hard cash they had received at the Chinese New Year. The full moon shone a brilliant orange over the "Black city" and its white stream and, on its banks, the splendid groves of Lombardy poplars which raised their leafless spires towards the stars. The men carried on the New Year's festival in their own tent with wine and song, jokes and laughter, and the gramophone played Strauss, Kreisler, Grieg, Beethoven, marches and Hawaii turn and turn about.

Effe had the invaluable habit of dividing his favours equally between the masters' and servants' tents, and displaying in both places an equally inexhaustible store of jokes and pranks. Every evening he kept the talk going among the men, from whose tent roars of laughter were always heard at a late hour, and in gloomy and critical times it was he who kept the men's spirits up. He was always singing, and knew all the tunes in the world—Chinese, Mongolian, Swedish and English. He and Georg had been born in Northern China and talked Chinese much better than Swedish. Their daily conversations on technical matters concerning the cars were always carried on in Chinese. Yes, Effe was indeed a priceless acquisition for an expedition composed of three peoples so unlike as the Swedish, Chinese and Mongolian.

We had about a thousand gallons of petrol left and could get about the same amount of paraffin.

At night the camp was guarded by three soldiers at the commandant's orders. So we were able to sleep peacefully.

On the night of February 28 the temperature dropped to 11·3 degrees. We found in the morning that the river had fallen nearly seven and a half inches.

The commandant's adjutant paid us a visit and informed us that he had been ordered to transport beams, logs and planks to the southern shore of the island and build there a quay and an inclined plane to get the cars on to the ferry-boats. The channel through the ice was completed, and we could begin to shift our heavy baggage to the embarkation quay. Two ferry-boats had already crossed to the island, one carrying twenty men, four horses, two cows, a donkey and a loaded cart, a weight of about two and a half tons in all. So that ferry-boat could easily carry one empty lorry.

Now things grew lively. "Edsel" was loaded with part of our store of petrol and drove it to the place of embarkation, and then the cars went to and fro between this point and the camp. The southern shore of the island formed a perpendicular drop seven feet high where the bank had been cut away by erosion. Here a dismantled ferry-boat served as a quay. The work of construction went swiftly, and the first lorry was taken over without any misadventure. Each ferry-boat was divided into two halves by two transverse bulkheads. A deck had therefore to be constructed over the whole vessel, on to which the cars were driven. A crossbeam astern prevented the vehicle from being driven overboard.

Some of us went over with the second empty car. The ferry-boat was warped a little way upstream along the southern shore of the island, and was then punted over with long poles. The crossing took eighteen minutes. When the right bank was reached, two big planks were laid out from the ferry-boat as gangways, and along these the car rolled quietly and modestly down on to dry land.

When we had returned to the island we sat for some time watching the movements in the ice which the channel had caused. Above the channel large cracks were found, and one ice-floe after another began to drift down with the stream. It looked as if they would close the channel, but they were swiftly carried out into open water, and the ice-free surface between the banks grew wider and wider.

One ice-floe had grounded on a sandbank a short way below the ferry, and on this there happened to be a black dog. When he discovered that he was quite alone on an island of ice, he began to howl miserably, but at last resigned himself to his lot and lay down in the middle of the floe, attentively watching our proceedings and the movements of the ferry-boats. Other drifting ice-floes chipped off one piece after another from the stranded floe, and this gradually grew smaller. The dog lay quiet, waiting for help from compassionate humans. But it was too difficult to reach him without a rowing-boat, and we felt that if he was too lazy to swim the ten yards or so which separated him from firm ice, he must look after himself. When darkness fell, a few square yards of the sheet of ice remained, and the dog still lay there waiting. In the morning neither he nor the ice was there. He had had his evening bath all right. Later he paid a visit to our kitchen tent, and got a bone as consolation for his sufferings.

On March 2 the river had fallen another two and three-quarter inches, and the temperature had risen to 12·6 degrees. The air was misty. Big patches of water lay ice-free round the channel.

In the morning Yew and I, with Effe as chauffeur, drove round to pay farewell visits to the authorities. The mayor had just returned from the ferry, where he had seen the two last lorries crossing the Khaidu-gol. He had done us splendid service. The men he had set to work had done together 140 man-days of work and got forty silver dollars, which was considered royal pay. He knew that merchants in the town had paraffin; the only difficulty was to locate their hiding-places. We paid a few hundred dollars on account.

The mayor told us that two months earlier war had still been going on between Turkis at Kucha and Ma's Tungans, but that all was quiet now. He advised us to ask at Kucha if the road to Aksu was safe or not. From Aksu to Kashgar the country was perfectly quiet.

We drove through the main streets of the bazaar. Most of the shops were shut, but there was plenty of life and activity. Food shops were open, and whole rows of freshly slaughtered sheep and oxen hung in front of the butchers' stalls. Ownerless dogs had assembled outside in numbers, and had not the sense to get out of the way of a car. But the people were polite and showed no curiosity. Most of them were Turkis and Tungans. We noticed many Torguts. We were told that only about seventy Chinese families lived in Kara-shahr, and that all of these had been compulsorily converted to Islam.

When all the obligatory courtesies had been got over, we drove to the camp, where the last packing-up took place, and then to the ferry, where traffic was in full swing, and long lines of carts, riders, small caravans and pedestrians waiting their turn. Twenty Torguts were acting as ferry-men. They had this privilege because they were considered more skilful than the Turkis and received fixed wages for their work. But they had also the right to take presents from their passengers. At the same time they were held as hostages for Ma's emissaries to the prince of the Torguts, nothing yet having been heard of these men's fate.

Once on the right bank, we drove to our new camp at a walled farm. In the afternoon the mayor brought us 500 gallons of paraffin, which cost 404 silver dollars. We had thus received compensation—if not full—for the eighty gallons of petrol out of which Chang and Yollbars Khan had cunningly cheated us.

Our plan for the immediate future was as follows. At Korla the expedition would be divided into two parties. Bergman, with Georg and some of the men, was to go to Lop-nor, while the rest of us were to drive to Kashgar via Kucha and Aksu. The cargo, therefore, was now divided between the two parties. The

Kashgar party took 400 gallons of petrol and 200 gallons of paraffin. If we reckoned four miles to a gallon, our three cars could travel 800 miles. It was only 650 miles to Kashgar, and there we could certainly get our fuel supply reinforced. Bergman received 550 gallons of petrol and 300 gallons of paraffin. From Korla to Lop-nor he had only 240 miles to cover. But in case we were detained at Kashgar for any reason or expelled to India or Russian Turkestan, Bergman must have sufficient fuel to get the whole way to Anhsi or Suchow. At Korla we would fix a time limit, beyond which he was not to wait for us.

Professor Li and his party, and the Poles, came to see us during our stay at Kara-shahr. The medical assistant Plavski now told us that he was an occultist and fakir and had studied in Calcutta. He was pretty tough, if what he said was true—that he could rip up his or someone else's belly, or cut off an arm or a leg and stick it on again in a moment. He could also put a seed into the ground and make the plant shoot up in half a minute with big juicy leaves and sweet-smelling flowers. He was going to give a performance at the commandant's that very evening, and invited us to it. But we had no time, and needed our arms and legs ourselves.

March 3 was our last day at Kara-shahr, and was entirely devoted to mixing petrol with paraffin and taking the cars for trial trips with this inferior fuel. Then both fuel and baggage were loaded up on to the cars, the different destinations of the two parties being taken into consideration. The tyres and spare parts, tools, arms and ammunition were also fairly distributed.

These tasks were far from being completed when the sun went down, and our mechanics and drivers worked till late at night by lamplight and moonlight.

A good part of March 4 too was gone before we started. A number of purveyors had to draw their money, and the silver coins shone in their horny hands. When we arrived at Kara-shahr a Mexican dollar had been equivalent to 30 liang or *sär*, as the Turkis call a Turkestan tael; on March 3 one could get 35 and on the next day 42 liang for a dollar. Thus the shoddy, dirty, tattered notes printed by General Ma were falling in value daily, a circumstance which showed that his star was declining and that fortune had deserted him.

While all this was going on, the doctor was besieged by sick people. Soldiers and poverty-stricken wretches crowded together outside his tent, and the boxes with the Red Cross on the lid stood open. As usual, patients were most numerous in the last few minutes before we were to start.

The four graceless Tungan officers, whom General Li Hai-jo at Turfan had given us for an escort, had a batman of the same calibre. This fellow suffered from infectious syphilis. The doctor did not want to have him on the lorries, because he might infect our men. We asked that the man should be left behind and replaced by someone else. But the four bandits refused their consent to this. It was a matter of prestige for them not to give way to foreigners, whom they hated like poison. It would have been of no use to apply to the commandant or the general of cavalry, who had their headquarters on the other side of the river, for the four carried with them written orders from General Ma Chung-yin to his army commanders at Kucha and Aksu, and could therefore mount the high horse and get their way. Accordingly we agreed to a compromise. The creature with syphilis was to be dropped at Korla. One of our Chinese servants heard the arrogant young commander say to his comrades, "When we get to Korla we'll teach these foreign devils to mend their manners!" We left Kara-shahr, therefore, in an unpleasant atmosphere of strained relations, and the journey to Kucha in company with that rabble seemed to us unbearably long.

We started on this momentous journey at 1.20 P.M. First we went down a long street through the smaller part of Kara-shahr which lies on the right bank of the Khaidu-gol, and where the tall, beautiful Lombardy poplars lift their heads to the sky. Blue-black crows, several hundred of them, were sitting in or circling round the tree-tops, uttering their metallic gurgling cry. We crossed several bridges, some of them newly built and provided with parapets. The last houses were behind us, and we were out on the high road, enshrouded in greyish-yellow clouds of dust.

The road was flooded in places. Reedy plains extended on each side. The first village we passed through bore the name of Kili Ata-mazar, after a saint's tomb which was there. Two more high bridges. The road was sunk three feet deep in the loose earth.

Danzil (the *"yurt"*)[1] was a big village.

The next bridge was unreliable, and we preferred to force the passage of the canal which it crossed—after the high rampart of earth that crowned the canal bank had been levelled with spades. In places the ground was damp and soft and covered with grass. There was a good deal of traffic. We met or overtook riders, small caravans of horses and donkeys, Turki peasants with oxen or carts, soldiers or poor refugees on foot.

Beyond a belt of high tamarisk dunes the road was sunk to a depth of ten or twelve feet, in other places only about three feet. It was easy to see that the road had been worn into the earth for centuries past by the soles of feet, the hooves of horses and cattle, camels' pads and cart-wheels. After the famous old Silk Road, which in the Han era ran right across the interior of Asia and connected China proper with the Imperial Roman world empire in the West, had been cut in consequence of the lower Tarim and Lop-nor shifting in a southerly direction, the silk trade sought a new artery from Anhsi and Tun-hwang via Hami, Turfan, Kara-shahr and Korla to Kucha. The road we were now following revealed that traffic had been busy and that bales of silk representing huge values had swayed along on camel-back or in carts. Now this classic road bears the stamp of poverty and decay, and only an utterly insignificant local trade moves in the tracks of the mighty silk caravans.

We sighted, some way off to the right, the reddish conglomerate hills where lie the caves of Ming-oi, or the "Thousand Houses". I made an excursion to the place on March 12, 1896,

[1] A Russian name given to the Mongolian felt tent.

accompanied by Kul Muhammed from Korla, the *aksakal* or "white-beard" of the Andishan merchants.

The next village was called Shorchuk (the "Salt-bearing") and was totally devastated. By the roadside sleep two mullahs, or priests, under their gravestones decorated with *tughs*—pennons and animals' tails on high poles. Such timber is spared, thanks to Mohammedan superstition, but no consideration is shown for telegraph posts.

Then follows a barren belt of thirsty sandy soil. Here and there rose *mesas*—yellow blocks, the remains of clay deposits left by erosion. We drove between two of them as through a narrow gate in a devastated town. Another natural gate of the same kind was so narrow that we had to go round it.

On our left hand, to eastward, we were getting nearer and nearer to the mountains, and we had mountains on our right too, the former in sunshine, the latter in deep shadow, and both chains barren. We were now approaching a gateway more imposing than those we had passed through—the ravine of the Konche-daria in the southernmost ridge of the Tien-shan mountains. To the left we saw a first bend of this river of historic importance, which is a continuation of the Khaidu-gol, flows out of the Baghrash-kul, joins the Tarim, passes near the ancient town of Lou-lan and terminates in the new lake Lop-nor.

We were now on the threshold of the mountain gateway, and the scenery was assuming savagely picturesque shapes. To our right the mountains rose very steeply, on our left we had the right bank of the river. Between the two there was only just room for the road, which had been cut out of the mountain-foot in ancient times. From the left bank of the river, where an uninhabited village was sighted in the valley, the mountains rose to ridges and peaks. On the bank of the stream itself grew stumpy twisted willows. A side-valley to the right gaped like an open door leading to mysterious chambers. A stream came rushing down across the road.

We followed closely at a few yards' distance the innumerable bends of the river. At each bend a new and astonishing view was revealed; pictures of wild romantic beauty replaced one another in quick succession. The gorge contracted to a corridor, the cliffs fell precipitously to the bottom of the valley. A few yards beneath us rushed the Konche-daria in foaming fury, its thunderous echoes filling the whole valley. The water was as clear as mountain crystal; it had stood and grown clear in the Baghrash-kul and had trickled through the filter of its reeds. It was a dark shining blue-green, marbled by the snow-white foam-wreaths of waterfalls. Now and again a light-green ice-floe came tumbling like a porpoise among the waves, diving beneath the seething foam of the rapids. The old black willows leaned out over the river in majestic calm, untroubled by the roaring masses of water and the warring men that passed them.

The ruins of houses heightened the romantic atmosphere. In and out, up and down we went, the Konche-daria always on our left. The road passed through a *pailou*, or gate, white-plastered, newly built and tasteless. More sharp bends, then the valley seemed to come to a dead end, and we wondered where the track went. Next moment we swung round a sharply projecting promontory of rock, and down the narrow corridor a new and splendid view lay before us.

The last gleam of sun faded on the flecks of snow to eastward; the twilight thickened, and mysterious darkness enshrouded us on all sides. The contours ran together, and still the river sang its age-long hymn. But no rifle-shots rang out, no highwaymen or robbers were visible on the track, so suitable for raids. Suddenly the road swung off to the right and ran rather steeply up hills and bare cliffs to a little ridge. On the other side of this we wound down to the river again. On its left bank, which here widened out a little, a *mazar* (saints' tomb) had been erected in a grove of trees—an enchanting place, where it would have been pleasant to stop for a while.

Again the road curved up the heights to the right. A difficult, steep piece of road with sharp-edged ledges brought us to a new ridge. Up on the top we got out and waited. The four motor-lorries were not to be seen. We sat on the scree and tried to penetrate the darkness and silence in the valley. A creaking noise and cries of exhortation were heard; a cart drawn by oxen loomed up and passed. The peaceful countrymen must have been alarmed to see the car like a black monster, and our dark silent forms. But they must have realised with a feeling of relief that we were neither robbers nor ghosts.

Now the faint noise of a car was heard in the distance, and a reflection was seen in the sky which must have been thrown by headlights. Then all was silent again, and no light effects were seen. But then there was a flash of light at a corner below. A car was working its way up the slope; the lamps shone like a wolf's eyes in the darkness, and ridges and rough places threw pitch-black shadows. Down there gleamed another pair of wolf's eyes, and farther off two more pairs. So they were safe. Thank heaven, the whole squadron was assembled.

We proceeded on level ground among the ploughed fields and farms of the Korla oasis, crossing canals and bridges and a few patches of swamp caused by flood water from the irrigation canals. We had passed the starting-point of these canals on the right bank of the river, and the further downstream we got the higher they were above river-level. The road ran along a willow avenue between houses, some intact, some demolished. The former had been inhabited by Turkis, the latter by Tungans. Hodja Nias Hadji had looted them.

This countrified road gradually became the main street of Korla. Here the houses were still standing. Here were bazaars with their timber façades, and with the colonnades and shops boarded up. Ancient trees rose here and there. Their trunks were effectively illuminated by the headlights. Crowds of men and boys stared at us.

Serat and Kung drove ahead, then Effe and Hummel. The small car followed them driven by Bergman, with Yew, Chen and myself as passengers. Then came Jomcha, and last Georg.

Again and again the convoy was stopped by soldiers in field-grey uniforms, who rushed into the middle of the road with rifles at the ready. Kung shouted to them: "We've got some of your officers here; speak to them!"

A colloquy followed, and we were given free passage till we were stopped by the next sentries. The soldiers were impudent, and were clearly itching to be allowed to fire. We could feel that the atmosphere was different from that of Kara-shahr. We felt that in this little town a rough, undisciplined, savage soldiery held sway, and we were prepared for the guns to go off at any moment.

At last the convoy stopped outside a yard gate. We inspected the place; it was pretty good, but had no space for the cars. Bergman, Yew and Georg went to some other premises belonging to a wealthy Turki named Abdul Kerim. Here there was a big yard and two Turki rooms. We drove into the yard. The cars were placed side by side in a row, the small car by itself next to the house. A small room with a *kang* built into the wall and a little wooden *kang* was just the thing for Yew, Chen, Kung, Bergman and me. Hummel took up his abode in a lobby leading through into the kitchen. Georg, Effe, Serat and Jomcha got a bigger room on the other side of the yard. Our servants slept in the kitchen. The yard was shut off from the street by a stout wooden entrance gate, and was made fast at night with a cross-beam. On the west side another gate led into a large open yard partly surrounded by walls of sun-baked brick.

Our host and a few bearded old Turkis received us politely and asked if we would like to drink some tea and eat some *ash*, which was already cooked and could be eaten either there or at the place we had visited first. Bergman, Chen and I drove back there, were taken across a little square yard and ushered into a middle-sized room on the left, where a candle was burning on a table.

To our surprise we found there the four Tungan officers who had come with us from Turfan. The leader of the party, that young Chang San-yun, who so badly needed a thrashing, sat down at the head of the table. We realised that this mixing was due to a mistake; but now it was too late, so we put the best face upon things and sat down at the table. There was no *ash*, but a pretty substantial Chinese dinner with many dishes. An army of invasion requisitions what it wants from the bazaar, and lives well without paying a farthing. We were taking part in a feast of the kind against our will. The commander Chang was icy cold and stiff, helped himself first to the dishes, and did not look in our direction; but Chen forced him into conversation.

As soon as the rice had been served, we got up and went to our own quarters, where Hummel, Yew, Effe and Georg had got the *ash* pudding that was meant for us all. We had been taken to our escort's quarters by mistake and had eaten their food.

Two of our Chinese comrades paid a visit to the mayor, who was a Chinese. He advised us to wait for a week till he was able to get information about the situation at Kucha, which he considered anything but safe.

We decided to follow his advice, which suited us particularly well because I should now be able to make a short tour along the Konche-daria, at any rate a few days' journey down the river to some point from which I could be brought back in the small car. There were no canoes or other boats at Korla. Georg was accordingly ordered to construct from our three large planks, eighteen empty petrol tins, boards and rope, a raft on which I, with two men and provisions, could drift downstream, the farther the better. Bergman, with Chen, Effe, Serat and a couple of Chinese boys, was to go with two lorries via Bujentu-bulak down to the new river, the Kum-daria, where we could meet if circumstances allowed. My trip to Kucha I should not undertake till later.

It would be a delightful voyage. When all the orders for the necessary preparations had been given, we went to bed. I dreamed of myself being borne by a kindly current down the river and out on to the new lake Lop-nor (the "Wandering Lake"), on whose northern shore the Silk Road ran two thousand years ago.

OUR LIVES ARE THREATENED

MONDAY, March 5, was a day none of us were to forget. I was tired and slept late. In the morning I inspected Georg's raft, which was lying almost completed in the middle of the yard. It was to have a trial trip in the afternoon.

But first one or two of us had to call on the mayor, an infirm old Chinese, who could not move without the aid of crutches. In his *yamen* we also made the acquaintance of the amiable, white-bearded deputy-mayor, who bore the same name as the Turki national leader Nias Hadji, but lacked his distinguished title of Hodja. We talked of our wishes and plans, and the mayor repeated his warning against a trip to Kucha, where he thought fighting was now going on. Both of them afterwards sent a few sheep and some bread to our quarters.

Then we drove to the commandant's *yamen*. We were received in the courtyard by an adjutant, who omitted the ceremony usual with distinguished guests of asking them to come in and drink tea. He informed us that the commandant had gone to Kara-shahr on horseback and would not return for some days. We left our cards, and later heard from the mayor that the commandant *was* in Korla. Why he should hide from us neither we nor the mayor could understand. The adjutant, a Tungan of the arrogant type, we met again that evening.

In the afternoon Bergman and I had gone to sit in the small car, where I dictated and he typed. We had not got far when Hummel and Yew came up to the car—the former to report that he had been sent for by the mayor to treat the trouble in his legs, Yew to tell me that he had been asked to go and see Chang, the commander of our escort from Turfan.

Chang had demanded, in an insolent and challenging tone, that one of our lorries should be placed at his disposal next morning, with petrol and a driver.

"You're going too slowly," he said. "My comrades and I had orders from General Ma Chung-yin to travel from Turfan to Aksu in six days, with his plan of operations. We have been on the road for eleven days now and are only at Korla. I've just had a telephone message from Kara-shahr with orders from Ma to take one of your cars and drive on ahead at all costs if I value my life."

Yew had replied that he would ask me. He did so, and agreed with me that we could under no circumstances hand over a car to people who would certainly never return it.

Now we understood the reason for General Li's exaggerated politeness to us at Turfan, and his repeatedly expressed wish that we should start for Korla and Kucha as quickly as possible. It was the result of special orders from Ma Chung-yin, who perfectly understood that he would require cars in his flight and that, before that, it might be a good thing to have one or two of them at hand for the rapid conveyance of orders to the officer in command at Kucha. The talk of the road between Turfan and Kara-shahr having to be cleared of robbers before we could travel was, therefore, probably genuine. Ma Chung-yin wanted to be sure that the cars would be at his disposal whenever he might need them. The object of the arsenal comedy had been to show us that he had thousands of rifles in reserve in addition to all the arms he had in the field.

At half-past six two officers came and asked for a final answer. They were invited into our comfortless room, and conveyed to me a request from Chang that he might have a car that same evening. I replied quite briefly that as we had been sent on a special mission by the central government at Nanking, we had no right to lend cars which did not belong to us. They rose, saluted and went.

We dined on fresh fish from the Konche-daria. At half-past nine I went into Georg and Effe's room, where Hummel and Chen already were. Georg's view was that we should take no orders from that rabble, but should reply that we would go on when it suited us, and that they could then accompany us to Kucha or Aksu, according to the Turfan agreement.

Ten minutes later Yew entered and said that two soldiers had come with a message that I was wanted on the telephone at the commandant's, because an important message for me had arrived from Kara-shahr. Objections were raised; it might be a trick. I took Yew and Georg with me as interpreters and Effe to drive the small car. In this were my diaries and manuscript, maps, etc., in an attaché case, and on the back seat my splendid Zeiss glasses. We got in. The two soldiers stood on the running-board and directed Effe—not to the commandant's *yamen*, where the telephone was, but to the house where Chang and the rest of the escort were quartered, and where we had had supper the evening before.

We were led diagonally across the yard to the room with the single candle and asked to sit down at the table. Tea, sugar and cigarettes were set before us. Half a dozen soldiers armed with rifles and pistols stood at the door, as many in the room, and in the yard, which was illuminated only by the light flung through the window, twenty or thirty men, all armed.

Chang now repeated his demand. A telephone message had arrived from Ma Chung-yin at Dawancheng, and written orders had been sent by courier to Kara-shahr. These orders were explicit. He *must* have a motor-lorry that same evening.

I replied firmly, emphasising each word:

"We are in the service of the central government. I am responsible for the execution of the government's orders. The motor-cars are not ours and none of them can be lent."

"Military matters come before everything else," Chang cried. "Nothing can be allowed to interfere with them. Nanking counts for nothing in a war in Sinkiang. For that matter, we are under Nanking too, and it ought to be in both your interest and Nanking's to help us."

"It is specially laid down in our instructions that we are not to take sides in the internal conflicts in Sinkiang. I therefore refuse to hand over any of our cars."

White with anger, and with clenched teeth, Chang answered in a low-pitched, trembling voice:

"It makes no difference what you decide or refuse. The orders I have received from Ma Chung-yin shall be obeyed. One of your cars shall be at my door this evening!"

I gave a contemptuous laugh, rose abruptly and went out without taking leave of them. Georg and Yew accompanied me. I showed the way with my electric torch. I came out into the street, where Effe was waiting in the small car, opened the door and took my place on the back seat. Yew had his foot on the step and his hand on the handle ready to get in, when three soldiers flung themselves on him from behind and forcibly pulled him down. He turned round and raised his arm to hit out in self-defence. I called out:

"Be quiet and go with them!"

So saying, I jumped out of the car. Two soldiers caught Yew's arms in an iron grip, and two others swept him back into the yard with their rifle-butts. I was hardly out of the car before I was surrounded by more soldiers, who seized my wrists and pushed me the same way. Effe also had jumped out and slammed the door; he was treated like us.

We were driven like cattle into the dark courtyard, where Georg already stood bound. There we three Swedes and Yew were surrounded by some forty officers and soldiers. Among the officers we recognised our loathsome escort from Turfan and the adjutant to the commandant of Korla. Probably the commandant himself was there—he who was declared to be at Kara-shahr. Chang, with rigid features and ashy pale, gave his orders curtly and sharply. He did not say much. Every soldier knew his part, which he had played many a time before and which had cost the lives of so many innocent people.

Each of us was surrounded by half a dozen soldiers. They were in a hurry. It all happened in a few seconds. When someone is to be shot, nothing is gained by dawdling. The quicker the better, and then it is over.

A horny hand wrenched the electric torch out of my hand. One of the minions unbuttoned my jacket with one violent tug and took it off, while another pulled my shirt up out of my trousers to draw it inside out over my head. One devilish robber held his pistol against my heart while this was being done. Strong hands seized my wrists and pulled them behind my back to bind them with a rope. Yew, Georg and Effe already had their hands tied behind them as in a vice and their chests bare. Each of them had one or several pistols an inch from his heart. The murderers had their fingers on the trigger. If one of them had tripped on the uneven surface of the dark courtyard, a round would have been let off and the signal given.

Meanwhile the rifles were clicking as the bolts were pushed home before firing. The soldiers formed a group to one side. They held their rifles aslant, with the barrels pointed at us. It only remained to give the orders: ready, fire!

In a moment the whole situation became clear to me. In one second my life flew past me; I thought of my dear home in the North, the young men for whose lives I was responsible, the expedition for which I should have rendered account to the central government. We were going to be shot in half a minute! Christ in heaven, it *must* not happen! My three comrades' lives and my own were worth more than one motor-lorry. Quick as lightning I cried to Georg:

"We'll be shot! Promise them the car to-night!"

Georg, a head taller than anyone else, translated my words in a quiet, low-pitched voice. The psychological current changed. Taut muscles slackened; the rifles assumed more vertical positions. A new word of command rang out:

"Take the old man in, keep a tight hand on the young ones."

The soldier who had made the first turn round my wrists dropped the rope and released my hands. Two soldiers jostled me into the room and drew a chair up to the table on which the candle stood. I sat down and was about to light a cigarette. My cigarette-case was missing, as well as other things I had had in my pockets.

Curiously enough my watch was still there. The others lost theirs.

The minutes which followed were like eternities.

"Aren't the others coming?" I asked the guards who stood watching me like wolves.

"They're coming!" they replied.

But they did not come. I sat in a terrible stage of tension, expecting every moment to hear the three volleys which would announce my friends' death.

"Aren't they coming soon?"

"They're coming!"

But they did not come. Tortured with anxiety, I rose quickly, meaning to hurry out into the yard and see what had happened or was happening. The two soldiers placed themselves in my way like an iron wall and pointed to the chair. It was half-past ten. It had all happened in a few minutes. I remained outwardly calm, but feverish with anxiety.

Next moment Yew was thrust into the room with a violent push, crying:

"Their ultimatum is: yes or no about the car."

"Say that the car will be here this evening on condition that you and Georg and Effe are untied and the two Swedes brought in here."

Two men loosened the rope round Yew's wrists. He made a few motions with his arm, saying:

"They fastened the rope as tight as they could; my wrists hurt and my hands are quite numb."

Just then Georg and Effe were brought in, and Chang ordered them to be freed.

We were completely in Chang's power. The room was full of soldiers, and there was a sentry at the door. They all had rifles and pistols ready for use. Chang could dictate as he pleased.

"One lorry, one driver and enough petrol to get to Aksu. The lorry is to be brought here at once. Meanwhile you [Yew and myself] are my prisoners."

It would have been cruel to send one of the Mongols with that gang of robbers. Effe was only twenty. Georg was the only one who could possibly go; for that matter, he volunteered to go before I could give him any order.

Georg and Effe left the room escorted by soldiers. The small car could stay where it was, they were going to walk. Effe looked into the car to lock it. It was full of soldiers. I had asked him to see whether my attaché case was still there. If it was not he was to come back immediately and report. It contained my diaries, all our passports and other things of importance. He did not come back, so the case was not stolen.

When Georg and Effe had gone through the door of our yard and were making for the drivers' room, their escort shouted:

"Halt! If you move a step we fire."

They evidently feared that Hummel, Bergman, Chen and Kung, and the drivers and servants, meant to fire.

Georg answered quietly that if the car was to be ready it must first of all be unloaded, and then loaded with the petrol and spare parts and tools which were needed for the journey to Aksu. He must therefore have complete freedom of movement. They agreed to this. Two soldiers armed with rifles and pistols shadowed every step he took.

Bergman had already gone to bed on the *kang*. A soldier entered pistol in hand and shouted at him that he was to dress. Hummel was already in the yard. No one was allowed to remain indoors. They did not understand what had happened and were in mortal fear for Yew and myself, who had been detained unarmed.

For an hour and a half Yew and I sat as Chang's hostages at the table on which the candle stood. Pleased with his coup, and the way in which he had succeeded in coercing us, he gradually thawed. In the course of his talk he said:

"I haven't treated you like this for the pleasure of it. It was a matter of life and death for me to carry out Ma's orders. I am sorry your resistance compelled me to use force. Soviet Russia has just occupied northern Sinkiang, Ili, Chuguchak and Altai, and shot General Chang Pei-yuan, the military governor of Ili, who was an ally of Ma Chung-yin. Urumchi itself is occupied by the Russians. These events have made Ma's position extremely serious; it was vital for him to send his subordinates at Kucha and Aksu instructions in accordance with the new military situation, and so there was no choice but to take one of your cars. The order that came to-day by telephone was quite categorical, and it was the best thing you could do to give way. Otherwise anything might have happened. I have nothing to lose and nothing to hope for, and I shall soon be going to certain death at Kucha or Aksu. What I have told you is secret till I've been shot."

He sat for a long time in silent reflection, with a serious aspect. Then he said:

"My comrades from Turfan and a number of soldiers are leaving Korla to-night with your lorry and are going straight to Aksu. Your driver will be released there and can bring the car straight back to you. You can wait here if you like or follow us to Aksu if you prefer, but not for three days, or until the day after to-morrow at the earliest."

I objected:

"You ought to give us a receipt for the loan of the lorry, and you must compensate us for the petrol and paraffin you use."

Chang refused to give us a receipt, which meant that the car was lost to us. I added:

"I am astonished that, when General Ma has ordered that we shall be hospitably received everywhere in the country he occupies, his subordinates should use violence against his guests, and refuse to discharge such a simple duty as to write an acknowledgment of a loan of material belonging to the central government."

He shrugged his shoulders and repeated that it was war-time, and that in war-time no laws or obligations were respected. He had no choice but to execute Ma's orders.

At that moment the buzz of a motor was heard in the street. The motor-lorry stood at the gate. Georg and Bergman came in, the latter to persuade himself that Yew and I were really alive.

We rose. Georg got permission to return to our quarters and pack his own kit. Then he was to report to Chang immediately. Chang accompanied us out to the small car. We got in and drove home. Even now we had two soldiers on the running-board. The town was dead: not a soul was to be seen in the street; not a lamp was burning; not a dog barked.

In our quarters they were all sitting up in a state of breathless anxiety. They wondered why we were away so long. They could not conceal their joy at our return. Yew and I described the unpleasant incident in full detail. Our servants also heard about it, and were enraged against the Tungan soldiery, whom they consigned to the flames of hell for all eternity.

When we were being bound and partially undressed the soldiers had stolen our electric torches, one or two watches and cigarette-cases, even a thermometer which Yew had in his pocket; they had also taken my Zeiss glasses from the car. I complained to Chang that his soldiers had stolen these things. But I received the answer that they could not be found. This, however, was of comparatively small importance. We had reserves of everything, and I was glad they had not taken the attaché case—and still gladder that we had come out of it alive.

When our men called down wrath and damnation upon Chang and his gang of murderers, I replied that he ought to have a gold medal for having shown such great self-control as to refrain from having us shot in the dark courtyard. It had been a hair's-breadth escape. Yew, Georg and Effe were convinced that if I had not yielded the order to fire would have been given, in such a state of frenzy were Chang, the commandant and his adjutant. It would have been enough for Chang, in the extreme agitation of the moment, to have lost his head and shouted "Fire!" All the rest would have taken his side. No one would have reproached him for an act into which he had been forced by hostile foreigners when the rapid transmission of military orders, and Big Horse's flight, were endangered. If this final step had been taken, and we four had been shot, one more measure would have been necessary—to occupy our quarters and shoot all the others, masters and servants, and wipe out all traces of the dead. But then the cars would have been worthless—without drivers, except such as were to be found in Ma's army. It is possible that their urgent need of our fleet of cars helped to save our lives.

"If anyone lays a hand on me I'll shoot him down like a dog," Effe had assured me before that awful night.

"You go slow, my boy," I had answered. "Or you and all the rest of us'll be done for."

In the decisive moment on that terrible night my three companions preserved a magnificent coolness and an unruffled calm. We were unarmed, and our enemies outnumbered us by ten times and were all armed to the teeth. Yew was admirable in his icy self-control and showed not a trace of fear. At the height of the tumult, when he stood stripped to the waist with his hands tied behind his back, he had shouted:

"You're a lot of cowardly swine! How dare you lay your hands on the representatives of Nanking and Ma Chung-yin's guests? You'll pay for this!"

"You've been arrogant and overbearing here and on the way here. Now it's our turn!" the soldiers who stood round had answered.

We were sitting on the *kangs* in our room. The night wore on. It was one o'clock now. At two Georg was to be back at Chang's quarters. From time to time soldiers came with fresh orders. Just before two o'clock one came and said that Georg might sleep till four. They probably only wanted to make sure that he did not make a bolt and that we did not disappear with the four cars.

No one went to bed as long as Georg was still with us. We were all convinced that we were seeing him for the last time. Among the Tungans, he could not avoid witnessing things which must not be made known on the fugitives' line of retreat. He would, therefore, be put out of the way as soon as he had conveyed his barbarous passengers to their destination. Georg himself did not think he would ever see us again. When the moment

Photo by Bergman

A CAR HAS STUCK FAST, THE BAGGAGE HAS BEEN UNLOADED, AND EFFE, YEW AND A TUNGAN SOLDIER—
ONE OF THE ESCORT FROM HAMI—ARE TAKING A SIESTA ON A BUNDLE OF SLEEPING-BAGS AND TENTS.
ON THE LEFT IS THE UNLUCKY SHEEP-DOG PAO

Photo by Bergman

INTERESTED TURKIS AT SU-BASHI; IN THE FOREGROUND ONE OF MA CHUNG-YIN'S TUNGAN SOLDIERS IN
THE ORDINARY LIGHT GREY UNIFORM

JOMCHA'S LORRY STUCK ON THE SHOCKING ROAD AT SU-BASHI

THE SÄNGIM VALLEY AND ITS DANGEROUS ROAD

ONE OF THE DANGEROUS BRIDGES AT SÄNGIM–AGHIS

YOLLBARS KHAN, THE "TIGER PRINCE"—THE MOST POWERFUL MAN
IN HAMI

TOMBS IN THE MAUSOLEUM OF THE KINGS OF HAMI

AMIN HODJA'S MOSQUE AT TURFAN (EIGHTEENTH CENTURY)

Photo by Bergman

KARL EFRAIM HILL (EFFE), FROM FENG-CHEN, MECHANIC AND DRIVER

MAMESJER AHUN, A MAN OF SEVENTY-SIX, WHO IN HIS YOUTH
WAS IN THE AUTHOR'S SERVICE

BOGDO-ULA, GOD'S MOUNTAIN

THE CARS PARKED: EFFE AND CHIA-KWEI ON THE TOP OF A LORRY

SAINT'S TOMB OUTSIDE TOKSUN

Photo by Bergman

ICE-CRUSTS IN THE SU-BASHI VALLEY HAD TO BE LEVELLED WITH SPADES FOR THE CARS

THE ROUTE THROUGH THE VALLEY ABOVE SU–BASHI IS ONE OF THE
WILDEST AND MOST BEAUTIFUL IN CENTRAL ASIA

ENTERING A DESTROYED AND ABANDONED VILLAGE

of parting was approaching, he asked me to read a few Swedish hymns, which I did.

One natural consequence of the events of the night was that our plan of dividing the expedition between Lop-nor and Kashgar was abandoned. It was quite clear that we must keep together and not weaken our position by splitting.

The new plan was this: the whole expedition was to follow the tracks of Georg's lorry till we found him, alive or dead.

Georg insisted with almost monomaniac obstinacy that the expedition, for its own safety's sake, should flee as quickly as possible to the Lop-nor desert and thence endeavour to reach Tun-hwang and the Imperial Highway to Lanchow. "It is better", he held, "that *one* man should be sacrificed to save the rest, than that the whole mission should be killed."

Not one of us, Swedish, Chinese or Mongol, would hear of anything but reunion with Georg. But it was impossible to convince him, even when I said that what he proposed was the kind of thing which is not done by gentlemen. One does not let a man fall overboard without trying to save him. If we left him adrift on the western front the whole world would call us cowards.

None of us slept any more that night. Later in the morning Georg went to his room and waited for the fatal message. At seven a soldier appeared and summoned him to Chang's quarters. I was still awake, and heard him come into Hummel's room, where he had a cup of coffee. He had not slept a wink. I called to him. A last vigorous shake of the hand, and "God keep you! You'll wait for us at Aksu; we start to-morrow."

We heard his footsteps crossing the yard. The gate was slammed behind him, and he departed into the unknown.

IN SEARCH OF GEORG

O N the morning of March 6 Yew and I went to call on the mayor, who had already heard of the night's adventures and asked if anyone had been injured. Then we went to the commandant's adjutant to report that we intended to drive to Kucha the following morning. It would be best to lay all our cards on the table, otherwise they might detain us as prisoners. That scoundrel of an adjutant, who had been the real instigator of the previous night's outrage, put a good face upon things and declared that there was no obstacle in the way of our journey. Diplomatic wisdom bade us accept the two sheep and six chickens he sent us as a present.

Our yard was full of curious spectators, mostly old men and boys. Some of the Turkis were not afraid to say what they thought. "These Tungan soldiers", one of them said, "are a scourge and a plague to us poor people. They're sucking our life-blood and we're dying of hunger."

The worthy mayor had painted the following inscription in Chinese characters on the wall of his *yamen*:

"Commandant! You can kill me and I shall die gladly. But I beg you to spare my people."

In consequence of this an order had been issued that everything requisitioned should be paid for. But no one paid any attention to the order. The men stole and plundered as before, and so the shops in the bazaar remained shut and barred.

Another old man said: "They take our wheat and our rice, our eggs, fowls, ducks and sheep, our donkeys, cows and horses, and never pay a cent."

It was said that two or three hundred Turki families were now living in Korla; there were also fifty Tungan families, but no Chinese.

The whole day was spent in preparations and purchases. We left Korla on the morning of March 7. Effe had been appointed to succeed Georg as chief of our mechanics and drivers. A lot of people were out in the streets staring at us. We passed the main guard, at the gate of which no sentries were now posted. The bridge over the Konche-daria, which we had tested for the first time in the dark, had now been examined by Kung. He had guaranteed that it would bear us. It was packed with spectators, but the crowd thinned as we approached the border of the oasis. Willows, elms and poplars stretched their boughs across the road and formed an arcade.

We were out on the high road. Behind us lay Korla, that little town which we should never forget. As long as thirty-eight years before I had had an adventure with soldiers in Korla. My caravan master Islam Bai had been sitting in the bazaar chatting with an Andishan merchant when a party of soldiers rode past. Then all the Turkis had been obliged to rise as a sign of submission and obedience to the Son of Heaven. Islam Bai, who was a subject of the White Tsar, remained seated. The group of soldiers had stopped, and one or two of them had seized and beaten the offender. I had complained to their commander. His judgment was that Islam himself should point out the man who had beaten him. This was done, and the fellow indicated had had a dressing-down as the penalty of his error. Where was he now? Islam Bai was dead. And now it had been my turn to get into trouble with undisciplined soldiers at Korla.

And further back in time, in 1877, the conqueror Yakub Beg, after his defeat at the hands of Tso Tsung-tang, had taken his life in the little town on the Konche-daria.

Serat stuck on the flooded road. While he was being dug out a crowd of people collected again round the cars. A humorous dervish was given a piece of bread. He seemed to be a philosopher. It was all the same to him who won; he had nothing to lose, and would remain as poor as ever whoever held sway over Eastern Turkestan.

An old man gave us a cake and got five liang. An old woman stretched out her skinny hands, praying that God might grant us a prosperous journey. She received the cake the old man had just given us, and hastened to conceal it in her bosom before some other starveling got hold of it. Our profit on the deal was the old woman's blessing.

People came and went; women with children riding on donkey-back, people who had been in the bazaar trading, aimless wanderers, beggars, dervishes, villagers and fugitives returning home. All stopped and stared a while before continuing their journey. But no countrymen were seen selling sheep, poultry or grain. What would be the use of it, since everything was stolen by the soldiers? Better to hide the food one had, so as not to starve to death.

The only person who remained immovable was Serat. His back wheel had sunk in up to the axle. Not surprising, seeing that we had now only three lorries with cargo for four. We had successfully passed the rickety bridge and the insolent sentries. Now it was the mud of the high road which detained us in this awful oasis. But at last, with the help of matting, we succeeded in getting Serat going again. We went on, and the inquisitive crowd was scattered.

The convoy passed a Chinese temple, over the main door of which was inscribed: "The temple of the mayor of spirits". We left to our right the Konche valley road down which we had driven on March 4. Now we turned off along the high road to Kucha. Georg's wheel-tracks of the previous day had not yet been effaced by the scanty traffic. Not a soul was to be seen. Here were the dwellings of the dead, under the gravestones of Korla cemetery. In a number of fresh graves on the side nearest to the road, we were told, people who had been killed by robbers were buried.

Before us lay the desert, flooded with blinding light, splendid to look on—the silent, peaceful old desert where lived neither men nor devils. On my earlier journeys I had travelled along all the roads in Eastern Turkestan but this one between Korla and Aksu. Everything here was new to me.

Another *guristan*, or burial-ground, with five *gumbez*, monuments surmounted by cupolas, over *bais* (rich men). A flock of sheep was grazing among the common people's gravestones; it was often hard to distinguish the sheep from the stones that were as white as they.

A branch of a canal ran out here, betraying its presence by the rows of trees, willows and Lombardy poplars, which shaded its course. One or two houses were to be seen here. An old woman stood by the roadside offering eggs for sale. More burial-grounds, a serai with a resting caravan. Vegetation from the plain was being transported in ox-carts for use as fuel.

We had on our left a sharp westward bend of the Konchedaria and an oblong lake. After barely an hour's drive we passed the end of the canal among farms and trees. We were just fifteen miles from Korla. Then we rolled along a good but sandy road out into sheer desert. We had thus left the area of the Korla oasis.

We met a military convoy of twenty-one carts loaded with uniforms for Ma's army, escorted by thirteen soldiers on horseback. A solitary Turki lay on his face by the roadside. Was he dead? No, he got up as we hurtled by. All the way from Korla even the telegraph poles had lain on the ground, but now they were upright for some distance ahead. To our right the mountains drew back. The desert was absolutely level to the eye, but it falls imperceptibly towards the Tarim.

Here was a belt of vegetation-clad mounds nine feet high, among sand dunes. Then the way ran through an open wood of poplars, and at places was sunk six feet deep between the overgrown mounds. We were now on the genuine ancient Silk Road. A herd of horned cattle hurried off at our approach.

The village of Charchi was inhabited by twelve Turki families who were sowing wheat. Six cavalrymen had established themselves in its tea-house and were laying their hands on all there was to take.

Open poplar copses and tamarisk dunes were common sights. Now and again we crossed the dry channels of streams from the mountains. Sometimes the soil was sandy, at others it was mere dust, which swirled behind the cars. A few people were living in the village of Eshme.

After this the road became unpleasant—sand and whirling dust. An alley of stumpy old trees led to the village of Chadir. Its watercourse forked into a number of canals. The village, with its pretty groves, made a pleasant impression. Woods were visible to the southward at a great distance.

The plain continued westward and the road was good. A little later we crossed several strips of water.

Our camp No. 47 was pitched outside the village of Karasach-khanem, called after a mausoleum that is situated there. There were twelve families in the village. We had driven seventy-three miles and were about 3250 ft. up.

We had fried fish and soup with eggs in it for dinner. Our old stove had been scrapped and we had a brazier with red-hot embers instead. The people in the village were friendly, and we were supplied with quantities of eggs. When we asked the price, we received the reply: "You are visitors from distant countries and must be fed free of charge." We ourselves fixed the price.

The Tarim is hereabouts called the Chayan-daria (Scorpion River) and in the direction of Aksu the Musart-daria. A villager told us that he and thirty-three others had driven 12,000 sheep to be sold to Kirghizes and Russians in Western Turkestan, whence they had returned two months before: they had been well paid, but the money had been confiscated by the authorities. They declared that there were only two hundred Tungan soldiers at Kucha and that two thousand *chantous*, or Turkis, lived in the villages round about. The latter were mounted, but had only *kara-multuk*, or "black rifles", good enough for hunting but not for war.

I asked why we met no caravans or merchants, and was told that these were going by a desert route for fear of the soldiers.

The thermometer fell to 24.3 degrees in the night. We started at 9.42 A.M. on March 8, across bush-covered plains, over a fair-sized bridge and several smaller ones. We were driving all the way along an avenue of picturesque old trees.

It was not far to the bazaar of the village of Yangi-hissar, where we bought bread, meat and nuts. Many shops were shut, but there were a lot of people about. Outside the village a good-sized bridge crosses a canal.

Not far from Yangi-hissar the road runs for about three-quarters of a mile through a continuous salt marsh, where snow-water and spring-fed streams from the mountains percolate through the level earth and keep it continually moist. Despite fairly deep ditches and many bridges this is an unpleasant bit of road, and our three "elephants" sank in and stuck time after time. But the countrymen went to fetch their *ketman*, or spades, and helped us, and at last this obstacle too was surmounted.

Then the trees stopped; there were only tamarisks and tussocks of herbage, and the country became more desolate. Now and again we crossed a bridge. Local trade was being carried on between the villages on a very small scale; but we saw no caravans, only a few donkeys or horses, and occasionally a cart.

We crossed a few streams; and then came another stretch of salt plain. In places the soil was absolutely barren. Then came another string of bridges and an avenue of splendid trees which led into the bazaar of the large village of Bugur, to the Chinese Lun-tai. Here there was almost a crowd. The covered bazaar made an impression of prosperity, and all the shops were open. Caravans, riders, beasts of burden, buyers and sellers, noise and movement.

We did not stop now, but drove on so as to reach Kucha before dark. Georg's tracks had been visible the whole way, and villagers we asked told us that a car had passed along the road the day before.

So on we drove, through avenues and over new canals with bridges. Another belt of annoying wet salty soil, in which we stuck time after time. At one burial-ground *tughs* with tails and horns had been erected. It was no use trying to count the bridges; they followed one another too closely.

We stopped for a while on the bank of a river, close to a solid bridge, and had a modest lunch, with tea out of thermos flasks.

We had just driven through the bazaar of the village of Chompak and were proceeding westward. It was ten minutes to four when Bergman, who was sitting at the wheel of the small car, cried:

"Here comes Georg!"

"What? Georg! It's impossible; he only started the day before yesterday. It *can't* be him!"

At any rate surging white clouds of dust, which could only be caused by a swiftly moving motor-car, were visible between the willows which formed an avenue along the road. It was not far away; the trees had hidden it.

"He's got soldiers with him," said Chen.

"No," said Yew, "those are only the flags."

We had the flags of China and Sweden on the front of all the cars, the Swedish to show that we were foreigners and therefore not to be molested.

In a minute Georg had come up to us and jumped down. We had stopped. Bergman hurried to meet him with arms out-stretched. Then the prodigal son advanced towards me.

"Thank God you're alive, Georg! What's happened? How did you manage to get rid of them so quickly? Tell us all about it!"

"Well, after I left our quarters at Korla on the morning of March 6, I went straight to Chang's house, where we had been tied up the night before. The whole escort, the five fellows from Turfan, were to come too, and seven others. They got up on to the lorry at once, and didn't take any kit. I drove off as hard as I could over hard bits, bumps, canals, bridges, so that the passengers were chucked all over the place and had to hold on like grim death. They got a regular knocking about. All but two were sick and spewed like cats. Chang himself succumbed, sitting by my side in the cabin, and made an awful mess all round him. It was fun to think that I was kidnapping him now. He was so tame that I could have tied him up and heaved him into the ditch. But although they were having such a bad time they stood to their guns; after all, they had said themselves that they were in a fearful hurry to take Ma's orders to Aksu.

"I couldn't help pulling Chang's leg and asking him if he didn't think it was a lovely trip and a beautifully smooth road. . . . But I spoke my mind to him too, and told him straight out that their violence against the head and three other members of our mission would become known all over the world, and absolutely disgrace them and damage the prestige of General Ma Chung-yin, in whose service they were. They would get a bad reputation both in Asia and in Europe.

"Chang said, 'We don't care a hang about our reputation; we had simply to obey orders.' 'Well,' I said, 'I'm telling you straight out what I think of you. Here I sit, alone and unarmed, among twelve soldiers armed with rifles and pistols. You can shoot me if you like, I don't care; but as long as I can speak I'll tell you the truth. . . .'

"On the evening of the day before yesterday we got to Bugur. They were so done up by the awful drive that they had to stay the night there and have a good rest. Chang had a long talk with the officer in command and other Tungan officers and heard a lot of news about the war. Then we sat by the fire for some time talking.

"Chang said to me, with surprising frankness, 'I've heard that we can't get any farther than Kucha. The road to Aksu is blocked. You can certainly go back to Korla from Kucha; we don't need you any longer.'

" 'Will you give me that in writing?' I tore a leaf out of my diary, and he wrote on it: 'Georg Söderbom is authorised to drive his lorry to Korla; no troops on the road are to interfere with him.' Chang stamped the paper. I took it as if it was of no consequence, but hid it away well. . . .

"Yesterday morning I drove them to Kucha; we got there at twelve. We stopped outside the door of the main guard's *yamen*. Here I chucked them off—as a matter of fact, they were in a terrible hurry to jump down and rush in to hand over their orders, hear the war news, get some tea and have lunch.

"The minute the last thief had disappeared through the doorway I turned the lorry as quickly as I could and raced back out of the town like an arrow the same way we had come. Seven and a half miles out of Kucha the engine broke down and I couldn't move. Then I thought I was lost. I hadn't got permission to leave the town, and in all probability fresh despatches about the new military situation were to be sent to General Ma as quickly as possible. I couldn't do anything with the engine. I worked for dear life all day with my heart in my mouth, but I couldn't get the engine to go. But when it grew dark I had repaired it at last. I was astonished that nobody had come along and interfered with me, from either east or west, and I thought of going on during the night, but I didn't dare turn on my headlights—they might have given me away. My start from Kucha had been a regular flight, and my passengers must have been furious when they found I had cleared out. Their not sending men on fast horses after me at once must have been the result of the experience they had had on the way out, for we had really stepped on the gas. . . .

"I was so tired that I slept a bit, but uneasily, because I might expect to have them on my back at any moment. My own belief is that they had had such terrible news from the garrison at Kucha of crushing defeat and headlong flight that they forgot both me and the lorry, and thought of nothing else but saving their lives by bolting, anywhere on earth only not eastward, where they would meet Ma in all his fury. . . .

"When I woke this morning, it was all quiet. I started early and reached the outskirts of Chompak about three. There I had lunch. The eating-house keeper told me that four cars had arrived in the country about Yangi-hissar the evening before. So I was certainly less surprised than you at our meeting here."

Georg had finished his story. He was the hero of the hour as he stood there quietly smiling and smoking a cigarette. We had all got off. He narrated for our benefit in English, for the Mongols' and boys' in Chinese. To me it was a disappointment not to be able to go on to Kucha, Aksu and Kashgar, and dispose of this part of our programme now that we were so far on the way. But according to Georg this would have meant captivity or death.

He had learned from the Tungans' conversation and other informants that Ili and Kulja had been taken by Sheng Shih-tsai's White Russians and that the military governor of Ili, General Chang Pei-yuan, had committed suicide; we had heard before that he had been killed. General Chang's troops, however, had gone forward and reached the road between Aksu and Kucha in the neighbourhood of Bai, whence they might possibly advance towards Kucha and farther east. In Kucha fresh slaughter was expected.

Georg hoped that we should sooner or later get to Kucha, which was a fascinating town with picturesque streets and pleasant houses, bridges and gardens. He could not have visited the solitary Swedish woman missionary, Miss Engwall, without risking his life and the lorry.

On the other hand, he had heard that there was not a drop of petrol in the town. All the promises which had been given us of the repayment of our loan of petrol were therefore sheer humbug; for that matter, we had never expected anything else.

Georg had also received the definite impression that Ma's situation was hopeless and that he would probably be taken between two fires. In such a position, would he retreat via Hami or Korla to Anhsi?

Here, in the Chompak oasis, we stood as it were at the parting of the ways. If we went on to the westward, we should have to cross a front at Bai; according to Georg we should be fired upon, taken prisoners and robbed of our cars. If we turned eastward, to Korla, we should in all probability meet Ma Chung-yin, his staff, and his army fleeing in wild disorder. It would be more dangerous for us and our convoy of cars, now again complete, to fall into the hands of a beaten than of a victorious army.

We were truly between two fires, and it was not easy to guess in which flames we should be done the brownest. We now felt more clearly than ever that we had got into the middle of a Central Asiatic war in all its barbarous brutality. Nor was that all; we were near the hottest part of the theatre of war, and that in the war's last and decisive stage. For the moment we were surrounded by an ominous calm. Here countrymen and carts went about in the roads as in times of the most profound peace. But there was a feeling in the air which suggested that this was the calm before the storm and that the decision would be just here, between Korla and Aksu, on the ancient Silk Road, where in olden times immense caravans had journeyed with precious cargoes towards the western world. It was for us to take wise and well-weighed decisions, otherwise we were doomed to certain destruction.

It was five o'clock before, as a beginning, we decided to sleep the matter over and to spend the night at Bugur, seven and a half miles on. We had not stopped there on the previous day to avoid an unnecessary halt when we wanted to find out as quickly as possible what had happened to Georg.

We could hardly get to Bugur before dark. We knew the road; it was wretched. We turned the lorries right about and drove in our own tracks. After a quarter of an hour Jomcha got stuck in the mud, and then one or two of the others. It took an hour to get them out again. The twilight came creeping up. So we must encamp wherever we could find a dry patch of ground. A friendly old man helped us. Our tents were pitched in a field.

The old man got us fuel and eggs. He also mobilised four Turkis to keep guard at night in turns. The site of our camp No. 48 was called Shoyachi and belonged to the Chompak district. Our old man did not quite know what to make of us.

"One car went by here yesterday," he said, "and four to-day.

And this evening all five have come back. What is it? What has happened? Is there fighting to the west? Have you been obliged to turn back eastward?"

Naturally rural labourers and farmers were alarmed by our movements to and fro, and were afraid that something had gone wrong. Our old man told us that it was already difficult to get fodder, because merchants and countrymen preferred to hide what they had rather than take it to the bazaar at Bugur to be sold. "The soldiers take our grain and our cattle," he said, "and pay nothing."

The *aksakal*, or headman, of the village informed us that there was a road down to the Tarim which was good going for carts and free from sand. By the Tarim there was *abad*, or cultivated land with villages; the population consisted of Lopluks and owned boats, horses and camels. They put together several canoes and covered them with planks, and on these ferry-boats they could carry carts and goods.

After 24·3 degrees in the night we made an early start on the morning of March 9. Each morning I wondered how the day would end, and what would be the subject of the next chapter in our story.

We drove into Bugur and stopped outside the mayor's gate. We handed in our cards, and were escorted to the Beg's reception room, which was furnished in Chinese style. He was a man of fifty or so, with a full beard and turban and the melodious name of Jemaleddin Hadji. He had, therefore, been in Mecca and seen a part, indeed the cream, of the Islamic world.

The Beg offered us tea and cigarettes. It was a couple of hours before the lorries arrived. Serat's air filter was giving trouble, and had to be repaired by a smith in the bazaar. The others bought rice, flour, eggs, bread and twenty gallons of paraffin.

I wanted to hear Jemaleddin's view of the situation, but he was, and had to be, diplomatic. He did not say a word to betray what he knew of Ma Chung-yin's probable defeat, for even if he was convinced of it he must hold his tongue so long as the big village, whose highest Turki official and Beg he was, had a Tungan garrison loyal to Ma.

I explained our mission and how we had involuntarily got into a rat-trap, which we must at all costs get out of alive.

"What would you do in such a position, and what do you advise us to do?" I asked, and received the answer:

"You are great and powerful men, I am small and weak. You know much more than I do. You come from the heart of things, away to the eastward, I sit here and know nothing. But whatever you decide, I shall do everything in my power to serve you."

"Well, do you think we can drive to Kucha to-day?"

"Yes, to the village of Dushambe-bazar, outside Kucha. No one will dare touch your cars."

After further reflection he added:

"Don't go to Kucha to-day. I sent a scout there six days ago. His orders were to find out exactly what the position was and to come back here in two days. You would do well to stay and wait for my messenger."

Hours passed, and the convoy was not ready to start. The Beg asked us to stay and eat *ash* with him. I was on tenter-hooks, for I felt that we were losing valuable time, and that with every hour that passed the probability increased of our meeting Ma Chung-yin as he and his defeated army came sweeping like a hurricane along the Silk Road from Korla to Kucha.

The main road, the road the army would take, was the most dangerous of all to us. I therefore considered the possibility of extricating ourselves by driving down to the Tarim, crossing the river and hiding in the woods till quiet had been restored.

I asked the Beg about this, and he said that the road from Bugur down to the Tarim villages was waterlogged and impossible for cars. And even if we succeeded in getting the cars down there, the boats were too small to carry a lorry. He added that one came first to the Ugen-daria and then to the Great Tarim, which ran into a considerable lake; from this an arm of the Kum-daria issued. A hundred and sixty yoll (about fifty miles) below Charchi was the village of Sai-kichik, by the lake Bot-kul. "You ought to be able to drive there and wait to see how things turn out," the Beg said.

Again hours slipped by, and Serat was still waiting for the smith. Some of us went for a walk in the bazaar and saw some popular life. About half the shops were open, the other half shuttered up. Food of all kinds was being offered for sale—meat, bread, flour, rice, nuts, vegetables and dried fruit, especially raisins and apricots. In the restaurants which opened on to the streets of the bazaar the cooks stood with their ladles stirring the pot or dishing up *ash*, *mante*, *kebab* and *shislik* on wooden dishes, while fragrant vapours whetted the customer's appetite.

Sheep's carcases hung in the dust of the street, the first flies swarming round them. In some shops boots and shoes were sold, in others caps and embroidered head-gear of all kinds. There were cigarettes—a small packet of ten cost a dollar! Women with the white veil over or under a black head-dress were strolling in the bazaar, and in the prostitutes' alley the unveiled, crudely painted beauties stood at their doors and enticed their lovers with smiles.

We could see that the costumes were old and worn. Once red, blue, black or striped *chapans* were dirty and faded, so that their colour was hard to distinguish. The usually shining soft boots were worn out and shabby. People could not afford to buy new things; trade was paralysed, and the merchants had no desire to risk their capital. There was war in the country. One must get on as well as one could for the time being. Only the beggars and dervishes were dressed as in time of peace, ragged, poor, half-naked and hungry.

In addition to all caravan animals, which were for sale—besides cattle, sheep, fowls, ducks and geese—the zoological gardens of the bazaar included pigeons, dogs and cats.

We returned to the Beg's house, which had formerly been the Chinese mayor's *yamen*. We gathered that 180 Chinese had been killed at Bugur at the Chinese New Year, 1933. Only five were left; they seemed to enjoy the protection of Jemaleddin Hadji.

When changing money we got only twenty taels for a dollar. The Beg gained on the deal.

In the evening there was dancing and music at Jemaleddin Beg's. Two Turkis danced to a slow, monotonous rhythm with uplifted arms and bent knees, rotating round one another and pirouetting. They also sang to the music of a *dutar*, or two-stringed zither, and a *dak*, or tambourine. Dinner consisted of mutton, rice, onions and tea.

We did not succeed in getting our repairs done and making our purchases. We had to stay at Bugur, and were put up free of charge in Jemaleddin's *yamen*. His earnest desire that we should stay a few days made Yew think that he wanted to detain us, and meanwhile had sent mounted messengers both to Kucha and to Korla with reports on our movements and plans. He was bound for his own safety's sake to be loyal to the power of the moment, General Ma Chung-yin.

An old Turki who was present at the musical evening told me in a whisper that the Beg had heard that two thousand Tungans belonging to the late General Chang's force had just arrived at Kucha. He said there were still a few thousand Chinese at Dushambe-bazar.

On the night of March 9 the minimum thermometer fell to 34 degrees. I had given orders for a start to be made at six, but "Edsel" gave trouble and would not start, and we had to wait again. We lost a whole day and night at Bugur. What this meant to us was seen next day.

Jemaleddin Hadji had asked in the evening if he might drive with us to Yangi-hissar, where he suddenly had something important to do. Certainly, with pleasure! Later he asked Georg cautiously if he could be sure of being put down at his destination, and that we should not drive through the bazaar at lightning speed without letting him get off. When it came to the point, and we were ready to get in, he excused himself, saying that he had got extra work on hand and could not start before twelve o'clock, when he would ride to Yangi-hissar. We were as little inclined to persuade him as to wait. It had probably occurred to him that no one could know which side we were on—that is to say, whether we belonged to Ma Chung-yin or Sheng Shih-tsai. In the latter case it might cost him his life if he drove in our cars.

The outer courtyard of the *yamen* was packed with curious spectators when we started. There was almost a crush in the bazaar, and it was pleasant to come out on to the airy high road among fields and trees.

Outside Yangi-hissar Georg and "Edsel" went into a three-feet-deep ditch, and it took a good three hours to get them out again. It seemed to be written in the stars that we should arrive too late for something important farther east.

Among the people who collected round the waiting cars were some talkative Turkis. Several of them were refugees from Korla, who lamented that their town and oasis, once a fertile garden, had been completely devastated. Seven months before Hodja Nias Hadji had come to Yangi-hissar with seven thousand Turkis, mounted but unarmed. All who had served under him and all who had helped him had been amply rewarded. He had got money from Urumchi. Where he was now no one knew, and about Yollbars Khan they would say nothing. One old man said:

"When you drove past here the day before yesterday, going west, we hoped and believed that you had been sent by Nanking to make peace between Hodja Nias Hadji and the Tungans, and we were all glad. Now that you are turning back eastward again, we are all sorry, for we understand now that we have nothing more to hope for."

Another said:

"We who have come up against the Tungans have lost everything. The only things we have left are our souls."

The friendship between the Turki and Chinese Mohammedans is not worth much. Hodja Nias Hadji, after some wavering, finally joined General Sheng Shih-tsai at Urumchi.

While we were stopping the Beg of Yangi-hissar rode past, accompanied by five horsemen. He was pleasant, courteous and genial, and told us among other things that the Ugen-daria, a stream I had known since 1896 and 1899, was now dry, and that all the water from Yarkand, Kashgar, Khotan and Aksu was now flowing into the Chayan-daria, but could never reach the Charkhlik region as it formerly did.

The air was not clear. The mountains to the northward were invisible. A kind of mist lay over the earth, both actually and figuratively.

At Karasach Khanem-mazar, where we had had our camp No. 47, we stopped for a time and chatted with our friends, who were astonished that we had turned back so soon.

At Chadir we rested for a while at a little tea-house close to the road. Here the mysterious fakir Plavski reappeared. He had arrived two hours before us and had come straight from Korla. He now told us that on the day we left Korla the whole garrison, 150 strong, had suddenly started off northward in full marching order, and had entered the ravine along the Konche-daria. Plavski had asked some of them what was happening, and had been told that they were on their way to a battle which was raging twenty li from Korla. They did not know against whom the fight was.

When the garrison set out, the civil population of Korla had been terrified and had fled headlong towards the mountains and into the deserts, avoiding the high roads. The few shops which had been kept open were shut before the exodus began. On the morning of March 8 still more had fled. Plavski was a doubtful source, but the news he gave us did not seem improbable.

In one village Georg, who was driving a long way behind us, had met three soldiers, who told him that they had come straight from Kucha and the military conference which had been held there about three days earlier. They were now on their way to Kara-shahr and Turfan with letters. To Georg's question about the situation at Kucha they had replied with an ironical intonation, "All quiet". But they had added that we had been wise to turn back eastward, "for to the west only Turkis live, and they are much worse than we".

It was important that we should reach Korla before these messengers. They were on horseback and required two days to get to Korla. We ought to be there about noon next day. We therefore made our stay at Chadir as short as possible.

But when we were already sitting in the cars, it struck me that Plavski had said he was on his way to Kashgar, the journey to which place he estimated at twenty days. I warned him, telling him about Georg's experiences and the front at Bai. He smiled, and assured me that he would get through by using side-tracks, not roads on which battles were being fought. Well, he had made his way from Tonkin to Chadir, so perhaps he could manage the next stage as well.

I therefore wrote as quickly as I could a letter to the British Consul-General at Kashgar, telling him in a few words how I had come to Chadir and asking him to send off a telegram (which I enclosed) to my sisters in Stockholm. I said in the telegram that we were on the way to Lop-nor, that no news of us could be expected for several months, that everything was going well, and that my representative in Peking (Dr. Erik Norin) should arrange to have a thousand gallons of petrol sent to Anhsi.

The letter was entrusted to Plavski, who received ten silver dollars for his trouble. The telegram never reached Stockholm, nor Plavski Kashgar. It was hard luck on our relations at home to have to await news of us for further anxious months. But it was good luck that the order to send the petrol miscarried. For otherwise Norin, with his irrepressible energy, would have gone to Anhsi himself with camels and petrol, and would have had to wait there for six months without any news at a time when we did not need a drop of petrol from China.

As for the fakir, he had met with insuperable obstacles on his way to Kashgar and, just like us, thought best to turn back. He had given my letter to a Turki who had sworn by Allah and all the joys of paradise to deliver it into the British Consul-General's own hands. *Habent sua fata libelli!* It would be amusing to know what became of this letter. Possibly the Turki smelt a rat and burned the letter. Possibly he was killed before he arrived at Chinne-bagh, where the Consul lives, and where in old times I was so often the guest of my old friend Sir George Macartney. Or perhaps the Turki letter-carrier was seized by Tungan guards, who searched him, found the letter in his girdle and used it for cigarette papers or something even worse. For it is quite out of the question that the Consul-General should have omitted to send the telegram and hidden the letter away as a curiosity in his collection of documents.

In the meantime we took leave of the fakir, whom I blessed in my thoughts for the message of relief which was going through his agency to our dear ones in Sweden, and the cars rolled away from the little open inn of Chadir. It was already late, and evening was casting its shadows over the earth. That everything disappeared from our sight was of little consequence; we had seen that road already. It was past nine when we reached Charchi, having covered sixty miles. The village was our camp No. 50.

So far the country had been absolutely quiet, and we had met only a few travellers. Traffic was quite dead. No heralds loomed up out of the darkness, the outriders of a beaten general in flight. The sentries had no cause to wake us. So long as I was awake I could hear the sentry singing under his breath, his quiet steps, and his ringing blows on a piece of wood with a hammer to frighten thieves and show that he was awake. The grave-like silence which otherwise prevailed seemed ominous. We still had all our cars. Should we succeed in driving through depopulated and unguarded Korla unnoticed and unmolested? Should we reach the peaceful desert to eastward, where the Tungan robber hordes could no longer reach us?

THE CONVOY IS ATTACKED AND FIRED ON

MARCH 11. The thermometer touched 34 degrees during the night. The air was grey and damp, and we could not see far. Mist hovered over the earth as usual in winter in Eastern Turkestan. We could hardly realise that there were mountains to the north, although they were so close to us.

It was a quarter past ten before all was ready. We stopped for a few minutes at the first serai to pump a rider who had arrived from Korla the day before. He confirmed what we had been told—that the whole Tungan garrison had marched out northward a few days before, bound for Kara-shahr, where a battle was in progress.

"Between whom?" I asked.

"Between Tungans and Kalmucks," he replied. Kalmuck (Kalmak) is the Turki name for the Mongolian Torguts. These were said to have made an attack on Kara-shahr to cut off Big Horse's relief and flight.

In a belt of saksauls among low dunes to the south could be discerned a few antelopes, untroubled by human enmities.

After an hour and a half's drive we met a young Turki driving three donkeys.

"How are things in Korla?" I asked.

"Quiet and peaceful. The whole garrison went off three days ago. We heard yesterday evening that four hundred soldiers from Hami had arrived at Konche. They were to be at Korla this morning. Peasants south of Korla had seen them yesterday and some had reached the town already. These had given orders that barley, maize, flour and other supplies were to be bought up in as large quantities as possible."

"That's good; have you heard anything more?"

"No—yes, they say that the Kalmucks round Kara-shahr are fighting Ma's Tungans."

129

He received a coin and looked astonished. Doubtless he thought that he had let his tongue run away with him.

Another quarter of an hour's drive and we met an old man on foot, escorting his old wife on a donkey. They were from the western outskirts of the little town.

"Is all quiet in Korla?"

"We know nothing, but have heard that soldiers came to Korla to-day from the desert."

We now had the gardens and avenues of the oasis on our right. By one farm several men were standing, including one or two strongly built Tungan peasants.

"Is all quiet in Korla?"

"Yes, very quiet."

A little later we met a cart with an arched roof of straw mats. Probably some well-to-do family, fleeing they knew not where. Several fugitives passed bound westward. The town was being evacuated.

Several villagers came along the road; they had been in the bazaar and were now returning to their cottages.

"What news? Is all quiet?"

"They say in the bazaar that Kara-shahr is besieged by Kalmucks, Russians and Turkis and is being bombed from the air. There isn't a Tungan soldier left in Korla. We were told in the bazaar that over ten thousand East Turkis are on the march to Korla from Cherchen and Charkhlik. They've got to Tikenlik. What is certain is that the mayor of Korla has had orders to have all inns, offices and private houses ready to receive guests from the south under the command of Hodja Nias Hadji."

Aha! so it was for the Hodja they were waiting. He was the liberator, a new Atalik Ghazi, a new Bedaulet, like Yakub Beg in 1865!

At half-past one we passed the cross-roads and put behind us and to our left the fatal road to Kara-shahr, where a decisive battle was evidently raging. It was probable that Ma Chung-yin, after having evacuated his positions at Dawancheng, had been shut up in Kara-shahr. If he was beaten there too, his next stage would be Korla, and the little town would be flooded with his fleeing troops. Then the first shattered hordes might burst in at any moment. Our only chance of safety was to hurry through Korla and make for the desert to the eastward at the swiftest pace the vehicles could stand. There was no way round Korla. We *must* cross the river. There is only *one* bridge over the Konche-daria, and that is in the middle of Korla.

A beggar sat by the wayside.

"Give me a little bit of bread; I've nothing to eat."

And a farmer was ploughing with his oxen. He was a real fatalist, and would not let a war disturb him. We left to our right the fort of the town, with walls and moat.

Another conversation. An apparently calm and sober Turki answered my usual question:

"Yes, the garrison has left Korla. But there is talk of a small body of cavalry having orders to requisition as much flour, rice and corn as can be had from the outlying villages, and to return to Kara-shahr this evening with its haul. A battle has been going on there for four days."

"Have you heard anything about a Turki force from Charkh-lik?"

"Yes, *mehman* [guests] are on their way here."

"Are they under the command of Hodja Nias Hadji?"

"Yes."

"Is he with them himself?"

"No."

"Are there no guards in the town?"

"Yes, ten Tungans, but only two of them have rifles."

Another informant declared that there were twenty-two guards, all armed.

The intelligence we were obtaining was contradictory. Our anxiety grew more intense. Should we succeed in driving through Korla unhindered?

Now we had reached the bridge. There were no soldiers there, only a few ragged boys. The timbers bent, the cars swayed over the bridge. It held. The whole convoy was over.

At half-past two we stopped at the mayor's house and left our cards. The mayor, the sickly old Chinese, received us at once, and the deputy-mayor, the white-bearded Nias Hadji, was with him. The usual questions were put. The two answered cautiously and knew nothing definite. We could see that they were acutely uneasy. I felt sorry for them. We should soon be far out in the eastern desert, but they were tied to their chairs of office. They were serving under Ma Chung-yin. He might come at any moment. There might be bombings, a siege, street fighting at Korla as there had been at Kara-shahr. Then the victors would enter the town. Was it strange that they now trembled for their lives, on the verge of that supreme moment when all old accounts would be settled?

They gave us neither advice nor warnings when we told them our plan of disappearing into the desert. They were irresolute and dared not take any line. We rose to go. They pressed us to have a cup of tea. Nias Hadji went out, but returned immediately and sat down by my side. A servant appeared at the door of the room which opened into the courtyard and said a few words about a new visit or message.

Nias Hadji turned to me with assumed indifference.

"There are some soldiers in the courtyard, and they say they want to speak to you. Will you see them?"

"Yes, let them come in."

Four Tungan soldiers, with slung rifles and Mauser pistols at their sides, entered and stood by the door. They had probably taken part in the horrible kidnapping on the night of March 5. They were cocksure in bearing and speech, but polite. Their leader, a non-commissioned officer, asked:

"Why have you come back here, and where are you going now?"

"We wanted to avoid the battle front in the west. We are going to Hami now by a roundabout way and shall return here when all is quiet."

"How are things at Kucha?"

Georg had to answer that question, and he assured them that all was quiet at the moment. The leader then asked Georg:

"Did you take Chang and the eleven others safely to Kucha, or did something happen to them on the way?"

Georg is a giant, but it was too absurd that they could suppose he had lured their comrades into a trap. He replied with an ironical smile:

"I was alone and unarmed; they were twelve men armed. Of course I obeyed their orders."

"Can you give us proof that they arrived safely at Kucha?"

Georg held out, with an airy, superior gesture, Chang's guarantee, signed by Chang himself and bearing his red stamp, which he had shown us by the camp fire near Bugur. The leader took the paper and talked with his men. None of them could read. The mayor offered his services and read aloud. The soldiers nodded their satisfaction, and asked if they might keep the guarantee. This request was firmly refused, and the paper returned to Georg's wallet. The men smiled, bowed and departed.

Hardly had they disappeared when we rose, thanked the two mayors, and went out to the cars. In the courtyard Georg observed:

"Now the four soldiers will go straight to the main guard and telephone to Ma at Kara-shahr. If we lose any time we'll be caught."

Something had happened behind the scenes during the half-hour in which we had been sitting with the mayor. Nias Hadji had sent a message to the main guard. That was why the soldiers had appeared at the right moment. The two mayors did their duty; they thought above all of their own skins. The consequences of their proceedings were soon to show themselves.

Serat and Georg drove ahead; then came the small car with Hummel at the wheel, and last Effe and Jomcha. At the south gate of the town a cube-shaped, deep-sunk stone stuck up out of the ground, to support the two halves of the gate when they were shut at night. The small car could not clear them. The right wheel must go right over the stone, and short inclined planes of stones had to be built up on both sides to a level with its top. This was successful, but took time. The wretched stone was not meant for motor-cars, only for carts.

Outside the gate we were checked by a high wooden bridge over an *arik*, or irrigation canal. It was cleared, but a little farther on a lorry stuck in the mud on a flooded stretch of high road. Further delay. The cars that followed made a detour over a ploughed field with nasty ditches.

It was four o'clock when we approached a fresh canal bridge, rotten and weak. It had to be strengthened with our rough planks. It creaked, but held. Another flooded piece of road. The small car got water in its engine, and was towed out on to dry land by a lorry. We moved like a funeral procession along the willow avenue. There Georg stuck fast and took a quarter of an hour to get free.

Before us we had another bridge over a canal five yards wide, whose maximum depth was 4 ft. 9 in. while the speed of its current was 2 ft. 7 in. per second. The canal carried nearly 150 cubic feet of water a second. It starts above Korla, and its surplus water goes back to the Konche-daria below the town after the ploughed fields have received their allotted share.

The bridge was not bad. It rested upon three solid timbers placed lengthways; but the intervals between them were gaping holes which had to be filled. Our huge planks were again unloaded and the bridge strengthened. The small car went over easily. Then Serat tested the bridge with his car. It held. The three others followed. It was five o'clock. We had only a few hundred yards to go to the next bridge, the last in the Korla oasis on this side. Then we should be out on *gobi*, hard barren gravel desert, and could drive hell-for-leather to the village of Shinnega. But Serat had inspected the last bridge and reported that it had collapsed. We had, therefore, either to build a new bridge or drive across the deep irrigation canal over which it led.

There seemed to be a curse upon us. It had taken us two good hours to go two miles and a quarter, and now we were stopped by a bridge which was unfit for use! We had seen many wretched roads since we left Kwei-hwa, but this road beat all records. And this at a moment when our lives might depend on our getting out into the desert before the Tungans could mobilise their horsemen to pursue us.

The road up to the last bridge was dry and good. On either side of it narrow irrigation canals ran between raised banks about a foot high. Along the edge of the canals willows grew, forming an avenue. The road between the inside banks of the canals might have been ten or twelve feet wide. Beside the road were ploughed fields with scattered bushes and young trees.

Four Tungan soldiers on white and brown horses came riding along among the bushes to our left. Several more followed them. Another party appeared to our right. They were riding parallel with us, at a distance of about two hundred yards, and soon disappeared into the undergrowth alongside the road ahead of us.

"There are Ma's cavalry come to requisition wheat in the villages."

"No," I replied, "they're shadowing *us*!"

At that moment a shot rang out.

"They're firing at us," Bergman cried, and took up his rifle. "Get out, quick!"

We crawled out of the car, doubled up. I got out last. We took cover by the canal wall, with "Edsel" as our nearest neighbour. All our marksmen had their rifles in their hands.

"Don't fire!" I shouted.

They held their rifles in readiness, but did not fire. It was eleven minutes past five. The bullets were whining round us now. Before Yew and Georg, who were standing side by side, could lie down under cover, a bullet hissed past between them. Fresh shots came whistling from both sides. Again and again we heard the dull thud of a bullet striking a willow trunk. A bullet snipped off a willow twig just over my head. Others passed through the cars and the provision cases; one went right through a box of melons. Another, after striking some hard object, was found lying flattened on a petrol tin. Luckily none of the petrol tanks were holed.

When the bombardment began I was terribly anxious. If they were firing at us they must mean to destroy us. They were only waiting for us to reply; then they would go on firing, protected by the undergrowth, as long as there was one of us left alive. Then the whole expedition would be swept off the face of the earth, and Ma might possibly have in his army enough drivers to manage five cars. I only waited to see someone's head fall against his breast. But all our men lay motionless under cover of the canal bank. I counted fifty shots, Yew fifty-five. The marksmen were invisible; they lay hidden in the undergrowth. Only their horses were seen here and there.

When we did not answer the fire, it gradually diminished, and when the last shot was fired it was twenty minutes past five. The bombardment had lasted nine minutes, but those minutes seemed hours to me, seeing that our lives hung by a thread.

The pause grew longer and longer. What was going to happen now? We waited for a new volley. But it did not come. We raised ourselves cautiously. A soldier was approaching from the left. He was on foot and was unarmed; evidently a negotiator. He stopped a stone's-throw away and shouted a request that one of us should go and talk to him.

Kung asked if he might go. Certainly he might. He walked straight up to the soldier with his hands in his trouser pockets, smiling and looking at the ground. While they were talking several others joined the party. We could see soldiers in all directions; they had completely surrounded us. In a few minutes Kung came back to us. Their ultimatum was as follows:

"According to express orders from General Ma you have no right to leave Korla. If despite this you try to escape, we have orders to stop and arrest you at all costs and detain your cars. It is clear that you meant to get away from the oasis unnoticed, as you did not even call on the commandant. You must return to the town instantly!"

I asked Kung to give the negotiator this answer:

"We did not call upon the commandant partly because he did not receive us on our first visit, although—as we heard from a reliable quarter—he was in the *yamen*, not at Kara-shahr as was pretended; partly because of the scandalous treatment we received at Chang's quarters in the presence of the commandant's adjutant. We have no objection to returning to Korla, but as the drive is very dangerous in daylight, it will be impossible in the dark. We shall therefore encamp here. The road is too narrow and the canals too deep for the cars to be able to turn. You can post as many sentries as you like. We shall drive into the town at sunrise."

Kung delivered the message and came back with this news:

"They insist on our going back to Korla this moment."

It was only a little after half-past five when the retreat began. We had all cause to be thankful—no one killed, no one wounded. Our hope of finding peace and quiet in the Lop desert had been shattered. Fate was casting us back into one of the hottest places of the war on the old Silk Road. To all human judgment it looked as if our destinies often depended on pure chance. If Georg had been detained at Kucha, we should not have stopped till we had found him; and then we too should have been taken and driven by stages to Kashgar with Ma's fleeing army. There we should have been suspected of belonging to Ma's army, and in the most favourable event sent to India or Russian Turkestan. If we had not lost a day at Bugur, we should probably have succeeded in withdrawing to the Lop desert. Our oil supplies would have allowed only one or two cars to get to Tun-hwang.

Meanwhile the cars were turned right round with much trouble, and the convoy moved back towards Korla in its own tracks, but in reverse order. The sun sank, twilight fell and it grew dark. The bridges were now far worse and more dangerous than in daylight. Several soldiers had clambered up on to the lorries, and a score of horsemen swarmed round the convoy, all holding their rifles menacingly in their hands. Effe's back wheel cut through a rotten bridge and his vehicle was left hanging. Another bridge broke under Jomcha's lorry, which was unloaded and towed up out of the canal. The cars that followed had to go the same way with fearful jolts, and it was a miracle that no springs were broken.

When the convoy had passed this horrible place, it was half-past nine already and darkness had fallen. The cavalrymen's rifles shone in the light of the headlamps. Again and again they urged the drivers to hurry up. Perhaps the drivers thought subconsciously, "If Ma is to take the cars anyhow we may just as well smash them ourselves". But they made every possible effort. All the bridges were strengthened with our planks, and where it was necessary the car was unloaded.

The mixing of petrol with paraffin caused little explosions which sounded like rifle shots. Until the soldiers grew accustomed to these detonations, they started and thought we had begun to shoot. Later they pretended that it was these explosions that had caused them to open fire in the willow avenue.

After long delays at the last bridges and the stone at the town gate we drove into Abdul Kerim's courtyard, our old quarters. The lorries were drawn up in a row on the right. It was half-past ten. We had taken five hours to cover two miles and a quarter. We were all dead tired after the hardships of the day and the fearful mental strain. We were content with some tea, bread and eggs, and longed for our sleeping-bags.

We had no longer any freedom of movement, but were entirely in Ma Chung-yin's hands. We now had it in black and white that it was our cars he wanted. When, before we left Kwei-hwa, he told General Fu, the military governor of that town, that we were welcome, he doubtless thought that our convoy might be a good thing to have whatever turn the war took. The hurrying-on of our departure from Turfan seemed suspicious. But the firing on the convoy was the final proof. His calculations were exact almost to the day. By means of the attack he had got possession of the cars just at the moment when he most needed them.

So our first captivity began. On March 12 I was awakened by Effe with the message:

"Big Horse has fled from Kara-shahr and come to Korla."

"How do you know that?"

"They say so in the bazaar."

"Then it's only a rumour. We shall see."

Nothing was heard from the commandant, who we had been told the day before was so annoyed at our not having called upon him when passing through. I sent Georg to his *yamen* to ask when he received visitors. An adjutant replied:

"He cannot receive you till he has been told over the telephone from Kara-shahr how he is to treat you."

If General Ma was really in Korla, no orders by telephone from Kara-shahr were needed. The story sounded all wrong. A Turki who had arrived from Kara-shahr told us that the commandant of that town, our friend Hwang, had his headquarters on the right bank of the Khaidu-gol.

We had no occasion to call upon the two mayors, and simply sent our cards and a few trifles as an expression of thanks for the sheep and food they had presented to us.

Two soldiers kept guard at our gate. About twelve o'clock fifteen men marched into the courtyard, most of them with rifles. Things looked critical again. But they explained that they only wanted to see the doctor. One of their comrades, whom they had helped to our quarters, had got a bullet in the right shoulder and was now suffering the most fearful pain. Three medicine chests were taken out and a table was placed outside our little verandah. On the latter Hummel arranged his packets of bandages, bottles, basins and all the necessary apparatus. The wounded man was laid on the table; he really looked exhausted and moaned pitiably. He had pain all down his arm. Hummel washed and dressed his wounds and put on a spotless white bandage. Then he gave the man an injection of morphine. In a few minutes the wounded man told his comrades with a smile that the pain had completely disappeared and that he had a pleasant feeling in his arm. The fifteen laughed delightedly, raised their thumbs in the air and cried:

"You're a good doctor!"

I expect they thought we were curious people, to revenge ourselves thus for the attack of the day before.

The treatment was hardly finished when a boy of sixteen, who had got a bullet in the chest, was brought to the doctor's field hospital. No operation could be prepared without X-rays. But the boy was treated as carefully as the first man, and the fifteen were just as interested.

Then came a third, with syphilitic sores on his neck. The most interesting thing was to watch the spectators. Their hard, brutal features lightened and softened, and something like a spark of gratitude appeared in their eyes. The lessons in savagery, cruelty, sadism and bloodthirstiness they had learned in the gallant Ma Chung-yin's school had made their features hard and animal. But now they began to thaw, and human nature asserted itself. The doctor did not give them a glance; he did not notice that he had spectators. But they devoured the doctor with astonished, friendly looks. They could hardly have been more impressed by the first flying machine they saw than by this superior, quick, clean and effective medical treatment. When the wounded men had been attended to, and shown how to look after their wounds in barracks, they bowed to the doctor and withdrew politely and in silence. The whole garrison would know that the convoy they had fired upon from an ambush the day before contained a wonder-working doctor.

Early in the morning the adjutant had brought us an order that the cars, after we had removed our personal effects from them, might not be touched or kept ready to start. But when the doctor began to rout among the baggage in one or two of the cars, not one of the guards or of the other men said a word.

Once more the air was full of rumours. One said that Ma had

come and would at once go on to Kucha, Aksu and Kulja and take command of the Ili army. We hoped this was true, because in that case we should have Lop-nor and the Silk Road to Tun-hwang all to ourselves. Others declared that Ma would lead the Ili army to Korla to meet and defeat Hodja Nias Hadji, which might be dangerous for us.

The atmosphere around us was insecure and uneasy. Georg was very pessimistic. "We ought to be thankful if we come out of this purgatory alive." I replied: "What does it matter if they take the cars and the whole of their cargo so long as they spare our lives?"

The wind wailed and howled, the air was chill, grey and misty; everything seemed gloomy and futile as the hours slowly passed. The doctor's soldier patients afforded us a welcome distraction. A new syphilis patient certainly betrayed a military secret when he cried to the doctor:

"I've been ordered to go to Kucha to-morrow with General Ma Chung-yin. So you must cure me at once."

Everything indicated that Ma was approaching and in retreat. It looked as if the negotiator of the day before had spoken the truth when he said that Ma had ordered our cars to be detained at all costs. That circumstance was more significant than all the rumours of his early arrival at Korla. We had a disagreeable presentiment that we were condemned to imprisonment in this town and in our cramped, uncomfortable quarters for an in-definite time.

At five o'clock we had a none too welcome visitor, the courteous general Hwang Wen-ching, commandant of Kara-shahr. He had just arrived. We invited him into our poor room, where all the seating accommodation on the two *kangs* was occupied by my bed and those of the three Chinese, with an oblong stool between them.

Hwang seemed tired, but fairly calm. He put forward a firm request for the loan of three lorries, which were to be sent to Kara-shahr that evening to fetch wounded officers and men. It was just for the journey there and back, and the cars would be back in our yard in the course of the night. I replied that I had no objection to lending the cars provided that he gave me a written undertaking that they would be returned. He faithfully promised this.

A good hour later Hwang came back to tell me that the trip to Kara-shahr could not come off until early next morning.

At eight o'clock Hwang sent a young officer with a request that he might borrow all four motor-lorries the following morning. They were to fetch General Ma Chung-yin himself and his staff of twenty-five from Kara-shahr to Korla. Again I said yes, against a guarantee that I should get them back. The messenger replied that I could be perfectly easy in my mind, because General Hwang himself was going with twelve men. They would probably be back in the afternoon or evening, and immediately after their arrival General Ma Chung-yin, according to what he had said on the telephone, would come and call on us in person.

When Hwang first asked for the loan of the cars, I wrote the following "open letter" in Russian, which Georg might need if he, his comrades and the cars should fall into the hands of General Sheng Shih-tsai's victorious army on the way to or in Kara-shahr:

"The bearer of this letter, Mr. Georg Söderbom, has been in my service from October 21 till now. He has been compelled against my will to go to Kara-shahr to take some wounded soldiers to Korla." Then followed an account of the expedition's aims and plans, and I concluded: "Our expedition is, therefore, under the protection of the Chinese Government and has no political character of any kind. Accordingly I beg you to treat Söderbom kindly. The expedition is at present at Korla."

It was not easy to find out what had really happened at Kara-shahr. Some said that a thousand Torguts had assaulted the town in alliance with Russians, Turkis and Kirghizes, but had been driven back by Ma's garrison, which was only three hundred strong. Hami, Turfan and Toksun had been taken by the northern army. Hummel's patient, the cavalry general Ma, had been carried on mule-back from Turfan to Korla, where he had just arrived in the company of the chief of staff, General Li.

During the siege of Urumchi, which had been raised a month before, Ma had taken an armoured car from the northern army. This clumsy vehicle, which had been constructed by White Russian mechanics at Urumchi, had been driven by a Chinese chauffeur by way of Dawancheng and Toksun to Su-bashi, where the supply of petrol had run out and the armoured car had been smashed up and left by the wayside.

This same day, March 12, this driver came to our prison and gossiped. He assured me that Kara-shahr had fallen and that Sheng Shih-tsai's victorious army would enter Korla in a few days. Ma Chung-yin's defeated army had that very day begun to stream into the town in groups. Possibly they would continue their flight to Kucha at once—what luck that we had not met these wild, starving bands on our return journey to Korla! As the main body of Ma's army would swamp Korla at any moment, general looting might be expected.

"It would be best for you to keep your gates barred," the driver observed. "And when the northern army comes in pursuit of Ma, you'll be in a hole, for you'll be regarded as enemies," he added. The driver was no fool. He understood the situation perfectly.

We asked him if he had heard what had happened to the five hundred young Turki recruits we had seen at Chi-ko-ching-tse, and the hundred or so whom we had seen at Turfan setting out to join Ma's army.

"Yes," he replied, "they were all taken by the northern army and cut down to the last man."

We heard later that this information was untrue. The recruits had indeed been captured, but had immediately been sent home to their villages.

In the evening two fresh soldiers announced themselves, in full marching order. They had orders from the commandant Hwang to supervise the unloading of all four lorries and to sleep on two of them during the night.

Now it happened that the greater part of our funds, several thousand silver dollars, was kept, in tight rolls, in two secret drawers in the bottom of lorry No. 1. So if Ma took all the cars we should lose our silver. How could we save it from the soldiers' vigilance?

All the baggage was taken off and piled in stacks in the yard. The soldiers saw that all was going well, and their attention flagged. When it had grown nicely dark, Georg asked the two supervisors into the drivers' room, treated them to tea and cigarettes and told them hair-raising stories of adventure. One or two of the engines were set going "to see that everything was in good order till Ma took them", as he explained to the soldiers, but really so that the roar might drown the noise which could not be avoided when the secret drawers were broken open. When this had been done, the silver rolls were taken, a few at a time, to a big lumber-room with an earth floor beyond our kitchen and buried by the light of lanterns in a hole in the middle of the room. The hole was filled up, the earth floor trodden level and a ragged straw mat placed over it.

The manœuvre succeeded, the noise of the motors was silenced, and in its place the long-drawn, deep snores of the soldier supervisors resounded through our prison yard. I suspect that the beverage Georg had given them was not merely tea.

MA CHUNG-YIN TAKES OUR LORRIES AND KORLA IS BOMBED FROM THE AIR

MARCH 13 had come! To judge from all that we had seen and heard already, this day was to be a critical one for us. We had also heard more than we had seen with our own eyes, especially from General Hwang. We were prisoners, and could only hear through gossip what was happening in the little town.

I was awakened with the news that machine-gun fire had been heard to the north-west. But when I had my breakfast at half-past seven everything was quiet. We all realised that this quiet could not last long in a situation like ours, and we waited anxiously for what was to come.

A few soldiers who did not belong to our guard went straight into Georg's room and asked for food—they had not eaten for several days. He gave them a few cakes, but when they made themselves too much at home and appropriated a teapot, he turned them out and threatened to report them to Ma.

The doctor nailed a big red cross on white cloth to the wall of the verandah, and fresh wounded or sick soldiers came to his field hospital for treatment.

A young officer entered by the yard gate and went straight up to Hummel.

"General of cavalry Ma Ho-san is ill and would like the doctor to come to his quarters at once."

The patients had to wait while the doctor got his bandage and medicine chest ready and accompanied the officer to the general. This was the same Ma who had had a shell splinter through his thigh and had been treated before by the doctor at Turfan. Yew went with them as interpreter. Headquarters were in the finest Chinese house on the main street, north of the bridge. On their way there Hummel and Yew found the bazaar and the principal arteries of traffic swarming with soldiers, refugees, camels, horses, and loads of hay and straw on ox-carts, and received the impression that the defeated army was really overflowing Korla. A certain degree of order prevailed, and one could not say there was any panic, though everyone seemed to be in a hurry.

A fairly narrow passage, only four yards long, led from the street into a smallish, rectangular courtyard, surrounded on all four sides with wooden houses in the Chinese style. In one of the rooms the wounded general was lying on his bed. The wound was treated and dressed again carefully, and the general did not know how to show his gratitude.

Yew did not miss the opportunity of asking what was going to happen about Ma Chung-yin requisitioning our lorries. The wounded man replied:

"General Ma Chung-yin arrived here on horseback a few hours ago and will come at any moment to ask for the loan of your cars."

"Our motor-lorries are the property of the Central government," said Yew. "If we are compelled to hand them over by superior military force, we protest at any rate against their being used for the transport of war material."

"If they are loaded with war material it will be because our camels have been left some way outside the town to rest and graze. As soon as the cars get there the arms will be taken off the lorries and put on to the camels. Then wounded will be carried in the cars."

"Does Ma Chung-yin mean to return them?"

"Yes, you can be quite at your ease about that. To show my gratitude for the doctor's excellent treatment of my wounds I shall, if necessary, demand that they shall be sent back as soon as they are no longer needed. My bed will be fixed up in one of them, and I shall stay in it as long as the cars are under our control. It is of the greatest importance both to Ma Chung-yin and to me to get a good reputation in the world, and it is therefore in our interest to help you. We understand that you are going to make known what you have seen and heard during the campaign."

"As far as what place does General Ma require our cars, and for how long?"

"As far as Kucha, possibly Aksu."

"So it will be sufficient for you to have enough petrol to get to Aksu and the same quantity for the return journey?"

"Yes, that will do."

"Will you promise that no more petrol than is necessary will be taken from us?"

"I guarantee that."

They rose and left. In the narrow passage they met a tall young officer of agreeable, energetic appearance. He looked at them closely but did not salute. Both Hummel and Yew had seen Ma's portrait in the rooms of Pai, his representative at Peking, and recognised him. In a second he had disappeared.

While Hummel and Yew were visiting the sick, we had a message from Big Horse requisitioning a lorry to take him to Kucha at once. A few minutes later a fresh messenger arrived and requisitioned all four motor-lorries and as much petrol as possible.

Georg had already put aside the supply of petrol which four cars would require to get to Aksu and back. The tanks were filled; 428 gallons was considered to be the necessary quantity. On his first drive to Kucha Georg had done seven and a half miles per gallon with his light load of twelve passengers. The distance from Korla to Kucha is 165 miles, from Kucha to Aksu 136 miles.

While the drivers were putting the drums of petrol on to the lorries, one or two soldiers entered the yard and demanded on the highest authority that all the petrol we had should be taken. Luckily Yew and Hummel had just returned from the sick-bed. Yew declared with impressive calmness:

"You won't get one drop more than General Ma needs."

"We've orders; they must be obeyed."

"General of cavalry Ma has just fixed the amount that is to be taken. Go and ask him if it is true."

The soldiers hurried off. When they came back they began to unload all the superfluous petrol.

Our yard was now swarming with Tungan soldiers. The gate stood wide open. They came and went, bringing machine-guns, old field-guns, rifles and ammunition on horses, mules or carts; and the lorries were loaded up with the stuff as it came in. Several officers stood round and superintended the work.

It was twenty-three minutes to twelve when ominous organ music was heard faintly to northward, and someone called out:

"Three aeroplanes are coming."

Quite right, there they were, flying at a height of perhaps 1600 ft., but slowly descending to 1300 ft. or lower. Now they were hovering over the town. Three minutes had passed when a heavy explosion was heard to the south of our quarters. It was tragi-comic to watch the soldiers round the cars. They looked up in the air, and in a few seconds the yard was empty. They vanished as by magic. Where did they go?

Bergman spread out our largest Swedish flag in the middle of the yard. Then he and all our men went and sat down under the willows in the large back-yard which marched with ours on the west. I took up a position on the farther side of the wall that divided the two enclosures and noted times and explosions. It was a few minutes before the next bomb exploded, also to the south of us. Then seven bombs fell at short intervals, most north of us. We assumed that they were meant for the cross-roads where the high road to Kucha turns off, and where there were crowds of fleeing soldiers, carts, horses and mules laden with wounded, ammunition and supplies.

The six next bombs fell to the south of us. We had heard talk of four hundred Russians having crossed the Kuruk-tagh to Tikenlik on the road to Korla, and of Hodja Nias Hadji's army from Cherchen and Charkhlik. Perhaps the bombs which had been dropped to southward were meant for them.

Then came the detonation of a bomb in the northern outskirts of Korla. The machines were cruising over the town and the

Kucha road. But they were coming nearer to us. The seventeenth and eighteenth bombs burst to the north of us, only a few hundred yards away. One fell on an outhouse, which blew up in a dark-brown cloud of dust and smoke. The three next were still nearer to us. The airmen were coming lower and lower and were approaching our quarters. They had seen our convoy already when we were going to Toksun, and could not fail to detect the five motors in our yard. Presumably they thought the cars belonged to Ma Chung-yin, and therefore aimed at them in the hope of destroying them and delaying his flight.

Three bombs fell just east of us, about a hundred and fifty yards away. We heard later that large parties of Turkis, with women and children, were fleeing westward, but not along the high road! What were they going to live on, poor creatures? During the actual air raid most of the Turkis sought shelter in their houses, thinking it was sufficient to be under a roof. They were terror-stricken, and doubtless thought their last hour was come.

At five minutes past twelve the twenty-eighth bomb fell to the north of us. After that no further explosions were heard. The airmen departed and disappeared to the northward in the direction of Kara-shahr, where they probably had a temporary aerodrome.

Hardly had all become quiet again before the doctor was standing at his operating table, taking a splinter of shell out of a warrior's arm.

The soldiers crept out of their hiding-places again and crowded round the cars, and the loading of the war material was now completed.

The moment of separation was approaching. Our spirits were low; we felt that something disastrous was about to happen. It was like the last minutes before an execution. We knew that Ma Chung-yin was ruthless and cared little how many human lives he sacrificed if it served his own ends. The war was lost, but there was still hope, and he was famous for attempting the impossible. We did not think our drivers' lives were worth much in his hands, and it would be impossible for Georg to get away this time, since the road along which he must retreat was filled with fleeing soldiers.

For that matter, we did not see much of Georg, Effe, Serat and Jomcha during the last hours in the prison yard. They had to pack their kit in a hurry after the cars had been given a final look over and provided with spare parts and tools. They took with them only a minimum of bedding and clothes, a cup each, coffee, tea, flour, sugar and a few tins of preserves. A fairly large supply of cigarettes and matches was not forgotten.

Meanwhile I wrote for each of them a testimonial in Russian.

Soldiers and officers came several times and urged them to hurry up. Georg replied as quietly as ever:

"If we start before everything is ready we shall get stuck on the road."

At a quarter to one came our friend from Turfan, Chang, the commander of the training corps, smiling and polite as ever, and informed us that it was time to start now. But there cannot have been such a terrible hurry, for when we asked him if he would have some tea, he said yes. He stayed for a quarter of an hour, and told us that he was going in the car which was to serve as an ambulance for the wounded General Ma Ho-san. General Ma Chung-yin had left Korla an hour earlier on horseback, accompanied by a few mounted men. The motor convoy would soon overtake him, and he would then get into one of the cars.

It was nearly one o'clock when Chang rose. The drivers had reported that everything was ready. I repeated to Georg what I had said before—that his and his three comrades' lives were infinitely more valuable than the cars, and that none of them was to do anything foolhardy to save our vehicles. "We can always get on without cars, but not without you!" Each of the drivers received a vigorous handshake and a "God be with you, come back soon!"

They jumped into their drivers' cabins, the motors began to hum, and one after another they disappeared through the gate.

The crowd of soldiers who had taken part in the loading went off, and the curious dispersed. Then the gate was shut again and we went to the field hospital, where the doctor was occupied in bandaging a patient.

I have never experienced a more sickening feeling of emptiness than on that afternoon, March 13. The lorries on which we had driven the whole way from Peking, across half Asia, were gone; only the small car remained. In Ma Chung-yin's hands the lorries were lost. The yard was empty and desolate. Now we were really prisoners. We had no means of getting away.

Georg, Effe, Serat and Jomcha, who had performed their duties and tended the cars so faithfully and untiringly, were gone. They belonged to our brotherhood no longer, but to Big Horse and his fleeing army. An atmosphere of stifling gloom weighed upon our spirits. Should we ever see them again?

We walked about, loafed, talked and made notes. How long was this going to last? Something must happen soon. The commander-in-chief and his staff had fled, and we had helped him and accelerated his flight. We were therefore compromised in the eyes of the northern army. We could fairly be accused, or at least suspected, of being among Big Horse's adherents. Not only were we in mortal fear for our drivers' safety and for our cars; we had also all possible reason to wonder how the victorious generals would treat us. Our position was more than critical. The expedition was split in two. One half, consisting of four men and four cars, was threatened by Ma Chung-yin, the other—twelve men and one car—was threatened by Sheng Shih-tsai. The whole undertaking was being ground between millstones. At that moment it did not look as if much of it would be saved.

It was said that crowds of fleeing Tungans on horseback were passing the cross-roads north of Korla every minute. An unbroken stream of refugees was flowing westward. They came from Turfan, Dawancheng, Toksun and Kara-shahr.

Several Turkis came to our quarters and expressed in cautious language their anger at the bombing and at Ma having taken our cars. The mayor had sent us two Turkis with orders to be at our disposal for shopping in the bazaar, fetching water, getting fuel, and other things. They were fully charged with stories, and told us that the airmen had dropped manifestoes urging the people to join Urumchi, which would give them peace and quiet.

Ma was said to have issued a proclamation declaring, "I am king of Alti-shahr" (The six cities, or Eastern Turkestan). But the people said, "It is he who has made Sinkiang a desert. Before we had more than enough of everything, now there is nothing. All are poor and hungry."

Of Hodja Nias Hadji it was known that he had 15,000 men at Aksu, all armed with Russian rifles. His army had 60,000 sheep and 40,000 cows.

In all the towns we had touched, as well as at Dawancheng and on the road to Urumchi, a large part of the population consisted of Tungans. One Tungan soldier came into our yard anxious and depressed. He had served in Sheng Shih-tsai's army, had been taken prisoner by Ma and now wished to return to Urumchi, where his wife was. At Korla he had got mixed up with another woman, whom he now wanted to get rid of. He wondered whether we could help him. But we could not. Why, we were prisoners ourselves.

To inspire the people of Korla with respect we had the Swedish flag hoisted on a staff over the gate, and on the outside of the two halves of the door a red cross on a white ground with an inscription in Chinese:

"Suiyuan-Sinkiang highway expedition under the Ministry of Railways of the Central government."

This was repeated on a placard in Russian nailed to the door.

The day before the motor-lorries were driven away we had placed on each of them a red cross on a white ground to show that they belonged to the medical service. For we had been told that the cars were to be used to transport wounded. To our astonishment they were used instead to carry war material. I related above how the wounded General Ma had explained the position to Yew. At the last moment Georg was ordered to remove the red crosses if the cars were used for the transport of war material. He did take them away. None of us would sail under false colours.

AN ANXIOUS NIGHT

MARCH 14 and the night that followed it are among those memories of our journey in Sinkiang which will fade only when long years have passed, and can never be quite forgotten.

Weary after the trying events of the previous day, we had meant to sleep our fill, but at seven o'clock we were waked by San Wa-tse, one of our servants, who announced that four soldiers, two with rifles and two with horses, were asking to see our belongings.

We got up. It was pleasant to emerge from our poky, dank dungeon into the fresh morning air, whose temperature had risen only slightly above the night minimum—30·2 degrees.

The four soldiers walked about indifferently looking at our stores, but without lifting the canvases and straw mats which covered our boxes and cases.

"What do you want?" Yew asked.

"Both our horses are worn out. We want to exchange them for two good horses. We're looking everywhere and wondered if you had any."

"Do you think we've got horses in our boxes? Besides, if we had any, we wouldn't exchange for your wretched screws. Go and look somewhere else!"

This talk of exchanging horses was only a pretext. They were spies, come to see if it was worth while to plunder our quarters by night. Now the supreme authority, under whose protection we had been, had gone off to Kucha—with our cars—and there was no one in Korla who cared a straw what happened to us. Without lorries we were valueless; we did not count. Even the sentries, who had been posted at our gate on March 12, had disappeared.

As the four drivers were now gone, and our boxes seemed to be an object of interest to the undisciplined soldiery of the town, we did some furniture removal in the hovels in which we were imprisoned. All our private boxes and suitcases were placed in a protected room under lock and key. The provision boxes and a few good-sized cases were piled up under the projecting roof supported by wooden posts, on the north side of the yard. The whole pile was covered with tarpaulins and straw mats. The petrol which remained—nine thirty-gallon drums and two or three dozen five-gallon tins—and a few drums of paraffin were rolled into a little enclosed side-yard which had served as a stable. The door leading into this yard was locked.

Hummel, Bergman, Yew, Kung and I had our sleeping-bags in the room described above, at the western end on the south side of the yard. Chen was sleeping in the little passage room leading into the kitchen. So long as Georg and Effe were among us, the cook Chia Kwei and the boys San Wa-tse, Li, Chokdung and Liu Chia slept in their large room; but after the previous day's experiences they did not dare sleep on the opposite side of the yard, cut off from us, and begged to be allowed to move across to the kitchen. And there they were now lying like sardines in a tin. Immediately behind the kitchen was the big lumber-room, where the silver treasure and wireless apparatus were buried.

I am now about to describe the day after Ma Chung-yin's flight and the aerial bombardment, and the course of our life during the slow passing of the hours. It may seem superfluous to repeat all the gossip that was dinned into our ears, but even gossip is part of the story; it reflects both the Easterner's powers of imagination, more lively than ever in war-time, and the mental strain under which we lived during our first imprisonment.

In the morning no more Tungan soldiers appeared. We had the impression that the whole crowd had fled westward, and thought the doctor's field hospital had outlived its usefulness. But about noon a stream of Turkis started, men, women and children of the civil population of Korla, seeking remedies for aches and pains of all kinds, and the hospital was hard at work again. Hummel was the only one of us who had no need to complain of lack of occupation. If we could believe the young Chinese driver in Ma's service, who had come to see us a few days before, and had been ordered to join the motor convoy as a reserve driver at the very moment when he was attempting to escape from Korla—not one, but fifty doctors and surgeons would have had plenty to do on the route of the defeated Tungan army. He himself had travelled from Toksun to Korla, via Kara-shahr, and told us that wounded, bleeding soldiers lay in multitudes all along the road, waiting for death. In Ma's army they were not coddled by doctors; they knew no such things as medical orderlies, surgeons or nurses. Only death, the most drastic of all doctors, could free them from suffering and torment. Even the Chinese driver, who was certainly none too sensitive, assured us that it was painful to hear their cries and groans and prayers for help, or at least for a bowl of water.

At half-past ten two distinguished-looking Turkis with greying beards and decent *chapans* were announced. They wished to speak to me. The elder, who acted as spokesman, was called Turdu Ahun, and was *hsiang-ye* (headman in a village or quarter of a town); the name of the other was Rozi Ahun, and he bore the title of *hsiang-chung*, or head of a district.

Turdu Ahun said that we were known to be distinguished visitors, and he therefore wished to tell me a few things about the actual situation.

When the Tungans left the town the day before, hundreds of marauders roamed through the streets and bazaars and stole and looted everything they could lay their hands on. The civil population was utterly terrified; people sought refuge in the houses, locked the doors and barricaded them as well as they could. Everywhere were heard cries for help and anguished lamentation. The leader of one band of looters had told Turdu Ahun that his people were hungry and must have food, and they understood that there were quantities of provisions in our quarters. They therefore intended to plunder us. Turdu Ahun had said that the

Tungans had better leave us alone, for in the first place we were distinguished strangers, who ought to be protected, and in the second place we were heavily armed. This news had made them cautious, and they had selected other fields for their activities.

Hundreds of Tungans, in bands and unorganised crowds, were roaming through the outer parts of the oasis and making their way westward. But the hungriest went into the town demanding bread and meat. If people refused, they raised their rifles or pistols and got what they wanted. They were *haram*, or unclean, like dogs and pigs. The people were being sucked dry and would die of hunger.

Up till now about fifteen hundred Tungans had left the town by road in the direction of Kucha. The Turkis hoped that soon none of the rabble would be left in Korla.

Turdu Ahun and Rozi Ahun were well informed about our experiences both on March 5 and March 11. They knew a number of details which we had not heard before of the attack in the willow avenue. The party of cavalry which had fired on us was not in the town when we arrived with the cars and called on the mayor. The four Tungans, a *fu-kuan*, or adjutant, and three privates, who came in and questioned us, had reported our flight through the south gate to the commander of the party of cavalry on its arrival a few minutes later. The commander had at once given orders for our pursuit. "You were surrounded on all sides except on the north, towards Korla," the Turkis said.

Turdu Ahun's information made it clear to us that the chain of events on which our destinies hung would have been quite different if we had not lost a day at Bugur. Yes, if only we had saved a few hours on the way to Korla, we should have got out into the belt of desert south of the town before the band of horsemen arrived. Our start would have made it too risky for them to pursue us when they themselves were in wild flight and had the northern army's advance-guard hard on their heels. But we did not know at all whether it would have been to our advantage to get away and reach the desert and Lop-nor. By shooting at our convoy the Tungans themselves had testified in fiery writing that they regarded us as enemies, and that might be a mitigating circumstance for us when we were called to account for our actions before the commanders of the northern army.

Turdu Ahun confirmed a lot of gossip we had heard before from other sources. The main body of the northern army, he thought, was not coming straight from Kara-shahr to Korla, but was marching to Balguntai in the Yuldus valley, three days' marches west of Kara-shahr, and thence through the mountains to Bugur or Yangi-hissar. The army was believed to be seven thousand strong: Torguts, Turkis, Kirghizes, Taranchis from Ili, and five hundred White Russians. All these people had now united in a common cause—to drive Ma and the Tungans out of Sinkiang. Turdu Ahun regarded Ma's position as hopeless. He was completely surrounded. To westward lay Hodja Nias Hadji with a large army. From eastward the victorious northern army was advancing from Kara-shahr, the Ili forces were coming from the north, and there were said to be troops to southward too, at Shah-yar, near the Tarim.

Indeed, Turdu Ahun even knew something of which certainly no one else had any idea, not even Nanking or Urumchi—namely, that an agreement had been reached that Sheng Shih-tsai should become supreme ruler north of the Tien-shan and Hodja Nias Hadji south of the same mountain range. The Hodja was to be *wang*, or king, in Alti-shahr, Eastern Turkestan, a new Atalik Ghazi, a new Bedaulet like Yakub Beg. The Hodja would assemble his people, all its tribes and clans, under the prophet's banner, and all that was Tungan in the province would be uprooted like weeds out of the earth.

Nor would the position of the Chinese be enviable, to judge from the way they had been treated by the Turkis in Alti-shahr in 1931–33. As in Yakub Beg's days, they were killed in thousands; only those who had themselves circumcised and embraced Islam were allowed to live in poverty and misery. When the Holy War rages, the Eastern Turkis, usually so peaceable, rage like wild beasts. And what more could one ask, seeing that the Book of Books, the Koran, commands them to spread Islam by the sword and slaughter? If you cut the throats of ten infidels you make sure of Bikesht, paradise and its joys—beautiful women under rustling palms on the banks of murmuring watercourses.

Finally Turdu Ahun and Rozi Ahun proposed to send us two reliable men—a day and a night watchman named Haushim, to guard our quarters. We could be quite easy in our minds, they would protect us! How this would turn out we were soon to learn.

When I expressed my wish to return Turdu Ahun's call, he begged me not to do so. Savage Tungans were still roaming about the streets like ownerless dogs, and no one was safe from them. The sight of well-dressed foreigners would only aggravate their lust for plunder.

We had heard that proclamations drafted in Turki in Arabic character, as well as in Chinese, had been dropped on the town in masses from the aeroplanes of the day before. I asked Turdu Ahun to get me one of these documents, and it was not long before it was in my hands.

The proclamation contained an admonition to the people of Korla to keep quiet. The bombs which were dropped on the town were not intended to injure the Turki population, but only to hasten the evacuation of the town by the Tungan troops.

One of the doctor's patients, who had to undergo a minor operation, had in his pocket a leaflet which had been dropped by aircraft at Kara-shahr, and which also was drafted in both Turki and Chinese. Yew translated it as follows:

Open letter to the Turkis.

I understand very well how the bandit Ma has endeavoured to make you the poorest of the poor. At present his forces have been greatly diminished; indeed, destroyed. But he is still trying to compel you to fight on his side. In his hands you are lost. But I shall do my utmost to assure your rehabilitation and the safety of your lives and your property. If you make genuine submission to me, you shall live in peace and quiet and receive all that you require for your maintenance.

TUPAN SHENG SHIH-TSAI.

The sheet bore the general's red stamp. "Tupan" is the Chinese title of a military governor-general.

At one o'clock the menacing hum was heard again from the sky, and an aeroplane came hovering from north to south. I was sitting writing when the doctor looked in and asked me and the others to assemble round the Swedish flag which was spread out in the yard. He wanted to take a photograph of this memorable episode. I was just finding the airman with my field-glass when the doctor took his snapshot.

Twenty minutes later the airman returned, and now he dropped two bombs at short intervals. He cruised over the town, and when he passed over the northern part of it, where there were probably still Tungan troops in the old fort, he was fired on with machine-guns. In all he presented us with only seven bombs that day. I do not think any damage worth speaking of was done. The day before only two Tungans and a cow were killed. The intention was no doubt that stated in the manifesto—to hasten the evacuation. Leaflets had been pasted up on many house walls, especially in the bazaar. They seemed to think in the northern army that Korla was not yet cleansed of Tungans. The dropping of several bombs on the southern outskirts of the town indicated that troops were hiding in the houses there.

Many Tungan soldiers had grown tired of the war, and were going to the mayor of their own accord to surrender their rifles to him. They said they no longer wished to serve under Ma, and asked to be allowed to return to their villages and families. About a hundred rifles had thus been handed over to the magistrates.

A few Tungan surgeons who had been working in the hospital at Turfan came to see the doctor, and told us that when that town fell there were eight or nine hundred wounded in the hospital. The surgeons had to leave the wounded and accompany Ma's fleeing army. They did not know what had happened to the poor fellows.

The hours passed, and rumours flew in at one ear and out at the other. It was a quarter to ten when the night watchman Haushim reported that three or four soldiers were knocking at the gate and demanding to be let in. Yew and Kung went to the gate without opening it, and asked what they wanted.

"We want to come in; don't be afraid," the men answered.

"Our Swedish doctor doesn't see patients at night. Come again to-morrow morning at eleven."

"We don't know anything about the doctor, we want to come in," they said.

Then an animated conversation between the soldiers was heard. But the voices grew fainter and fainter, and at last they died away down the street. It was an advantage that our quarters were some three hundred yards from the main artery of the town, so that only roaming marauders and plunderers strayed our way.

An hour later the night watchman Haushim looked in again and reported in a trembling voice that a crowd of soldiers had collected outside the gate and were hammering on it with their rifle-butts and shouting "Open the gate at once!"

Our Chinese, Bergman and I had just gone to bed in our clothes, but Hummel was still up and hurried out. In a little while he came back and called to us inside:

"Come out at once. It sounds threatening."

We hurried to the gate, where the watchmen were also. A large party of Tungan soldiers were making a noise out in the street, talking excitedly. We could not tell how many of them there were. They were bumping and rattling their rifles. We too raised our voices and spoke in threatening tones. One of the men banged on the door with his rifle-butt and shouted:

"Open at once, or we'll fire."

"This gate isn't opened at night; Europeans live here!"

"We want to speak to you. One of you must come out here to us, or else we'll fire."

"One of you can come in to us."

"No, we won't send anyone alone. We must all come into your place and see who you are. You needn't be afraid to open the gate; nobody's going to take you prisoners."

"Well, and nobody's going to let strangers in here at night, either."

"Where do you come from?"

"Nanking."

"Where did you come here from?"

"Turfan."

"What day did you leave Turfan?"

"The 22nd of February."

"Were you with that motor convoy which went off from Turfan?"

"Yes, certainly."

"Show us your passports."

"There's no need. Ma's men have seen them already. You can have a card if you like."

My visiting-card was thrust out through a chink in the door and held in the light of an electric torch. None of the men could read. Yew read out my description—head of the road-making expedition in government service. Again they talked eagerly among themselves and went off in the pitch darkness without making any further demands. We heard their footsteps dying away in the direction of the main street.

We assumed that they were only going to fetch reinforcements, and that next time they would answer our refusal to open by smashing the gate into fragments and bursting into the yard, brandishing rifles and pistols. Then they would go further on the path of violence than on the night of March 5. At that time they were under the command of Ma Chung-yin. Now Ma was on the road to Kucha, and his power was broken. The faint glimmer of organisation and military discipline which before had controlled them to some degree had now disappeared. The fugitives, numbering some hundreds, who were still in Korla were under nobody's command. They were simply gangs of marauders, not a scrap better than common robbers and bandits. They had nothing to lose, were exposing themselves to no risks, and could not be punished for their actions. What were they but the dross of a beaten army, poor leaderless devils who had been seduced into an unsuccessful adventure, in flight they knew not where, tired, hungry and desperate?

We knew that the plundering of Korla had begun when Ma left the town with his staff and our cars. There was no commandant, no authority but the magistrates, who were powerless. No orders had been given to hold the town and defend it against the pursuing northern army.

Now they had been roaming about in small parties during the day and the earlier hours of the night, and plundering. Korla was sucked dry. Nothing more eatable was to be had. But everyone knew there was a house where rich Europeans and Chinese lived, and where whole stacks of boxes were piled up. There was food in those boxes.

"If there are enough of us, we can storm the place and plunder the stores," they must have said.

On their first visit they had threatened to fire. Next time they would translate the threat into action. Nothing else could be expected of starving madmen and ruffians. They were sharks who broke in wherever there was any swag to be got. And now three of our best marksmen were away—Georg, Effe and Serat.

We went in again. We should have to keep guard for the rest of the night. Hummel and I undertook that duty. We sat up and wrote. The others lay down on their sleeping-bags in their clothes, with their pistols within reach. Bergman had his rifle beside him. It could hardly be called resting. Not a snore was heard. They were lying awake waiting for the next robber band.

The atmosphere was depressed and nervous. We could not work quietly either. We thought of the peaceful winter nights in the Gobi desert, where nothing happened and no night guards were necessary.

The watches of the night passed. The hours went horribly slowly. I wrote a passage that seemed very long; but when I looked at the clock again only a few minutes had passed. Ordinarily time flies, and one cannot manage to get through all one wants to do.

Our Turki night watchman had a piece of wood and a peg. He was to strike two blows every two minutes to show that he was awake. After ten o'clock not a single blow was heard. Presumably he thought it wiser to keep quiet than to attract attention to us. We let the watchmen do as they liked. We could be sure that spies were standing outside the gate all night.

We had three men keeping guard. The day watchman and the water-carrier were keeping the night watchman company. Did they sleep? No, on such a night they needed no special stimulus to keep them awake.

Now it was twelve o'clock, the hour of ghosts and unquiet spirits! We calculated that if nothing was heard of the robber band before one o'clock, they would hardly come again that night, but would wait till the next. But perhaps they were thinking that a few hours after midnight we should be so worn out with sleeplessness that we could not keep awake. Then would be the time for them to attack and loot us.

A quarter-past twelve. The doctor and I went out into the yard to see how the night watchmen were getting on. One was lying asleep, the two others sitting by a fire they had made up as far from the gate as possible. Beside them bubbled a *chugun*, or tea-pot. The flames had gone out, only the embers shone red. They laid fresh fuel on the fire and the end of a whole trunk, which was to be pushed in above the embers as the fire burned lower. There was no object in having too big a fire. Its flames would produce a fiery reflection on the upper floor and its wooden columns on the north side of the yard. This might attract fresh bands to our quarters, and on such a pitch-dark night even the dimmest light was visible a long way off.

We went in again. Half an hour had passed. Again and again we started at some unusual noise—aha, there they were!—no, all grew quiet again. We listened. All the dogs in the town were barking frantically. A regular dog concert was going on without interruption. I asked the night watchman if the dogs of Korla always made such a noise at night.

"No, for the last four days the dogs have barked and howled like mad all night long, but it's never been so bad as to-night. They're barking at thieves and robbers who are hanging about, and to some extent at people who usually sleep indoors, but are keeping guard now out in their yards. It's pretty quiet at night in Korla as a rule."

I went out for a bit and walked up and down between the gate and the fire for a little while. I said to Kader Ahun:

"To-morrow morning you'll go to Turdu Ahun, who is *hsiang-ye* in this town, and tell him that I want to have a talk with him here or at his house. He promised to set a guard over our quarters now that we no longer have any military guard. As long as the motor-lorries were here they kept guard. Now we are outside the law. Tell Turdu Ahun that we don't want any more trouble such as we've just been having."

"Yes, *tura* [sir], to-morrow morning."

When we had been sitting in the room for a little while, Hummel went out, but soon returned and begged me to come out and listen.

"What is it?"

"There are voices quite close by."

We crept down to the gate. There we heard rough, hard voices speaking in dictatorial, quarrelsome tones. Other voices were heard farther away. The dogs were barking frantically. We fancied that by locating the barking we could trace the passage of a band of marauders. The barking became more violent as it grew nearer our quarters. A rifle-shot was heard some distance off, and a cry. We listened, holding our breath.

The sky was clear. The stars twinkled as calmly and peacefully as in the Gobi desert, where there was not a soul, and one slept in undisturbed peace. We had difficulty in making out the trees which rose like black spectres outside our wall. The atmosphere was nerve-racking—the mysterious darkness, the warning barking of the dogs, and the night watchmen squatting by the smoking embers, not daring to whisper or even stir their tea. We had a feeling that something was going to happen—something like the outrages of March 5 and 11.

We went in again and began writing. It was one o'clock. We had gained three-quarters of an hour by our tour of observation. Hummel went out to have a look at things. A few minutes later he came back and asked me to come and look at a curious light which was to be seen outside the street gate.

We crept back to the gate. Through its chinks we saw a light glide past from time to time, but could not make out whether it was an electric torch or a lantern. We listened, and heard steps and voices outside the gate. On the trunk of an elm just outside the wall of our yard we could see the reflection of lights being moved about. There too voices were heard. Something was going on just by our gate, and the dogs in the neighbouring yards were barking themselves hoarse.

"Now they're collecting. They'll break down the gate at any moment. Better call the others."

"Wait a bit."

The light passed by again. Then the chink remained dark for some time. We sat down by the fire. I had a chat with the night watchmen.

"What do you think of Ma Chung-yin?"

"We were so sick of Chin Shu-jen that we looked on Ma's arrival as our salvation. So he was welcome at first and was received as a liberator. But after his officers and troops had begun to ravage, loot, plunder and kill, we grew tired of them too, and now we want to be rid of them."

"How many Tungans do you think there are in Korla now?"

"Several hundred. Many of them are hiding in the southern part of the town. The troops which have gone west to Kucha already have horses, which they look after. Those which come here now are dismounted—scum, rascals and robbers. We long for the northern army to come; then there will be order in the oasis."

We went in again and continued our writing. We talked, too, of the strangeness of our position. How much had happened since we left Turfan on February 22! Only twenty days had passed since then! It seemed like an eternity. Yollbars and Li assured us that the whole country was quiet as far as Kashgar. Urumchi would fall any day; "then you can go there". And now! Urumchi was saved, Turfan taken, Toksun and Kara-shahr in the northern army's hands. The next step was Korla. Big Horse, the invader, was in headlong flight, and had taken our cars to get on faster. The night watchman peeped in at our door and whispered:

"There are one or two heads looking over the north wall."

We crept out. He showed us whereabouts he had seen them. He also said that he had seen one or two men crawl under the overhanging roof. We could not penetrate the darkness. The Turkis have cats' eyes; the lights and shadows caused by the star-light are enough for them.

We listened again. Nothing was heard. If the bandits meant to make their coup from the roof and the top of the wall, and were on their way already, they would stop when they saw that they had been discovered. They would lie still and wait.

But as nothing happened, we went in again.

At half-past two Hummel went out to reconnoitre. On his return he said:

"The dogs are barking less. Only one of the watchmen is on guard by the fire, both the others are asleep."

Bergman was snoring in his corner; the Chinese were awake.

At half-past three Hummel went the rounds again. His report ran:

"All quiet at the Shipka Pass. All three watchmen are asleep now."

"Let them sleep; they're tired."

After his last reconnaissance the doctor reported:

"It's getting light; the dogs aren't barking any longer."

And while the stars were fading, and the birds beginning their morning song, we too went to bed and fell into a deep sleep.

O<small>N</small> the morning of March 15 an educated young Chinese named Pan, who had been for two years in Chin Shu-jen's service, paid us a visit. He had come to Korla six months before from Kara-shahr, where he had been first secretary to Hodja Nias Hadji in July, August and September, 1933.

It was 10.42 A.M. We were sitting chatting in the yard when the ominous organ notes were heard again over Korla and an airman came flying from north to south.

Hodja Nias Hadji had been appointed by Sheng Shih-tsai ruler of southern Sinkiang, *i.e.* Eastern Turkestan and the Turfan basin. Ma Chung-yin tried every means to win him over to his side. But Pan, as secretary, advised the Hodja to try to do something for his tormented people, and not allow himself to be led away by the inducements the invader proffered and the promises he made.

(At 10.47 the airman retreated in a north-westerly direction.)

Pan tried to make it clear to the Hodja that if he stood loyally by Sheng Shih-tsai there would be peace in the land; otherwise the whole province would be bled to death by continually recurring war.

While the Hodja was at Kara-shahr he received every day, or every other day, long letters from Ma Chung-yin, who then had his headquarters at Turfan. In these letters Ma portrayed the advantages the Hodja would gain if he joined the Tungans and fought for their cause. Pan had read all these letters, and at last had a pile of them in his office a foot high. Their contents showed Ma to be a fairly accomplished diplomatist. But it was noted that he did not rely upon his own strength, and saw that he could not carry through his ambitious plans without the help of traitors and deserters within the province.

Pan said to the Hodja, "You must think in the first place of your own people and help them to get peace. Have no faith in Ma Chung-yin's promises." And the Hodja had remained loyal to the provincial government.

(At eleven o'clock two bombs burst north-west of our quarters. "So it's beginning again," we said.)

The Hodja had instructed Pan to draft the replies to Ma's communications. He had couched the refusals in very sharp language.

(At 11.2 three bombs fell, probably meant for the rearmost parties of Ma's cavalry which were fleeing to Kucha.)

Hodja Nias Hadji set out with his troops in July, 1933, to attack Ma Chung-yin in the defile near Arghai-bulak, where we had seen so many soldiers' bodies and dead horses.

(At 11.5 two more bombs fell, likewise aimed at the cross-roads quite close to and north-west of Korla.)

The Hodja detached another contingent of his Turki army to a pass above Ushak-tal. He was thus attacking Big Horse from two directions, but was defeated by Ma at all points and retired to Korla in September, 1933.

(At 11.6 another bomb fell.)

In comparison with the brave, audacious, dashing Ma the Hodja was a clumsy, inexperienced beginner. His right-hand man was Mahmut, and Ma's second-in-command was called Ma Shu-mien. The Hodja managed to hold the passes for a month. After the retreat he stayed for a month at Korla.

(At 11.7 the airman flew over the town and departed southward.)

The Hodja sent out small forces to the south and west to get fodder and food supplies. When the southern contingent returned from Konche, it found that Ma had occupied Korla in the meantime. It therefore attacked the town, but did not succeed in recapturing it. During the battle Pan fled to a little lake on the banks of the Konche-daria, south-west of Korla. This was evidently the same Bot-kul by which Jemaleddin had advised us to hide. He lay hidden in the jungle for a whole month in the hope that the disturbance would come to an end during his absence.

Pan now hoped for a speedy peace. The Turkis had formerly hated the Chinese and killed them in multitudes. The Hodja had given orders that all Chinese should be spared and treated with respect. In Pan's opinion it was Hodja Nias Hadji's attitude which decided the campaign in Sheng Shih-tsai's favour—a view the accuracy of which is very doubtful. It is more likely that he, who had not the faintest idea of making war, and his troops, which had never had any training and, moreover, were more than defectively armed, played no part worth mentioning in the war.

It was amusing to hear Pan talk about the campaign and politics in Sinkiang. He could find no words to express his contempt for the late governor-general Chin Shu-jen (who had resigned). When Chin, in the hour of danger, clambered over the back-yard wall of his *yamen* in nothing but his shirt, he had thought more of his own skin than of the thousands of men whom in the days of his power he had squeezed, punished with death, or driven to rebellion and war in conditions of unspeakable misery. As an official Chin had been impossible. He had filled all the high posts with countrymen of his own from Kansu, especially from his native district of Hochow. A popular lampoon in Urumchi ended with the refrain: "In the morning learn the Hochow dialect, and you'll get a fat job in the evening". Tailors, cobblers or bakers became senior officers in his bodyguard. Efficiency and suitability were of no account. Capable officers did not get promotion if they were from other provinces than Kansu. Titles many hundreds of years old, held in honour among Turkis and Torguts, were abolished, which only increased the general indignation.

The day passed unusually quietly in conversations of this kind, under a bombardment of flying rumours. We were waiting for the northern army and wondering why it had not come already. We were between two millstones, but the space was so wide that we were for the moment in no risk of being ground to powder. The one army had fled, the other had not yet come. Our most serious anxiety was for the drivers. Where were they? How had their journey gone with Ma Chung-yin as a passenger? And how had he treated them when his destination was reached? If the northern army accelerated its pursuit of the defeated general, might it perhaps save our drivers and lorries? And how would the northern army treat us, who had assisted Big Horse in his flight? The tension in which we now lived was of quite a different kind from that we had experienced during the preceding days and nights.

The approach of the northern army was also the subject of rumours. Representatives of Konche (Yü-li-hsien) and Korla were said to have just set off northward along the Kara-shahr road to welcome the northern army. Others knew that 1500 men of the victorious army had already reached the outskirts of the Korla oasis.

One informant explained the delay as follows. In August, 1933, when Hodja Nias Hadji had been beaten at Kara-shahr and had withdrawn to the right bank of the Khaidu-gol, a number of Torguts, with their wives and children, had taken all the ferry-boats that were to be found and let themselves drift down the river and out on to the Baghrash-kul, in whose reed-beds they had lain hid and evaded the war. New ferry-boats had accordingly been built. When Ma Chung-yin and his troops were defeated close to Kara-shahr a few days before and had crossed the river, they burned all the ferry-boats on the right bank to delay the northern army's advance and pursuit. Whether Ma Chung-yin had made any attempt to barricade and defend the narrow valley of the Konche-daria, Bash-aghri, where Yakub Beg had had a fortress in his day, we did not know.

We heard, too, that 400 Tungan soldiers had now handed over their rifles to the magistrates at Korla and declared that they had been forced to serve Ma against their will. They were allowed to remain at liberty.

The civilian Tungan population of Kara-shahr had been com-

TURKI WOMEN TRAVELLING

CLEARING AWAY ICE-FLOES TO OPEN A CHANNEL FOR THE FERRY-BOATS ACROSS THE KHAIDU-GOL

Photo by Bergman

FERRY-BOAT WITH SMALL CAR ON BOARD HALF-WAY ACROSS THE KHAIDU-GOL. EFFE IS SEEN IN THE FOREGROUND WITH ONE FOOT ON THE BULWARKS, THE AUTHOR WITH STICK, AND YEW SITTING ON THE SPLASHBOARD

Photo by Bergman

THE AUTHOR, EFFE, HUMMEL AND LIU-CHIA IN CAMP ON THE RIGHT BANK OF THE
KHAIDU-GOL AT KARA-SHAHR

TWO OLD MULLAHS (MOHAMMEDAN PRIESTS) IN EASTERN TURKESTAN

Photo by Ambolt

Photo by Bergman

THE YARD OF OUR "PRISON" AT KORLA AFTER OUR CARS HAD LEFT FOR LOP-NOR. TO THE LEFT IS OUR BEDROOM, TO THE RIGHT OUR COMBINED WORK-ROOM, DINING-ROOM AND RECEPTION ROOM. THE DOCTOR HAD HIS FIELD HOSPITAL ON THE TERRACE-LIKE VERANDAH

GEORG SÖDERBOM, MECHANIC AND DRIVER

ENTRANCE GATE OF THE MAIN GUARD AT KORLA

MAIN CARAVAN ROUTE, THE ANCIENT "SILK ROAD", NEAR CHADIR

STREET IN BUGUR

Photo by Bergman

BRIDGE AT KORLA WHICH, STRANGE AS IT MAY SEEM, SUPPORTED THE WEIGHT OF OUR HEAVY LORRIES

Photo by Bergman

OUR INTENDED ESCAPE FROM KORLA WAS DELAYED BY SEVERAL MISADVENTURES. SMALL CAR BOGGED
IN A POOL ON THE ROAD

THE LAST BRIDGE BEFORE THE ATTACK SOUTH OF KORLA, MARCH 11, 1934

Photo by Hummel

Photo by Hummel

ROAD WITH WILLOW AVENUE SOUTH OF KORLA, WHERE OUR CONVOY WAS ATTACKED AND FIRED ON, MARCH 11, 1934. TO THE RIGHT IS SEEN ONE OF THE CANALS BETWEEN ITS LOW RAISED BANKS, WHICH AFFORDED US COVER AGAINST THE BULLETS

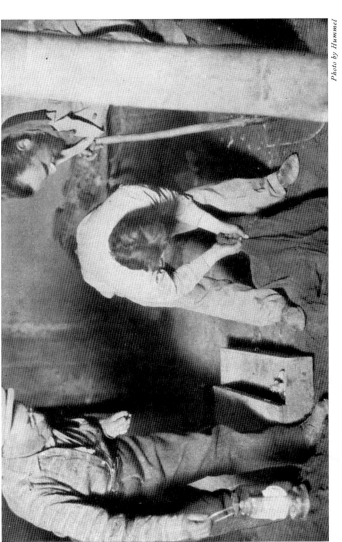

Photo by Hummel

EFFE BURYING SILVER, BERGMAN ON THE RIGHT, THE AUTHOR WITH LANTERN ON THE LEFT

Photo by Bergman

GATE OF "PRISON YARD" AT KORLA, SEEN FROM THE STREET. HOISTING
THE SWEDISH FLAG. NOTE THE RED CROSS AND THE TWO NOTICES IN
CHINESE AND RUSSIAN

pelled to fly with the defeated army and had taken with them as much of their property and their food as they could carry. The soldiers stole the latter.

When Hummel and Kung went for a walk in the bazaar, they found it crammed with thousands of Tungan refugees from Kara-shahr with horses, donkeys and baggage. All the food shops in the town had been plundered the night before, when we heard the barking of dogs from every direction. Only shops where caps, boots and articles of clothing were sold were untouched. An unbroken stream of human beings was moving towards Kucha, but the number of soldiers remaining in Korla was still estimated at 1300. They were said to have three headquarters, and might go out on fresh raids on the following nights.

The doctor had his hands full all day long in his field hospital. Five persons had been killed by aeroplane bombs, but, so far as was known, no one wounded. Among the patients a boy of twelve was noticeable, son of the deputy-mayor Nias Hadji. He had a tumour on his breast. It could not be operated on if the father was not present. The father was sent for; the son was agitated when he saw the knife, but the operation was carried out and the wound bandaged. The father told us that the whole town had been looted the night before, and thought it marvellous that we had escaped. He himself had not been able to leave his house without an escort of two soldiers. That very day four Tungans had invaded his house, demanding two hundred horses and a large supply of wheat and maize. When he assured them that he could not provide what they demanded to save his life, they had struck him, dragged him out into the street and thrashed him.

"If you don't get what we want we'll kill you," they said.

He declared once more that he could not possibly help them, and was then beaten with whips on the palms of his hands.

"We'll cut off your head and fasten it to a telegraph post."

"Very well," he answered. One of the ruffians had more heart than the others and cried:

"He's an old man; let him go."

Then he was released and dragged himself back to his house, which he found looted and destroyed. The gang had stolen his four horses and everything eatable that was to be found, and his family had fled.

Old Nias Hadji had become ten years older; he was pale, emaciated, furrowed and bent, and looked miserable. One could see that he had been brutally treated. He begged our pardon for not having called upon us, but he had not dared to put his nose outside his own door. Again and again he sighed deeply and cried: *"Ya Allah! allhamdulillah rabel ahlemin errahman errahim, Allahu ekbar!"* ("Oh God! God be praised, the protector of the faithful, the just, the merciful! God is great!")

Our friends Turdu Ahun and Rozi Ahun, who had promised to protect our quarters, had not even been able to protect their own property and their own houses. When the town was plundered, they had waited for their turn to come at any moment. Late at night they had fled out into the country. They had returned in the afternoon to find their homes devastated and completely looted.

Nias Hadji was right enough in supposing that if the bombing aeroplanes had not come the whole of the fleeing Tungan army would have settled on Korla like grasshoppers, and then the town would have become an even worse hell than it was.

"I am under Allah's protection," he said, stroking his white beard with both hands. "No man can harm me. But these Tungans are no men. They are wild beasts roaming about the streets. It is lost labour to talk to wild beasts. They always have their rifles and pistols ready. They do not understand any other language. *Ya Allah! La illaha il Allah, bismillah rahman errahim!"* ("Oh God! there is no God but God, in the name of the just and merciful God!")

All day long the doctor, his patients and we witnessed moving scenes and heard tragic stories. A little Tungan boy unwound the bloody rags round one of his elbows and revealed a horrible septic wound. He had fled from Kara-shahr five days before with his parents and his brother, and taken the road to Korla. They had been attacked and all his family killed. He himself had escaped, but had been struck by a splinter from an aeroplane bomb. He had wound rags round the wound and come on to Korla, bleeding and in misery. The poor lad, who had lost all he owned on earth, was a lamentable picture as he sat staring hopelessly at the red cross nailed on the wall.

The doctor thought the prospects of saving him very poor.

The hours of the day marched on, and no agitating events occurred. Again evening approached; the sun went down, the shadows began to play their tricks, and a new night descended upon Korla. The stars came out in the sky, and the dogs barked on earth. They were fewer and less frantic than the night before. The Tungan soldiers who had remained because their homes were at Kara-shahr, Toksun or Turfan, had thrown away their rifles. They were sick to death of the wretched war, and longed to get home to their farms and fields. It was unlikely that they would venture out on any plundering forays that night. The three night watchmen were in quite another mood from that of the previous night. Now they sat talking loudly by a flaming fire, and enjoying long draughts of tea. I gave them orders that one man should always keep guard and give the alarm as soon as anything suspicious was noticed.

We went to bed early, undressed as usual, and at last had a whole night of undisturbed rest.

THE VICTORS' ENTRY

WE still had frost at night; this time the thermometer fell to 28 degrees. After a quiet night I was waked at ten o'clock by Chen, who reported that a Turki had come, sent by a *hsiang-ye*, with a message that the commander of the newly arrived Russian troops would like to speak to me.

I dressed, breakfasted quite at my leisure, and then set out on foot with the Turki, who took the road to the bazaar, over the bridge and on to the northward.

The main street, on both sides of which the bazaar merchants have their stalls and spread out their wares under projecting roofs resting on wooden columns, was full of life and movement on Friday, March 16. Korla had not seen its like since the May day in 1877 when Yakub Beg, the conqueror of Sinkiang, took his own life within its boundaries, or the October day in the same year when Tso Tsung-tang's conquering army made its entry into the little town.

Fifty-seven years had passed since then, and now it was granted us to witness the entry of another victorious army into the same town, in the days of peace so quiet, so pleasant, dreaming the time away in rustic innocence.

The whole street was packed with people and horses. There were not many Turkis, and those who loafed about and stared were those who through all the preceding days had kept indoors and as well hidden as possible. One or two Tungan civilians, natives of Korla, were also to be seen.

Far more numerous were Torguts from Balguntai, in the Yuldus valley west of Kara-shahr, and from Bajin-buluk, half-way between Kara-shahr and Ili, where their chief had his summer residence.

But the element that set its stamp most strongly on the narrow, dusty street—which on the previous days had made so sinister

176

and gloomy an impression, but was now transformed into an incomparably picturesque, richly coloured canvas — was the Russians, the Cossacks, who had just arrived on their triumphal progress from Dawancheng via Toksun and Kara-shahr.

Their horses stood packed closely side by side, as far as the eye could reach, with their heads inside the bazaar shops and their tails turned towards the street. The street is narrow, and there was not much space between the horses' tails. The Russian Cossacks sat on the low terrace-like projections in front of the shops, or stood in groups, smoking cigarettes and talking. Some were still in the saddle. They had arrived in batches, the first at half-past eight, the last so recently that they had not had time to dismount.

Some wore field-grey uniforms, others long cloaks, with broad leather belts round their waists. They carried carbines on their shoulders, pistols in their holsters. The saddles were solidly made; reins, harness, saddle-girths and saddle-covers, all were in good order, and behind their saddles they had their sheepskin furs rolled up tight in leather straps.

The men looked well and burnt. They were clearly in good spirits; they nodded, laughed and replied politely when I spoke to them. But how dusty they and their horses were! A layer of light-grey dust covered their faces and their fair hair, and really made it matter little what the colour of their uniforms was— the dust of the high road had coloured them field-grey anyhow. What an enormous difference between them and the starving ragamuffins we had just seen in Korla! But, to do Ma Chung-yin justice, it must be recognised that his main body also was composed of smart, well-clothed, well-mounted men.

We could see by the look of the Cossacks and their horses that they had travelled swiftly during the previous night, covered with dust as they were, and with every sign of having just arrived. The horses were still sweating, and stood champing their bits so that the froth fell to the ground in flecks as white as soap-suds.

For quite natural reasons I had taken no photographic apparatus with me. Here we had the advance-guard of a new army. We had clearly sided with the defeated Big Horse. What must they think of us! Were we enemies, spies or what? It was obviously to clear this up that the commander had asked me to go and see him. And now I was on my way to him, and should hear our fate in a few minutes.

Now the shops were being opened one by one and goods displayed. The Turkis walked through the open space between the horses' tails, driving before them donkeys loaded with goods, sacks of grain and fuel. Foodstuffs, especially wheat and maize, which had lain buried in well-concealed underground rooms, now emerged into the light of day, for it was understood that the victorious army which had swept down from Urumchi would not take anything from the farmers and merchants without paying for it honestly.

It was known also that Ma's paper money, which only a few days ago the people had been obliged to accept on pain of death, were now hardly worth the paper on which it was printed. These grimy notes, hand-printed on any kind of paper, had been thumbed by so many sweaty, sooty hands that they were of no use even for lighting the camp-fires.

Now we had arrived at the entrance to an unassuming Chinese house, with a narrow entrance from the street. I recognised the place to which Hummel and Yew had gone three days before to tend the wounded General Ma, and where, in the narrow passage, they had seen Big Horse for the first and last time.

A red cloth was hung across the street, a Turki sign of welcome —the only *pailou*, or triumphal arch, the people had had time, or resources, to erect. An equally red cloth had been put up over the door. The tributes, therefore, were in the colour of blood and Bolshevism, which, for that matter, is also the Chinese ceremonial colour.

Two soldiers stood at the entrance. They returned my greeting with dignity and took my visiting-card, English on one side and Chinese on the other, on which I was described as leader of an expedition in the service of the Nanking government—on the Chinese side in curious symbols.

I was told that General Volgin was expecting me, and was asked to go to his room. I went along the narrow passage, crossed the square courtyard diagonally and entered a fair-sized room. A table stood close to the wall opposite the door. At it sat an officer, smoking a cigarette. I saluted. He rose, held out his hand to me and asked me to sit down at the table. He was of medium height, strongly built, with pleasant features, and was as grey with road dust from head to foot, from his fur cap to the heels of his boots, as the Cossacks out in the street.

General Volgin surveyed me with a faint smile, as if he was thinking, "This fellow can't be a spy". He asked me why we had come to Sinkiang and what was our business at Korla. I told him about our task and our journey, and how we had been well and hospitably received at General Ma Chung-yin's orders the whole way from Hami via Turfan and Kara-shahr.

"Have you met General Ma yourself?"

"No, I'm sorry to say not. He left here three days ago and took our four lorries and four drivers against our will. Two of the drivers are Swedes, and *they've* met him all right!"

"Why didn't you go to Urumchi?"

"I asked if we might go there from Turfan; but the chief of staff General Li, after talking to Ma on the telephone, replied that Dawancheng was dangerous because it was in the front line, and that the road was almost impracticable for motor-cars."

"But why didn't you go by Chi-ko-ching-tse and Kuchengtse?"

"We asked if we might take the Kuchengtse road, but again they said no. The valley road was blocked by snow then, for that matter."

I thought—but did not say—that it was lucky for us that we had not been allowed to go to Urumchi. If the road had been opened to us, we should have got stuck at Urumchi, missed the fighting at Korla and never got on to the road to Bugur and Kucha. General Ma's hospitality had only one object—to get hold of our lorries if he should need them. And now he was driving in one of them. But none of this concerned General Volgin for the time being. It was enough for him and for me if I replied briefly and honestly to the questions put to me in the course of this impromptu orderly-room cross-examination.

He realised that we had not come to Korla for a pleasure trip when I told him what a narrow shave four of us had had of being shot.

General Volgin listened with keen interest and said:

"General Ma is hated and abused everywhere, and he has turned Sinkiang into a desert. But he is brave and energetic and sticks at nothing. He isn't afraid of anything, either aeroplanes or superior numbers. But now a new era has begun for Sinkiang; now there is to be order, peace and security in this province. General Sheng Shih-tsai is going to organise the administration and put everything on its legs again."

I replied:

"Yes, thank heaven you have come here! During the last few days we have not felt that our lives were safe; we have expected to be attacked every night. Tell me, General, what is Sheng Shih-tsai's attitude towards Nanking?"

"Perfectly normal. He takes no important steps without informing the central government. He intends in future to keep in close touch with Nanking."

"We have been anxious lest our drivers, if they get away from Ma alive and are able to return here from Kucha, should meet Ma's beaten army on the road and be robbed of their lorries again. And if they manage to escape the mobs of fleeing soldiers, they will come up against your men in pursuit, and the lorries may be taken for a third time."

"No, you needn't worry about us. We don't want them. We have lorries enough of our own. But if Ma has not destroyed them, we can get them back for you. How are you off for petrol—have you enough?"

"We saved 420 gallons at the last moment."

"How much is a gallon?"

"Three and a half kilos. We have ninety poods[1] altogether, sufficient to take us over 900 miles."

"That's bad. You must go to Urumchi; you'll get petrol there."

He did not ask about passports, but as I had taken them with me, I laid them on the table before him.

"May I keep them till to-morrow, so that I can take copies and send them to General Sheng Shih-tsai? I shall have them translated into Russian for myself."

"We telegraphed to Nanking and Stockholm from Hami and Turfan, but we don't know whether the telegrams arrived. Can we send fresh telegrams from here, with your help?"

"That will take some time. All the telegraph posts between Turfan and Korla have been burnt and miles of wire stolen."

"But I am detaining you. You are busy."

"Not at all. Your information is the most important thing for the moment. I have just got here after a hard ride, and I haven't even had time to have a brush-down or a wash. For that matter, we must have a bit of rest before we start again."

"There are four things we want before we leave Korla to go to Urumchi—to get back our drivers and lorries; to be allowed to go to the new lake Lop-nor and wait there till things grow quieter; to be able to carry out our road programme and go first to Kashgar, then to Ili and Chuguchak; and lastly, to get our telegrams and letters sent off."

"I shall tell General Sheng Shih-tsai at once of the information you have given and what you wish to do."

General Volgin did not make any notes, but three young officers were sitting by the two windows, and one of them at least had pen and paper within his reach.

Volgin continued:

"Does General Sheng know all about your expedition?"

"Yes, the central government telegraphed both to him and to General Ma that we were coming."

[1] One pood (Russian) = $4\frac{1}{2}$ gallons.

"I know that; but Sheng has no idea that you are at Korla. I hope you have seen enough of the country between Hami and Korla to have got some impression of Tungan methods of warfare."

"Yes, we have seen a fearfully devastated country and a plundered people. When I get home I am going to write a book about my experiences, and that book will be read."

"Excellent! It's a good thing that Europe should know how war is conducted in Central Asia."

After an hour and a half's conversation I rose and went back along the main street. The Cossacks and horses had now disappeared; they had evidently been conducted to the caravan-serais and houses where they were to be billeted. But the street was still crowded with soldiers, now without overcoats or rifles. What a change of scene! Only yesterday I was meeting Tungan soldiers, and now Russians!

I talked with some of them; others came straight up to me and asked who I was. One came up behind me and asked:

"Do you live here?"

Another replied to my question as follows:

"We have been coming here from Kara-shahr all day, troop after troop. Two thousand Russians arrived to-day, half White, half Red. There are a thousand Torguts here, and two thousand troops of all arms have gone straight on to Kucha to attack Ma Chung-yin without touching Korla. Most of the two thousand who are in Korla now go on westward to-morrow. We were five thousand strong when we started from Urumchi."

The speaker was a White Russian. He was pleased to find someone who would listen to him with interest. He bragged a good deal about the northern army's achievements.

"Wasn't it a rather difficult job to take Kara-shahr?" I asked. "We have heard that Ma Chung-yin defended himself bravely, and that when you had taken the town once, you were turned out again by three hundred Tungans."

"Not a bit of it, it was child's play. They fled across the river in the six ferry-boats and burned them on the right bank. Then we built pontoons strong enough to take two lorries at once."

This might be true. But when the Russian soldier said that the northern army had two hundred lorries, a hundred of which had now been employed to carry from ten to thirty soldiers in full marching order apiece, he was drawing the long bow. Only a few lorries were sent to Kucha and Kashgar during the campaign, and it was said that fifteen wrecks were lying along the road.

Another Russian told me that the battle at Kucha had begun as early as the 14th. If this was true, our drivers had got right into the thick of it, and then their position must have been more than critical. News of this kind increased our anxiety for their lives. In no circumstances would Ma let himself be taken without a struggle. We feared above all that he might have fled down the Tarim river, burned the cars and shot the drivers to conceal his line of retreat.

Yet another soldier whom I met and talked with said that a Russian force was already on the way to Kashgar, while three hundred Whites had arrived at Kucha two days earlier and engaged Ma.

On my return to our quarters I heard that the Russians had cleared the town and bazaars of Tungan soldiers and captured fifty with the first sweep of the net. They were sent back to their native districts; none were killed.

In the afternoon we had a visit from a White Russian of twenty-eight, who told us about his adventures.

After the revolution of 1917 he had moved from Alma Ata (Vernij) to Urumchi, but had returned home eight years later. In 1930 he had travelled to Moscow, but had found everything so poverty-stricken and hopeless that he had preferred Urumchi and returned to that place.

The news that pleasant people inhabited our quarters must have spread among the strangers, for one Russian soldier after another came in, sat down and chatted for a while. In this way we got a picture of the situation which was not always reliable, but was better than none at all. When we asked how it was possible for Reds and Whites to work together, a powerfully built, fair-haired fellow replied:

"Why, when we've got a common object we get on all right."

He added:

"In January and February we were in a terribly bad way at Urumchi, and we were expecting Ma to take the town at any moment. Then the governor-general sent a wireless message to Moscow asking for help. It came. If it had not, the town would have fallen and not one of us would have escaped alive."

There had been hard fighting at Dawancheng. The first three hundred Tungans who were taken prisoners were shot, because the fury against Ma was then at its height.

Some visitors were attracted to our quarters by the Swedish flag and the Red Cross. Mr. Kuroshka had been an apothecary and surgeon at Urumchi, and the doctor knew him well. Sobinoff, an *émigré* and a merchant in Chuguchak, had met us before. Our host at Chuguchak, in whose house we had stayed so many times, the young merchant Hohriakoff, was now adjutant to our friend General Chow. Chow had long ago been interpreter to Baron Gustaf Mannerheim, formerly Head of the State in Finland, when, as a young man, he travelled in eastern Tibet.

Matsuk had been an employee of the German merchant Schirmer at Urumchi. He now came to our house just as we were having supper. He was General Volgin's adjutant and asked on the general's behalf if he could borrow two lamps from us, because his own were with the transport, which had not yet arrived. Of course he got them at once, as well as a bottle of paraffin. We never got them back.

Matsuk had with him four Russian soldiers, who had been ordered to keep guard at our gate and in our courtyard. It was said that many of the Mongols who had arrived were little better than the Tungans, and that the general desired that no one should molest us. We thought the real object in setting this strong guard was to keep us under observation and find out whether we had any secret communication with the Tungans. At all events it was pleasant to be able to sleep quietly without having to fear any nocturnal raids. But our Chinese comrades regarded this supervision as a monstrous outrage. In the course of the day five unarmed Tungan soldiers had been shot because they had been caught red-handed looting and committing acts of violence.

In the evening I chatted a little with the guards. One of them told me that 3000 Tungans from Altai had marched south to join Ma Chung-yin. On the way they had to pass through a ravine between perpendicular cliffs, and here they had been surprised by Russian troops and taken in front and rear. Five hundred men had saved their lives by climbing through snow and ice to the top of the cliffs, abandoning everything—camels, horses, arms and food. The remaining 2500 had been killed to the last man by machine-gun fire.

The fact that our convoy had not once been attacked by marauders and robbers on the road from Turfan via Kara-shahr to Korla was entirely incomprehensible to our guards. They told us that the whole road was now infested with bandits. Neither civilian refugees nor small parties of soldiers were safe. The former were always plundered and often killed. They could only think that we had travelled under singularly lucky stars.

GENERAL BEKTIEIEFF

WE passed a delicious, peaceful night. In the morning a captain appeared, with seven soldiers armed to the teeth, and relieved the first party of four men. So the supervision had become stricter. Pan, a few of our tradesmen, and our barber, who came to see us, were turned away at the gate. We could not make the most innocent and necessary little excursion to the backyard without being escorted by a soldier carrying a rifle. All the rooms in our quarters, and all parts of the premises not occupied by us, were examined, presumably to make sure that we had no large store of arms and ammunition.

At eleven o'clock I reported to the two soldiers who were on guard at the gate that I intended to go to General Volgin to tell him about our supply of petrol and to show him the map of Lop-nor which he had asked to see. The guard replied that I must wait till the sentry on duty returned. He should be there within half an hour. At the end of an hour nothing had been heard of him. Four o'clock came, and still no answer. I therefore left the general to stew in his own juice.

Bergman had heared shots from three different quarters in the town—presumably looters being shot. One or two of our fellows who wanted to go out and look into the bazaar were forbidden to leave our yard. If there were any important errand to be discharged, the sentry must first ask permission from the general, and if this were granted everyone who went out was to be escorted by two men.

So our second imprisonment had begun. We had spent the first with Ma Chung-yin's army; now came the second, with Sheng Shih-tsai's. One day and one night of freedom had intervened between the two—a night in which we were threatened every minute by bandits and looters.

It must be awful to be in prison, when it is so excruciatingly tedious to be a prisoner in a courtyard, where at least one can sit out in the sunshine reading, or walk up and down.

I was just strolling between the back gate and the street gate when there was a knock on the latter, the sentry opened it, and two Russian officers entered. They came straight up to me and introduced themselves—Colonel Proshkurakoff, adjutant to General Bektieieff, and Captain Vassilieff, who was prepared to act as English interpreter in case none of us spoke Russian.

Proshkurakoff was tall and thin with a big red nose, but nevertheless looked very pleasant. He was a White Russian, had come to Urumchi after the Red revolution, and had earned his bread by opening a food shop in the main street of the Russian quarter. His shop was opposite the premises of the Russo-Asiatic Bank, where the members of our expedition had lived the whole time from February 1928 to 1931. In common with about 1500 Russian *émigrés* in Urumchi, Chuguchak, Manas and other towns of Dzungaria, he had enlisted in one of the three White Russian regiments which had been formed by Chin Shu-jen. When Chin treated them with superior airs they had besieged his *yamen* and driven him out. Now they were serving under Chin's successor, General Sheng Shih-tsai; they had, with a contingent of Soviet troops, been the first to take up the pursuit of Ma Chung-yin, and while thus engaged found themselves in Korla.

Proshkurakoff said:

"General Bektieieff, commander-in-chief of the provincial government's field army, who arrived at Korla to-day from Kara-shahr, asks to be excused for not being able to call on you in person, because he has got a headache from all the dust on the road. The general has ordered me to ask you a few questions."

"With pleasure! Will you sit down out here or indoors?"

"Indoors, if you please."

I asked the two officers into our simple bedroom, where Hummel, Bergman, Yew, Kung and Chen were introduced. Tea and cigarettes were offered. Proshkurakoff produced a white box containing cigarettes and offered them all round. And now the second orderly-room examination began.

"When were you last in Nanking—in Peking—for what firm are you travelling (!)—what is the object of your journey—how large is the party—what are their names—what are their professions—how many drivers—how many servants—which way did you come from Peking—what day did you arrive at Hami—how and by whom were you received here—what impression did you get of the country on the way here—what day did you arrive at Turfan—which of Ma's officers did you meet there—have you met Ma Chung-yin himself—what was your impression of General Li—how long did you stay at Turfan and how were you treated there—did you meet a couple of Poles—when did you leave Turfan and by which road—why did you not go to Urumchi—if the main road was blocked, why did you not take the road via Kuchengtse—when did you first come to Korla, and how far west did you go—why did you turn back at Chompak—when did you return here—how many rifles and pistols have you—how much ammunition—have you a wireless apparatus?"

I gave detailed replies to all his questions, and the captain took them down. Proshkurakoff told us that Yollbars Khan and Kemal had fled to Hami on the fall of Turfan, and were going to surrender to Sheng Shih-tsai.

The three young Russians we had seen at Turfan had been shot by Ma. The Turki recruits we had seen on the road had been sent home to their villages. The northern army shot no one but traitors, spies and those guilty of outrages.

The examination lasted an hour and a half. At first he put his questions in a brusque, curt, military style. Later he thawed, and even condescended to laugh at some comic situation. At the end he rose, became serious, and said in the tones of one making a formal pronouncement:

"I am ordered to convey to you General Bektieieff's great dissatisfaction and astonishment that you, who bear a well-known name and who are approaching the close of an honourable career, should have helped our and the provincial government's worst enemy to escape by placing your motor-lorries at Ma Chung-yin's disposal."

"Colonel, please ask General Bektieieff what he would have done if he, unarmed, had been fallen upon by forty Tungans with loaded rifles, holding pistols aimed at his heart—who presented their ultimatum the first time and fired on him from an ambush the second. You can console the general with the reflection that even if we had fired and, in consequence, been shot down ourselves to the last man by superior numbers, the lorries would have been taken anyhow and Ma would have used them to get away quicker. It is very easy to make complaints like this afterwards. But thank God that in those decisive moments we kept cool enough heads not to commit follies which might have cost us all our lives."

He answered with a smile, somewhat embarrassed:

"Well, I was only carrying out an order. . . . But the passports you brought from Nanking, which General Volgin has handed over to General Bektieieff and which have been translated into Russian, ought to have given you the authority you needed to be able to refuse to hand over your cars."

"Yes"—I was on the point of saying "cheesemonger", but substituted "colonel"—"you are quite right in theory. But do you know what the Tungans' answer was? They said: 'This has nothing to do with Nanking: there's a war on here and no passports are valid in war-time.'"

The Russians bowed, and I accompanied them to the gate and said:

"Will you ask General Bektieieff what time I can see him to-morrow?"

On the morning of March 18 the storm was whistling round the corners of the house, and the dust whirling in grey shrouds about our yard. Sky and earth alike were dark and bleak. The trees outside our prison walls bent like bows, and slender trunks threatened to snap. The guards were not visible. If we had really wanted to bolt, opportunity was not lacking now. Yes, at the street gate sat a Cossack, hunched in his overcoat, and at the backyard gate another. But the other five had taken refuge in the drivers' room, where they had made a fire in the middle of the earth floor.

In such weather anxiety is more oppressive than at other times. In sunshine and fine weather it is easier to see the future in bright colours. We had nothing to fear on our own account. But what was happening to Georg and the other drivers? It was six days now since they had left us. They must have arrived at Kucha on the evening of the 14th. We had heard that fighting was going on in that town, and that both troops and civilian refugees had arrived, across the Tien-shan. The drivers and lorries ran the greatest risk if they got right into the fighting line. If all had gone well, as on Georg's first trip to Kucha, they ought to have been back with us already. We counted the days and hours and listened to all unusual noises, wondering if we had not heard the far-off buzz of motor engines.

At eleven o'clock there was a knock at the street gate and Colonel Proshkurakoff entered, this time alone. We went into the house. One could not stand in the yard in such weather without getting one's mouth full of dust. He had been sent by General Bektieieff to ask if I had time to go to the general's headquarters.

"Of course; I have nothing to do but wait for our lorries."

We went through the town on foot. The main street was rather empty; the storm had driven most people indoors. But in the bazaars, which were better protected and built in, and partly roofed, there were crowds of strollers eager to make purchases, small donkey caravans, and riders. A few Russian soldiers were to be seen, but no cavalry horses. The squadrons which had arrived first had presumably been moved on to the Kucha front. A number of shops were open, and even foodstuffs were for sale. Many merchants had hidden their wares in underground holes and pits so successfully that they had not been found by the plundering Tungans.

We went to the house where Volgin had received me. He was already on his way to Kucha. A number of young officers and soldiers were in the courtyard. Bektieieff himself came to meet us and held out a muscular hand. He was of medium height, solid and squat in build; his appearance was attractive, and he wore a jovial smile. He greeted us courteously and presented a young officer with a well-tended black moustache, who also remained seated at the table in the middle of the room at which we sat down, and on which tea-cups and cigarettes were set out. And so the third long examination began.

This time I described events in greater detail than before. The general asked a few questions which had not come up during the interrogations by Volgin and Proshkurakoff.

"How was it possible", he asked, "that Nanking could send out a road-making expedition in the middle of a war?"

"Because Nanking had received pacifying assurances from Urumchi that the war was over and all rebellions suppressed. And the situation is different now from what it was last autumn."

"No, there has been war here the whole time, and the war is reaching its decisive stage just now. But why did you not inform the governor-general, Sheng Shih-tsai, of your arrival?"

"I knew from a telegram from the Ministry of Railways to Suchow, sent on by courier to my camp on the lower Etsin-gol, that the central government had called upon the governors-general of Kansu, Ninghsia and Sinkiang to give us their protection and help in case of need. I also knew that the governors of Lanchow and Ninghsia had replied that they would do everything to make us secure. As I was in the service of the central government, I had no right and no occasion to send private telegrams to the governor-general at Urumchi."

Then the vital question was repeated which Volgin and Proshkurakoff had asked already—why we had not waited upon the governor-general of the province first of all, but had joined his enemy. The answer was the same as before. But now I added that when we came to Hami, that town and the whole road through Turfan, Kara-shahr, Korla and Kucha was under Ma Chung-yin's rule and not that of Urumchi. We were neutrals, and had to adapt ourselves to the realities of the situation. If we had declared that we belonged to Urumchi, we should have been arrested. Besides, when we arrived at Hami the war was undecided, and we were assured that Urumchi might fall into Ma's hands any day. We had therefore to wait on events, and use tact and prudence.

"But now the war is decided, and I suppose the road to Urumchi is open. We want to go to the capital, with or without cars, and wait upon General Sheng Shih-tsai."

"I'll ask Sheng Tupan if he will receive you."

Then it occurred to me that perhaps, after all, it would be better to postpone the visit to Urumchi as long as possible. That Sheng Tupan was displeased with us because we had lent his enemy our cars had been made clear to us the day before, for General Bektieïeff was under the command of the governor-general, and his words were only an echo of Sheng Tupan's opinion. We did not know what would happen to us at Urumchi. Perhaps we should be treated as spies and enemies, be deprived of all freedom of movement and arrested for an indefinite period.

I therefore turned the conversation into other channels. The general became interested and listened attentively. I had taken with me a large general map of Central Asia and large-scale maps of the Lop-nor area. More than half of our three and a half hours' conversation was devoted to the great communications and canal problems in Eastern Turkestan. In stirring, glowing words I depicted the magnificent prospects of the old Silk Road, along which, two thousand years ago, huge caravans went to and fro through Asia, and on which countless bales of silk had been borne on camels from the land of the Seres to the Mediterranean coast, loaded on to triremes and taken to Rome. A government which in our time, so long after, revived this road, the longest road in the world—not for caravan traffic now, but for motor-cars and railways and locomotives—would achieve a work whose splendour would not fade when centuries had passed.

If we should be able to contribute in any degree to the solution of this great road problem, we should have fulfilled one of the tasks which had brought our expedition to Sinkiang.

"From the questions which have been addressed to me by General Volgin, Colonel Proshkurakoff and you yourself, General," I continued, "I understand that we are suspected of having some kind of relations with Ma Chung-yin and of being interested in the war which is now going on. I assure you that our aims are much higher than this miserable struggle for ephemeral power in the province of Sinkiang. From our point of view the war between Sheng Tupan and Ma Chung-yin is only a second ticked away on the clock of history.

"As we had got into the middle of the war, we had to watch its course closely for our own safety's sake. But we are sickened at the sight of devastated towns, burning villages, fields and gardens turned into deserts, and a people whose surviving fragments are doomed to die of starvation and disease. This wretched war has made beggars of a whole people, and pulled down what it had taken centuries and generations to build up. It has moved the borders of the Gobi desert hundreds of miles westward.

"I assure you, General, that neither I nor any of my staff want to have anything to do with this disastrous war. Our intentions are peaceful. Our task is to raise and help the people, its trade and the lines of communication between the oases. In the instructions which were given me by the Minister of Railways at Nanking, Dr. Kuo Meng-yü, it was categorically stated that it was the absolute duty of the expedition to keep out of politics altogether and to observe the strictest neutrality. It amazes me that anyone could think we came here to take part in a war which we thought was over, and the result of which does not affect our task in the slightest degree."

The general listened attentively. Then he said:

"How would it be if, as you are in the southern part of the

province already, you first went to the new arm of the Tarim and Lop-nor, then to Kashgar and last to Urumchi?"

"That would suit us admirably, and I should be infinitely grateful to you if you could get that programme sanctioned. The best proof that we are more interested in Lop-nor, the lower Tarim and the Silk Road than in the war was given when we tried to get away to Lop-nor during the evacuation of Korla by the garrison; it was then that we were fired on and forced to turn back. Since then we have been prisoners here, and can't move without our lorries."

"I'll ask Sheng Tupan if he has any objection to your going to Lop-nor, and let you know his answer as soon as it comes. He's not likely to advise you to go to Urumchi now, for the road is unsafe all the way. One of our patrols found eight cut-off heads yesterday between Kara-shahr and Korla—the heads of travellers, probably merchants from Turfan and Hami."

"Have you heard what happened to the three young Russian drivers at Turfan?"

"We have searched for them everywhere without finding a trace of them, and we are seriously concerned about them."

"How far are we at liberty here in Korla?"

"You must not go outside your gates. There are still Tungan desperadoes in the town, and bands of soldiers are still roaming about looting. Last night a guard post was attacked and fired on by about fifty bandits. The rascals had been scattered and disappeared before we could get reinforcements to the spot. It is best for you to keep indoors and avoid attracting attention."

"How do you think Sheng Tupan will receive us, General?"

"Most hospitably. He is an educated man, who has had his military education in Japan. He is the opposite of Ma Chung-yin, who is certainly a brave, energetic man, but cruel and brutal at the same time."

I told the general that Dr. Hummel had opened a field hospital in our yard, and had treated both officers and soldiers of Ma's army and many cases from the civilian population of Korla. The doctor, I said, lamented that the Russian sentries had turned away his patients and that he had thus been compelled to break off his philanthropic work.

"The sentries are obeying orders," Bektieieff replied. "In the present state of things the members of the expedition ought to have no contact of any kind with the inhabitants."

"Is there any objection to my killing time by drawing portraits of inhabitants of Korla and the country round?"

"Yes, you had better wait a bit."

General Bektieieff promised to take charge of our telegrams and proposed that I should write one immediately. He would send it by courier to Urumchi in five days; from that place the telegraph was working irreproachably.

He was going to Kucha in a few days' time, and asked if he might borrow our small car so long as he remained in Korla. I proposed that we should lend it to him for his trip to Kucha, and hoped that on that journey he might have an opportunity of finding out what had happened to our drivers, perhaps even helping them if they had got into trouble.

Last of all the general asked:

"Do you remember, Doctor, when we last met?"

When I hesitated to reply, he continued:

"In the autumn of 1928, when you were planning a trip from Urumchi to Lop-nor, I called on you at your quarters and asked if I might come too."

"Well, and what did I say?"

"You said the whole thing was undecided, and that Chin Shu-jen refused you permission. But it is no longer Chin who holds the keys of Lop-nor."

Bektieieff was well aware of my earlier activities in Eastern Turkestan, and I could see that he was willing to assist our plans. It was certainly a wonderful stroke of luck that we fell into his hands of all people's, and at the moment when we most needed him! He had reached a fairly high rank in the Emperor Nicholas's army and after the revolution had emigrated to Urumchi, where he had lived for thirteen years and kept himself by giving Russian lessons. On the outbreak of war in Sinkiang he had been appointed commander-in-chief of the northern army. He did not say a word about his displeasure, which Proshkurakoff had conveyed to us, at our having helped Ma with the lorries. He was pleasant, friendly and jovial throughout.

The question which lay nearest our hearts was the fate of our drivers. On my mentioning this, he replied:

"Of course their situation is very dangerous, and I am sorry not to be able to reassure you. But we shall do everything in our power to save them, and I shall let you know as soon as I hear anything of them."

Captain Vassilieff accompanied me home. He had been ordered by the general to take away our wireless apparatus, which we had buried in the ground in a safe place when we hid our silver. We would get it back when the war was over.

Evening was coming on again. The storm howled, the dust swirled round the courtyard, and the branches of the trees chafed against one another. We were sitting in our poky room eating soup with carrots, dumplings and potatoes when suddenly a motor-horn was heard from the yard. We all sprang up and hurried out. It could be no one but Georg. But the yard was empty. The puzzle was soon solved. Two of the guards had got into the small car and sounded the horn by mistake.

As usual in stormy weather, the thermometer was high during the night (34·2 degrees.)

At eleven o'clock next morning, March 19, General Bektieieff and his adjutant came to pay a return call. They were offered coffee and cigarettes. Bektieieff told us that when he arrived at Korla there had been 1600 Tungan soldiers in the town, five hundred of whom had been captured and disarmed, to be sent home later to their native districts—Turfan, Manas and Chugu-chak. He repeated that we ought not to show ourselves out of doors. One never knew what might happen. Several Turkis had been killed the last few nights.

The general took a brighter view of the drivers' fate than the day before. He did not think Ma would do them any harm. If he laid hands on European visitors it would cost him dear sooner or later, if he came out of the war alive. I objected that even if Ma himself did nothing to injure them, they were exposed to danger from his understrappers and soldiers. But he thought that when Ma had disappeared from the scene, the fragments of his army would be glad to save their skins and be sent home. Ma himself had no prospect of safety except to escape in disguise to Khotan with a score of followers and hang about in the bazaars there, waiting for a chance to get back to Tun-hwang and Anhsi by way of Cherchen and Charkhlik. But it was doubtful whether he would be welcomed in Kansu, if he ever got so far. He might possibly have one other line of retreat, but an extremely unlikely one—by boat and ferry along the Tarim to Lop-nor, and then through the desert eastward.

Ma was thought to have only about a thousand soldiers left; all the others had deserted to become robbers or return home. Kucha might fall within a week.

In the afternoon the colonel came with two mechanics, had a look at the small car and repaired some minor defects in the engine. When this was done, and he had got a hundred silver dollars for Urumchi tael notes, he got into the car and vanished in a cloud of dust.

It soon appeared that all our dealings with the White Russians were unprofitable. They ruined the wireless apparatus, we got the small car back distinctly sorry for itself, and it was stupid of us to get rid of silver at a time when the value of paper was falling daily. But we did not find this out until later. On March 19 the exchange rate was 25 liang to a dollar. We were to see the day when 400 liang could be had for the same value in silver. When Sheng Shih-tsai set a reward of two million liang on Ma Chung-yin's head, this sum was only 80,000 dollars. Later it became no more than 5000 dollars. But perhaps the price was raised after the fall in the rate.

In the country round Tagarchi we had seen burning houses and found a telegraph wire stretched across the road. We now heard that the day after we had passed through the village a number of such wires had been stretched across the road and Mongol robber bands had taken possession of it all the way to Kara-shahr. It was considered a positive miracle that we had been able to travel in those parts unmolested, and especially that we had come through Kara-shahr alive.

Our enforced inactivity was a sore trial to our patience. Nor could it be said that our guards did anything to cheer our existence, or shortened the slowly passing hours with tales of their experiences. They did not speak at all. In answer to questions they said either yes or no or nothing at all. I understood pretty quickly that the guards had been forbidden to talk to us. The idea that we might escape was absurd—with no cars or drivers, and with whole loads of possessions piled up under the roof of the colonnade. It would have been amusing to know why we should have escaped, and where we should have gone in a country which was everywhere full of bandits and ruffians. We were safest inside the wall of our own courtyard, and guarded by the seven soldiers of the northern army.

But inside that wall our days passed slowly and monotonously. We had really no peace of mind for regular work. We could only kill time in one way or another. The doctor, so skilful with his hands, made a backgammon board with paper dice and cardboard pieces, and Yew and I sat bent over this for many hours, while the others played bridge with home-made cards.

The only distraction we had was listening to news from more or less dubious sources. In the evening two Turkis announced themselves, who had come straight from Bugur. The sentry did not want to let them in, but they assured him that they had a message for us. They were allowed to come in, and while they were delivering their message two soldiers were present to make sure that it did not refer to some secret conspiracy against the existing order of things.

The Turkis knew, like the rest of the population, that Ma had taken our lorries, and they therefore thought it would interest us to hear that they had seen all four lorries with their own eyes four days earlier. The lorries were going to and fro between Bugur and a neighbouring village, carrying war material. We received the news as a hopeful sign and gave our informants presents.

Then Professor Li and three of his students reappeared on the scene. He told us that the day we left Kara-shahr orders had arrived from Ma Chung-yin that Li, his students, and the whole of our party should be arrested. But as we had already started for Korla, they contented themselves with arresting Li and the students, who were taken to Kucha under military escort.

They had passed Charchi. The escort were riding on horses, the prisoners on donkeys. The distance between guards and prisoners grew greater and greater. To avoid being shot at the next encampment, Li and his followers determined to escape into a desolate tract south of the road covered with steppe vegetation. They therefore sacrificed their donkeys, their luggage and their money—two hundred dollars—and ran for their lives in among the tamarisks. They lay hidden there till it grew dark, and then crept back by a devious route to Korla, where they arrived on the evening of March 17.

Li had seen with his own eyes Ma's orders to arrest the whole of our expedition. He said he understood why they had fired to stop us on March 11, when we were so near escaping. They had to keep hold of us at all costs, alive or dead. When we were once made prisoners, they felt easy about us. Our lives had hung upon a hair several times without our having an idea of it. At the time when our first captivity ended and our second began— that is, when we passed from Tungan into Russian hands—our lives were not worth much. If it had occurred to the Tungans that the Russians could get from us important information about the fugitives' strength and equipment, they would either have taken us with them or put us out of the way. But luckily we had the motor-lorries which were of such importance to Big Horse. If we had not had them, they would have plundered us and carried us off as they had done with Li and his students. It was my definite opinion then, and has been even more so since, that—apart from a gracious Providence—we owed it to the lorries that we came out of that horrible war with whole skins.

THE SECOND IMPRISONMENT

THE thermometer always falls after a storm. On the night of March 19 the temperature was 27·7 degrees.

The first rumour of the day was that there had been a fight between Tungans and Russians at Yu-li-hsien, on the banks of the Konche-daria. The Tungans were fleeing to Charkhlik, the Russians were among the four or five hundred who, we heard, had come over the Kuruk-tagh on their way to Tikenlik and Korla.

Our landlord, Abdul Kerim, who lived with his family on a farm on the outskirts of the oasis, sometimes came into town to see that all was well with his house. A large unfurnished room in the west wing was standing empty. We asked if we might lease it. But the room had no floor, holes in the roof and no windows. An *usta*, or carpenter, was sent for from the bazaar and instructed to make the room habitable. He laid down a board floor, repaired the roof and put in windows. The room was scrubbed, tables and chairs were procured, and our mess was ready. Henceforward we took all our meals in it, read, wrote, played bridge and back-gammon, and received guests. Of an evening the gramophone played "Du gamla, du fria", the Swedish royal anthem, "Sverige", classical music, Hawaiian tunes, Bellman, jazz, more dance music, and other things. When the music struck up, one or two of the Russian soldiers used to come in and listen.

Abdul Kerim had a fortnight-old calf, which was let into our yard every evening. Our dog Pao looked upon the calf as a wild beast which had no business in our quarters, and chased it round the yard. The calf stuck its tail in the air and kicked out with its hind legs, easily and contemptuously avoiding its pursuer. The soldiers who were walking up and down in the yard, or standing on guard at the gates, thoroughly enjoyed the daily repetition of this circus performance.

A new day, March 21. The air was still full of dust, but the sun forced its way through again, feebly. Our *okhrana*[1] was now five strong. The sentry on duty was standing at the back gate. I was walking in the yard. Two cannon shots were heard to the northward, and a rifle was fired just outside our wall.

"What's happening?" I asked the soldier.

"Oh, there's always a bit of trouble somewhere."

"Where's our car? Has the general taken it to Kucha?"

"No, it's in the yard at headquarters."

Aha, I thought, the trip to Kucha was only a blind to prevent us from sending any of our fellows to look for Georg. For they surely could not believe that we meant to bolt, abandoning drivers, lorries and baggage.

A tall, stout Tungan peasant living in the Korla oasis had a son who was a soldier. The young man had a horrid septic wound in the thigh, and the doctor had looked after him for several days. Now the unhappy father returned with his son on a stretcher. They were turned away by the sentry at the gate. I assured them that we only wanted to give aid to a wounded man. Then the two were let in. The doctor told us that the lad's condition was hopeless, and that he would die of blood poisoning in a few days. For a few days more the Tungan came with his son on the stretcher. The wounded man's condition grew worse, and one day the father came alone and weeping, to say that his son had died.

I asked at the main guard if it was by orders from headquarters that the doctor's patients were turned away, and was told that this was so. I expressed my astonishment at the prevention of philanthropic work, for which the population was grateful. It was a military order—and that was all!

As the guards never addressed us, and usually replied to questions with yes or no at the most, I asked a colonel one day if they were forbidden to speak to us, as I assumed that they were not deaf and dumb or idiots.

"Why, yes," he replied, "prisoners' guards are obviously not

[1] Guard.

allowed to speak to the prisoners they are set to guard, and least of all if they are political prisoners."

After that I treated the guards like shadows—I did not see them.

After all the information I had given two generals and a colonel, it was both ridiculous and insulting to treat us as spies. No attention was paid even to our passports from Nanking. The northern army treated us as if we actually belonged to Ma Chung-yin's invading army. We thought that the repairing of our new mess ought to pacify them, for they could draw from it the conclusion that we were settling down to a long imprisonment.

One rumour said that a Tungan general called Ma Yi-ching had gone over to the northern army with eight hundred men in a fight the other side of Chompak. It was calculated that Ma Chung-yin had lost nine thousand men killed and made prisoners on the way from Dawancheng to Korla. Generally speaking we did not hear much about the course of the war. We were hermetically enclosed. But we had a feeling that something was happening, or would happen soon. It was pleasant for us to be out of the game; we had had more than enough of the war. The only thing that tormented us unceasingly was our anxiety for the four drivers. We had not heard a word from them for ten days. How could I face Georg's parents and brothers, Effe's mother and sisters, and the two Mongols' families, if anything had happened to them?

At 2 P.M. on March 22 the temperature rose to 59 degrees. Spring had come. The trees outside our walls were in bud. The day was one of the greatest and happiest of our journey.

About midday Yew and I were sitting playing backgammon when one of the *okhrana* handed in a letter. It was written in pencil on a couple of leaves from a notebook, and I recognised Georg's writing. The letter was not dated. Bergman was able to decipher the document, which was written in Georg's peculiar Swedish. It read:

DEAR CHIEF,

After much trouble and hardship we have managed to get

203

away from the Mohammedan soldiers—when we got to Yangi-hissar we were well received by Torgut soldiers but now we are in the soup again—Serat and Jomcha have had strict orders to go east with two lorries—they don't say if it's Korla or not but we hope it is—Effe and I have got to go west with the Russians to fight Ma Chung-yin but they have promised we shall not go to the front.

We are glad—we have all prayed to God every day. He has preserved us all the way—Serat and Jomcha must leave here this instant so this short letter I hope will be greatly added to by explanations from Serat and Jomcha.

God be with us all—pray for us—greetings from Effe and us all.

GEORG

Our depression vanished like mist before the morning sun. We wanted to leap, dance and sing. The drivers were alive—they had managed to escape Ma Chung-yin's eagle claws. Now they were in Russian hands, and all danger was past.

But how had the letter reached us? Investigations were made, and it was discovered that Serat himself had knocked at our gate, but had been turned away by the sentry. The sentry had taken the letter and sent it in to us. Bergman and I were now graciously permitted to go to the garrison headquarters under military escort.

We sent in our cards. While we were waiting a Colonel Bukharin came up, newly arrived from Yangi-hissar, with a message of greeting from General Bektieieff. But he had no time to say more, for at that moment the sentry informed us that Colonel Nareika would see us.

We entered. The colonel received us politely.

"I hope," he said, "you will excuse the untidiness of my room, but we are on active service."

"You should see what our quarters are like," I replied.

The colonel went on:

"Colonel Bukharin has this very moment handed me a letter from General Bektieieff, in which, among other things"—he read from the letter—"he apologises for being obliged to use your lorries for three or four days longer. He asks me to tell you that Söderbom and Hill are well, and that all four lorries will be returned in perfect order."

"Thank you for your good news, Colonel. I would be glad if you would forward a letter of thanks which I am going to write to the General. Our Mongol driver Serat came to our quarters about twelve, but was turned away by the sentry."

"Curious! I gave your two Mongols a written order to the sentries to let them in. They had evidently been there once before they got the chit. Their lorries are in the yard next door."

A messenger was sent next door, but Serat and Jomcha had just gone—now provided with chits.

We therefore hurried home. On the verandah we saw a group of Swedes, Chinese, Mongols and Russians, in the greatest excitement. Serat and Jomcha were sitting down in the middle of the group, healthy, weather-beaten and serene. A bombardment of questions was being directed at them in Chinese and Mongolian.

"Are you hungry?"

"No; the Torguts at Yangi-hissar gave us lots of first-class food. At twelve last night we met a party of Russians and had a splendid meal with them."

In the meantime Colonel Nareika had already told me that the two drivers must return to Yangi-hissar with their lorries at twelve o'clock. It was now one. I asked one of the guards if the Mongols ought not to be sent back to the main guard.

"No, a messenger'll come to fetch them when it's time."

Half-past two arrived. One cup of tea and one roll after another disappeared into the Mongols' interiors. Two Russians, who had accompanied the lorries on their night journey, now approached the tea-party and announced that Serat and Jomcha were to go and set out on their journey from the main guard. Serat filled his eighth cup, clapped one of the Russians on the shoulder and said laughing, "Otchen khorosho" ("Very good"). Serat said that he and Jomcha had bought some black lamb-skins at Yangi-hissar; they had got them on a lorry, and therefore asked that our boys Li and Liu might accompany them to headquarters and fetch the skins.

Then they rose, took a note to Georg and Effe, shook hands vigorously and disappeared again through the gate.

Now we were alone again, discussing the great event of the day. From the stories of Serat and Jomcha we pieced together the following narrative.

The convoy had left our courtyard about midday on March 13, reached Chadir in the night, rested for a few hours and gone on to Yangi-hissar, where Serat had run into Effe's lorry in the dark and smashed his radiator. Accordingly he was left at Yangi-hissar, while the three others went on to Bugur.

Serat, feeling lonely and forsaken, went to see the local *hsiang-ye* and showed him a certificate of identity written by Yew. The *hsiang-ye* promised to help him, and he began to repair his lorry.

On the evening of the 14th a Torgut force, one or two regiments strong, arrived at Yangi-hissar. One of their patrols had come across Serat and asked who he was and what he was doing. He had shown them Yew's certificate and told them that he and three others, with our cars, had been forcibly carried off by Ma Chung-yin. His car had had a breakdown and he had therefore been left behind. The Torguts, who were searching for Ma Chung-yin, had nodded comprehendingly and said that they would return later.

Five Tungan soldiers were staying in the house in the yard of which Serat was repairing his car; they were discovered by the Torgut patrol and taken away.

But the Torguts did not return as they had said they would, and Serat, feeling anxious, went out to look for their leader. He found him and was well received—after all they were compatriots, Mongols, if their dialects were rather different. The Torgut chief gave him a pass.

Serat remained at Yangi-hissar for four whole days and nights. On the 18th he heard from a Torgut that another motor-lorry had arrived from the westward, but had not been allowed to enter the village. He asked if he might go out and look at the newcomer, and his request was granted. If the lorry, as they feared, was carrying Tungans, he was cautiously to entice them into the place with him and hand them over to the Torgut leader.

He went, and found that the newcomer was Georg, who told them that he had arrived at Kucha on the evening of the 14th and been well treated by Ma's men. On the morning of the 17th he had got permission to leave Kucha and return eastward. Near Chompak, Effe's back axle snapped. As all the tools and spare parts were in Serat's lorry, Georg had to go on to Yangi-hissar to fetch them. Meanwhile Effe and Jomcha were left on the road, fearing an attack at any moment.

Before Georg, Effe and Jomcha left Kucha they had got a pass from General Ma. When, on the return journey, they met and were stopped by parties of Tungan fugitives, Georg always replied that they belonged to Ma and were members of the same family. Then they were left in peace.

Three bridges on the road to Kucha had been burned by Ma and repaired by the Torguts. No houses had been destroyed. Our host Jemaleddin Hadji had fled in time and shut up his *yamen*, but Ma's men broke the seal. At Yangi-hissar a number of suspected Turkis had been shot.

Georg had returned to Effe and Jomcha and all three had gone back to Serat. On the 21st Georg and Effe received orders from the Russians to drive to Bugur and the two Mongols to go to Korla, where they arrived at eleven the same day. It was expected that Kucha would be bombed on the 24th. The Russians had ten four-cylinder Ford lorries, 1929 model, running between Korla and Bugur. They had wireless stations all along the road. Georg had bought three hundred gallons of paraffin at Kucha.

In a couple of hours' time Li and Liu returned with the black lamb-skins. They reported that when Serat and Jomcha returned to headquarters they had not set off again. Instead, a Russian officer had sharply interrogated them. He had asked them how it was possible that Ma should have let them go free at Kucha instead of shooting them or at least keeping them as prisoners. The only explanation for this curious state of things was that we were on Ma Chung-yin's side and were acting in his interests.

Six o'clock came, and we still knew nothing of Serat's and Jomcha's fate. Li and Liu said that the drivers were agitated by the suspicions of which they were the object. But the Russians' astonishment was explicable. I had just said to Hummel and Bergman that I could not understand Ma Chung-yin's behaviour. Even if he spared the drivers, he would, from a military point of view, have been acting in accordance with his rights if he had burned the cars. For if he left them undestroyed, they would be taken by the Russians and his flight would be impeded.

"He must have some kind of sense of honour," Hummel objected. "His friend, the wounded cavalry general Ma, gave Yew and me his word of honour that the cars should be returned within four days. This was done, and Ma could not help it if the Russians laid hands on our lorries later."

On March 23 nothing happened. Now and again rifle shots were heard—presumably plunderers being caught and shot. The temperature at night was 41 degrees. The poplar buds were out, and there was a scent of spring. We had fresh guards every day. Those who came on March 24 assured us that none of our cars were still in Korla.

Our two Turki night watchmen, Shamshin and Haushim, had been dismissed, but the water-carrier Kader Ahun was retained. Our servants had to cut wood; they had nothing else to do. Certainly Chia Kwei, the cook, was always occupied, and San Wa-tse washed our underclothing and hung up our sleeping-bags, turned inside out, on ropes across the yard. Splendid to get a little sunshine and spring breeze into our stuffy winter lair!

A pair of pigeons had their nest in our mess. After glass panes had been put into the windows they could neither come in nor get out. One pigeon flew right against a pane so hard that the glass was cracked. The bird must have been astonished at meeting such hard, ringing air! We moved the nest and young birds to another protected roof-ridge across the yard, and the pigeons reconciled themselves to the move.

The mess was smartened up more and more. The sketches I had made of Georg and Effe were put up on the wall, surrounded by Swedish and Chinese flags.

On March 25 a new and more humane sentry, who did not care a rap about the order not to talk to the prisoners, told us that Kucha had really fallen and that the whole of its garrison had been made prisoners. No one was killed; all the troops were sent home unarmed. The whole road from Kucha to Korla was swarming with fugitives or people, both civilians and soldiers, who had been sent home by the Russians with their women and children. Carts creaked along, drawn by oxen or horses and laden with lousy rags, pillows and blankets; poor mothers came riding on donkeys, with their children in their bosoms, sitting astride sacks and bundles containing their goods and chattels. Merchants and farmers were seen on horseback, and small donkey caravans were carrying grain, flour and rice to the bazaars, whose shops had been opened again now that the bloody business of war had given place to peaceful intercourse and trade. Kirghiz shepherds were driving flocks of sheep from the Tien-shan to the markets of the looted towns, where life and commerce would burst into flower again when the forces of destruction had beaten a retreat. Now and again a troop of Russian Cossacks, fully equipped, came galloping along the road in clouds of dust, or Torgut horsemen in blue or red fur-lined cloaks, riding the tough, thick-set horses of the Yuldus valley.

What varied scenes, and what a difference compared with our experiences a fortnight earlier, when this road lay as dead and silent as a desert! Now the beaten army had already passed in its flight or had been dissolved, and the northern army had stormed by westward. What unspeakable misery and confusion had been brought upon hundreds and thousands of homes by the avaricious governor, hankering after gold, and the ambitious general who thirsted for power over Sinkiang!

A driver in the service of the Russian staff, Anatoli by name, came to our quarters and told us that our small car had gone to Kara-shahr the day before with Colonel Nareika and had now come back to Korla. He asked for a few quarts of petrol to be able to bring it to us. It was like meeting an old friend again. But the left door had had a knock which had bent the hinge somewhat. Neither Anatoli nor the young chauffeur who drove the car to Kara-shahr pointed out the defect; the doctor discovered it. They were ashamed, and earnestly begged me not to complain to the general; if I did they were lost. There was a workshop in the garage at Urumchi where the door could easily be repaired. We found later that the engine also was badly damaged after the Russians' short but evidently reckless career.

In the afternoon a young lieutenant came in with two soldiers carrying our wireless apparatus in a box. Orders had come from Urumchi that it should be returned to us; it was only asked that we should not use it for the next ten days. Curious. Did this mean that the war would be over in ten days? They might just as well have said that we were at liberty to use it at once, for when Chen, our wireless expert, examined it, it was found to be destroyed and hardly usable.

The conversational sentry told us that Volgin, Bektieieff and Proshkurakoff were at Kucha, that the troops pursuing the retreating Ma had now reached the Bai oasis, between Kucha and Aksu, and that the whole general staff would be at Korla one day soon.

We did not know at all where we were to go. Kashgar or Urumchi? In any case we had not fuel enough. We possessed only 360 gallons of petrol and ninety gallons of paraffin. Anatoli betrayed the fact that thirty Russian lorries at Kara-shahr had no petrol and were therefore not to be counted. But large supplies were expected from Russia, and we hoped to get our share of this.

March 26 was a dark, foggy, windy, gloomy day—weather hardly calculated to cheer the monotonous life of prisoners. But we still kept our courage up, and of an evening, when the Pil-grims' Chorus, Händel's Largo, and the Barcarolle resounded from the gramophone in the mess, the strength of the notes seemed to burst our prison walls and bear us away to other worlds where a boundless prospect was spread before us. Night is our best friend. There are no fetters in dreams; all gates are open there.

On this day, March 26, the doctor woke us early with the following original message:

"It is such wretched weather to-day that you may just as well stay in your sleeping-bags."

I received a letter from a regimental commander named Feodoroff asking for a tin of paraffin and six candles.

A splendid commissariat! We, who had dragged our stores half-way across Asia, again and again had to help the northern army, which ought to have had a (for armed men) perfectly safe line of communication from Urumchi.

On March 27 we awakened to another day which was to try our patience. The worst time was getting up in the morning— the sudden transition from delightful dreams to the colourless truth. But when one had washed, shaved and dressed, drunk coffee and eaten eggs, rolls and orange marmalade, one saw life through rosier spectacles again, and the curious thing was that the day passed all too quickly. Before one could say knife it was time for afternoon tea. Then came the twilight. We were summoned to dinner; the cloth was taken off; we played patience or back-gammon, or read by lamplight to the notes of music. If we had had an exhausting time on the road from Peking to Korla, we had now had rest enough, willy-nilly!

Kader Ahun, our water-carrier, came and complained that Nias Hadji had taken his two donkeys to send them to Urumchi, and had not paid for them. It had happened many times before that I had been appointed supreme judge in disputed questions, and dispensed law and justice among the peoples of the East. Nias Hadji had been ordered to send to the capital as many donkeys as he could get hold of. He had collected thirty. I urged him to pay poor Kader Ahun, but I do not know whether he did. Both Urumchi and Korla seemed to be suffering from a shortage of four-legged asses.

Yew and I had just written a long telegram in English to Liu Wen-lung, the head of the provincial government, and Sheng Shih-tsai as general in command at Urumchi, giving an account of the expedition's task and expressing our desire to go to the capital. I had even translated it into Russian, and was just going to headquarters to get it sent off, when four Russian colonels came into the mess—Nareika, Salomakhin, Nikolaieff and Feodoroff.

They were asked to sit down at long tables, and tea and cigarettes were served. And now there happened another of those marvellous episodes, like an incident in a fairy tale, in which this expedition had been so rich.

Colonel Nareika, the four colonels' spokesman, assumed a serious mien, and said, looking at me:

"A wireless message has just arrived from Sheng Tupan, in which he says that he cannot take the responsibility for your going to Urumchi now, because Russian motor-cars are sometimes fired upon from ambushes among the rocks along the road between the capital and Kara-shahr. Your journey to Urumchi must therefore be put off. Sheng Tupan goes on to say that you and your expedition have the right to go to Lop-nor to investigate the possibilities of irrigation. You had better stay at Lop-nor for two months, and then you can go to Urumchi."

I could not believe my ears, and had to support my elbow against the table in order not to tumble off my chair. But I betrayed nothing. Taking from my pocket the telegram in Russian to Liu Wen-lung and Sheng Shih-tsai, I replied:

"What a strange thing! I had just written this telegram to Sheng Tupan, and was just coming to you to get it sent off, and now you come in with an answer from Sheng Tupan! Please read the telegram, which of course is now superfluous. As soon as our lorries and drivers have returned to Korla, we will prepare for the journey to Lop-nor. We shall stay there two months. Then we shall return to Korla, and I hope we shall then hear something further about Sheng Tupan's wishes and get the quantity of petrol we need for our trip to Urumchi."

"All the telegraph posts on the road from the capital to Korla," Colonel Nareika replied, "have been burnt by Ma Chung-yin's men, except those which stand on inaccessible jutting-out rocks. A new line of posts is now being set up between the two towns, and it will be finished in six weeks. So when you come back from Lop-nor you can get into direct communication with Sheng Tupan.

"As for the petrol question, this is how things are: the road from Chuguchak to Urumchi is thawing, and heavy traffic is impossible. It will be practicable in a month. Then large supplies of petrol will come from Siberia to Urumchi through Kazakstan and Dzungaria, and you can buy as much as you want."

"Wouldn't it be wise to order a certain quantity now, which can be brought here while we are at Lop-nor?"

"That can easily be arranged when you have returned to Korla."

"Do you think, Colonel, that we shall be able to make a trip to Kashgar in two months, before we go to the capital?"

"Probably. Kucha is taken already. Ma Chung-yin has gone off to the westward with his last troops, scarcely a thousand men, and is now surrounded at Bai. He is lost and cannot escape. You couldn't get farther than Kucha at present. When you come back from Lop-nor everything will be quiet and you can go where you like, assuming that you get Sheng Tupan's permission."

We heard, too, that Hami was not yet taken, but that the town had been evacuated by the Tungans and now lay desolate and empty. Five thousand refugees, men, women and children, were on the way to their homes in Manas, Chuguchak and other towns in Dzungaria. They were all weary of the war, and had found that Ma's promises were not to be relied on. They had not been at war since Yakub Beg's days, and hoped it would be sixty years before the next war broke out.

P

Finally, I asked the colonel if he would be kind enough to despatch some telegrams which I would send to his headquarters later. Of course, he would be glad to take charge of our telegrams and letters.

With that the colonels rose, took their leave and went away.

Yew and I wrote a fresh telegram to Sheng Tupan and Liu Wen-lung, saying that we should carry out the plan put forward by Colonel Nareika and thanking them for the kindness and help we had received.

We composed another telegram to Dr. Kuo Meng-yu, Minister of Railways at Nanking, telling him how the expedition was faring.

I told my sisters that all was going well, and asked them to stop the order previously given that petrol should be sent to Anhsi.

Our Chinese friends also telegraphed to their homes.

So ended this wonderful day. The time of captivity was past, and the prison gates were opened wide.

Had I not, in the autumn of 1928, begged and prayed Chin, then governor-general, to allow me to go to Lop-nor, and had he not replied to all my representations with an arrogant no?

And now his successor, General Sheng Shih-tsai, came and *asked* me to go to Lop-nor!

From every point of view this solution was the most fortunate possible for us. What should we have gained by a trip to Kucha? We had been there already, and could have got no further on the road to Kashgar. And the road to Urumchi was still thick with robbers and marauders; besides, I detested that town, where the patron and friend of our earlier expedition, Marshal Yang Tseng-sin, had been shot, and where the ruler of the Torguts, Sin Chin Gegen, had fallen by Chin's murderous hand.

On the other hand, the road to Lop-nor, and all that it meant, opened up splendid prospects. In the original plan which I submitted to the Nanking Government, I had taken up the question of the utilisation of the lower Tarim's new arm, the Kum-daria, to water the Lop desert. This plan was no Utopia. The country round this watercourse and the ancient city of Lou-lan had two thousand years ago been watered by canals, which had certainly conjured up gardens and fields out of the flats of alluvial clay. I had guessed this when I discovered the ruins of Lou-lan on March 28, 1900—thirty-four years earlier to a day. Why should not we in our time, with elaborate technical resources at our disposal, be able to do what the Chinese of those days had done?

Another fascinating problem, which also I touched upon in my memorandum to the Government, was the revival of the two thousand-year-old Silk Road, which went past Lou-lan and which, reconstructed for motor traffic, would be a direct and convenient channel of communication between China proper and Kashgar.

And last, there was the definite solution of the Lop-nor problem, a scientific question of geographical, hydrographical and historical significance, which had its origin in Prshevalski's momentous discoveries in 1877 and Richthofen's criticism in 1878. Dr. Erik Norin, Dr. Nils Hörner and Mr. Parker C. Chen in particular had made the most valuable contributions to the solution of this great problem. All that now remained was the survey of the new river, the Kum-daria.

I shall always owe a vast debt of gratitude to General Sheng Shih-tsai for his perspicacity and good-will, and to General Bektieieff for his part in the decision which opened to us the gates, so long shut, to the fairyland round Lou-lan and the "wandering lake".

THE DRIVERS' RETURN

GENERAL BEKTIEIEFF's friendly letters, and all we had heard about our drivers from the four colonels, were like balsam to our wounds and turned our anxiety into jubilation. We knew that our lads were on their way home under safe escort, and that we might hear their horns sound outside our gate at any moment.

The doctor was busy decorating the mess with a fiery-red table-runner and white curtains, and Chen pasted to the walls round the portraits of Georg and Effe whole swarms of bats (representing happiness) and symbols of long life, ingeniously cut out in red paper. The sensation of captivity, too, had disappeared entirely; instead, we had before our eyes boundless prospects of freedom in the unknown deserts of the east.

As if we had not had enough shooting and bombing, some of our fellows, on the evening of March 28, arranged a fireworks demonstration which, if luck had been against us, might have had unfortunate consequences.

Our supply of pure alcohol, which was used for zoological and meteorological purposes, was kept in a five-gallon tank. The tank was hermetically soldered up, and whenever bottles or jars were to be filled with a certain quantity of alcohol, Serat made a hole in the tank. This was carefully soldered up again after the alcohol had been drawn off.

The doctor, Chen, Yew and Liu Chia were drawing off a quantity of alcohol on the verandah outside the mess. I stood looking on for a little while and then went in to write.

I had hardly sat down when a fearful explosion shook the house, so that plaster fell from the roof. I thought the house had been hit by an aeroplane bomb, and looked out. The floor of the verandah and one pillar were blazing fiercely, and, worse still,

I saw Liu Chia running for dear life with tongues of fire flickering about his clothes. The doctor was close on his heels, crying:

"Knock him down, get his clothes off!"

The boy was mad with terror. By the time they had managed to pull him down and tear off his burning coat and trousers, he had got a number of burns all over his body, and seemed to have gone clean out of his mind.

I had rushed out and realised what had happened. As the alcohol tank had to be shut again, and the soldering outfit was in the cars, Chen tried sealing-wax and happened to let a drop of melted wax fall into the tank, which exploded in a few moments. It was an absolute miracle that he and the doctor escaped without the slightest burn. But poor Liu Chia, who was holding the tank at an angle, received the full brunt of the fiery douche. Luckily his baptism of fire caused him no lasting injury.

The fearful explosion had a comic effect in another way— our Russian guards thought our peaceful yard had become the scene of some horrible outrage, and hurried to the burning verandah rifle in hand. The fire was soon put out, and the doctor had got a new patient. The dog Pao, who must have thought we had gone as mad as the Tungans, vanished down the street and did not dare to associate with us till next morning.

At half-past nine on the morning of March 29 I was awakened by running about and shouting in the yard, and heard motor-horns in the street and the cry :"The lorries are coming! the lorries are coming!"

I shuffled on my slippers and dashed out in pyjamas. I got outside just at the moment when Georg drove in slowly and surely through the gate and took his old place on the north side of the yard. Serat, Jomcha and Effe followed. There stood the whole car-park, as if nothing had happened.

The drivers jumped out. There were embraces and vigorous handshakes.

"Thank God, you've got back alive! You can't imagine how worried we've been about you!"

Effe, as sun-burned and lively as ever, assured us:

"We've been all right, but it's been a narrow shave time and again."

"How are the cars?"

"First-rate, except Serat's."

Then followed a stream of questions and answers. What a running to and fro and noise and stir! We devoured the weather-beaten fellows with our eyes, wanting to take hold of them with our hands to convince ourselves that we were not seeing visions and that they were really back. The miracle had happened; they were alive. Ma Chung-yin had not shot them. God bless him for it. Never had our courtyard seen such excitement. It was Thursday in Holy Week. None of us had experienced such an Easter as this. They had come like men risen from the dead.

When they had removed the thickest layers of grease and high-road dust with brushes and soap, they were taken into the mess and were astonished at the splendour which met their eyes—flags, draperies and table-runners, and the symbols of happiness and long life round their portraits. The coffee-table was prepared with all the house could provide in the cake line. If we had had champagne they would have been greeted with fresh explosions. As it was, just a simple speech was made, testifying to our pleasure in having them back.

Two Russian soldiers, who had come in the lorries as escort to our men, joined us at the table. They were already old friends of Georg and Effe, and earnestly begged us to let them come with us to Lop-nor.

We talked for hours, and initiated our fellows into the new plans. About twelve Colonel Salomakhin, commanding the 3rd Regiment, entered. He was a pleasant, frank man. He had received orders from Sheng Tupan that an escort of four Russian Cossacks should to accompany us to Lop-nor. He assured us that this was being done only to secure our own safety. No doubt! But I am sure their real task was to see that we did not make a bolt across the desert to Tun-hwang.

"The order says that you must start for Lop-nor as quickly as possible."

I asked Georg. He needed three days to get ready.

"I beg you earnestly", said the colonel, "not to start later than the 1st of April. It is the 29th of March to-day. I must go back to Urumchi, but I must not leave Korla until you have started for Lop-nor."

"Colonel, we have had a melancholy experience of the bridges south of Korla. Thanks to them, we took five hours to go two and a half miles. They must be repaired."

"I'll give orders to the magistrates at once and send my own soldiers to help with the bridge-building."

"We need a tent for the escort and extra rations for it—rice, flour, tea, sugar, fifteen sheep and other things."

"Give me a list of all the things you want. And write down a note of the quantity of petrol and lubricating oil you want sent to Korla, and how much you would like to have when you get to Urumchi."

"Can you look after our letters and telegrams?"

"Get everything ready, and I'll take it all to Urumchi and hand over your letters to the postmaster, Mr. Kierkegaard."

"While we are away at Lop-nor we shall leave one car and all unnecessary baggage at Korla."

"Excellent! the garrison staff will receive orders to be responsible for all of it."

"We have 800 gallons of petrol and paraffin left, which is enough for the trip to Lop-nor, but not for the trip to Urumchi. Your people have borrowed 166 gallons from us."

"It will all be returned. And what you need for the trip to Urumchi will be sent here. Sheng Tupan is friendly to you and will do all he can to help your expedition."

After some consultation with Georg I said to Colonel Salomakhin:

"We must have a hundred poods of petrol and six poods of lubricating oil sent to Korla, and some spare parts. We need two hundred poods of petrol and ten poods of lubricating oil at Urumchi."

"Make a list of it all. When you come back here you'll find a hundred poods of petrol and six poods of lubricating oil at our headquarters. The rest will be kept safely in the capital. And you promise that you'll start for Lop-nor on the 1st of April!"

"We leave Korla on Easter morning. You can be sure none of us want to stay in this awful town one minute longer than we need."

Colonel Salomakhin thanked me, rose and went.

We spent the whole day talking round the big table in the mess. Time after time Georg and Effe cried:

"Is it really true that we're back, or is it a dream?"

Georg told us that after Serat had been left behind at Yangi-hissar, Big Horse and his people wanted to keep the three lorries and their drivers for their flight to Bai and Aksu. Georg and Effe succeeded in gaining Ma Chung-yin's favour and confidence by flattering him and comparing him to Tamerlane and Napoleon. He was delighted, and, despite the contrary advice given him by his staff, released them and let them return.

Georg was convinced that they were within an ace of being shot when officers on Ma's staff warned him of all the information they would give the pursuing northern army about Ma's strength, plans and routes, not to speak of the advantage it would be to the enemy to get three new motor-lorries. Here too all hung upon one psychological moment, as on the night of March 5 at Korla. At that moment Georg had been as convinced as on March 5 that he was going to be shot. That this did not happen must have been because Ma saw clearly that his game was lost, and that he would gain nothing by taking the lives of two Swedes and a Mongol. But if it had happened, Serat could have thanked his lucky stars that he had smashed up his car at the right moment, so that he had been compelled to stay at Yangi-hissar, where he met the Torguts' advanced troops and saved his life.

Georg brought with him a letter from General Bektieieff,

CHEN, YEW AND THE AUTHOR IN THE "PRISON YARD" WATCHING
BOMBING AEROPLANE, WHILE BERGMAN SPREADS OUT THE SWEDISH
FLAG ON THE GROUND

Photo by Ambolt

TURKI GIRL

TURKI FAMILY

Kader ahun, water...   Korla E Y mus

Drawn by the Author

KADER AHUN, WATER-CARRIER IN OUR "PRISON YARD" AT KORLA

Photo by Kung

HODJA NIAS HADJI, THE TURKI LEADER IN SINKIANG, DEPUTY CIVIL
GOVERNOR-GENERAL AT URUMCHI

PARKER C. CHEN, IRVING C. YEW AND C. C. KUNG, THE THREE CHINESE MEMBERS OF THE EXPEDITION

Chinese photograph

SHENG TUPAN, MILITARY GOVERNOR OF SINKIANG AND THE MOST POWERFUL MAN IN THE PROVINCE. DESPITE THE COURTEOUS INSCRIPTION "TO DR. SVEN HEDIN FROM HIS YOUNGER BROTHER SHENG SHIH-TSAI", I WAS DETAINED AT URUMCHI FOR FOUR AND A HALF MONTHS

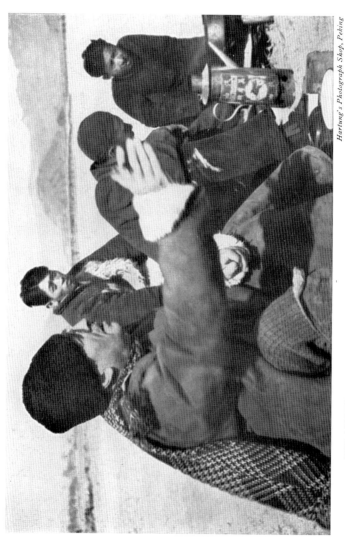

THE AUTHOR BY A FIRE IN THE OPEN AIR WHILE TENT IS BEING PITCHED

Photo by Söderbom

FOLKE BERGMAN IN SUMMER CLOTHES

Photo by Lieberenz

DERVISHES AT PICHAN

Photo by Bergman

JOMCHA, WITH CUDGEL, TELLS OF THE DRIVERS' ADVENTURES ON THEIR FLIGHT WITH BIG HORSE

MARSHAL YANG TSENG-SIN, FOR SEVENTEEN YEARS MILITARY AND
CIVILIAN GOVERNOR-GENERAL OF SINKIANG, WHO RESTORED THE
PROVINCE AND PLACED IT ON A FIRM FOOTING. ONE OF THE LAST
GREAT MANDARINS, WITH THE OLD-TIME ARISTOCRATIC DIGNITY OF
IMPERIAL CHINA

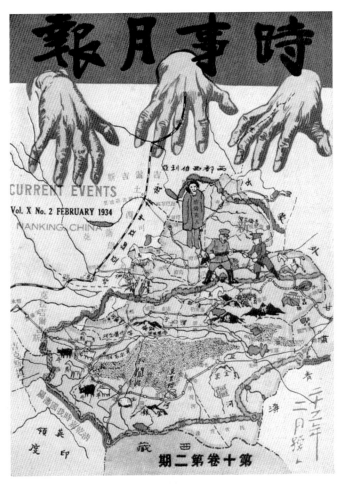

CHINESE CARTOON OF THE WAR IN SINKIANG. WHILE GENERALS SHENG AND MA FIGHT, WATCHED BY AN INHABITANT, THREE GREEDY HANDS ARE STRETCHED OUT TOWARDS THE PROVINCE: THE ONE IN THE CENTRE IS RED (SOVIET RUSSIA), THE TWO OTHERS BLUE (PRESUMABLY JAPAN AND GREAT BRITAIN). THE NATURAL RESOURCES OF THE PROVINCE ARE ILLUSTRATED BY HORSES, CATTLE, SHEEP, GOATS, JADE, GOLD, ETC.

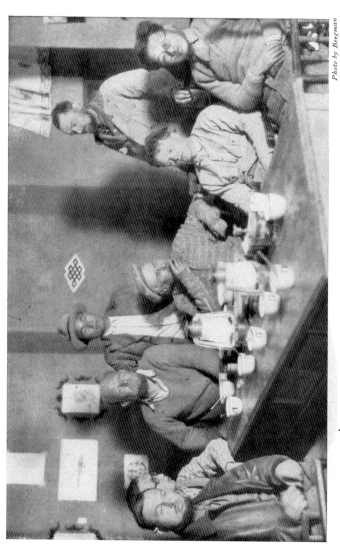

Photo by Bergman

AFTER THE DRIVERS' RETURN. FROM LEFT TO RIGHT: HUMMEL, YEW, GEORG SÖDERBOM, KUNG, THE
AUTHOR, EFFE, BERGMAN, CHEN

Chinese photograph

BIG HORSE

SERAT, MONGOL FROM ULAN-OBO IN INNER MONGOLIA. HE WAS IN
OUR SERVICE FROM 1927–35 AND HOLDS THE GOLD MEDAL OF THE
SWEDISH ORDER OF MERIT

which I did not read till the evening, when the place was quiet.
It ran:

Now that I am sending your cars back from Kucha, I thank you
for the kindness you have shown us and the help you have given.

I have received an answer from Sheng Tupan on the question
of your future movements. As the road to Urumchi is not safe,
the Tupan has decided that you had better go to Lop-nor for
the present and carry out there the investigations you wish to
make. By the time you have completed your work the country
will be quiet everywhere, and then you must go to Urumchi to
meet the Tupan, who has ordered me to convey this decision to
you, and also to let you know that to protect you and ensure your
complete safety four armed Russian soldiers will escort you to
Lop-nor and thence along the road to Urumchi.

This is all I have been able to do for you in accordance with my
promise. I wish you a pleasant journey and a prosperous return
from Lop-nor. I thank you sincerely for your kindness in letting
me make use of your mechanics, Mr. Söderbom and his friends,
who have done us such splendid service.

Hoping to meet you again soon in pleasant circumstances at
Urumchi,

I am, yours very sincerely,

GENERAL BEKTIEIEFF

I replied:

DEAR GENERAL,

I have received your letter and thank you heartily for the
services you have done me and the expedition.

I cannot find words to express my gratitude to you for having
secured permission for our expedition to go to Lop-nor. It is
most interesting to us to be able to go there, and I shall be glad
to be able to wait on the Tupan at Urumchi later. Please convey
to General Sheng Tupan the heart-felt gratitude of myself and
the expedition.

Thank you also for your kindness in detailing an escort to protect the expedition.

I owe a great debt of gratitude to you and the Tupan for your kindness and help.

Yours very sincerely,

SVEN HEDIN

Our position was now really promising! Georg and Effe, by their tact and diplomatic shrewdness, had managed to extricate themselves from under Big Horse's iron hooves, and we had had all possible success in our efforts to win the confidence of the high command of the northern army, to which, being absolutely neutral in politics, we were entitled. The passage from the one camp to the other, which had often seemed to us almost hopeless, was now successfully achieved.

As long as I live I shall be profoundly grateful to General Ma Chung-yin for not having let himself be persuaded, in his hour of sorest need, to kill our drivers, and for having chivalrously restored to them both their liberty and the cars.

Likewise I am infinitely grateful for the kindness and generosity which was shown us by General Sheng Shih-tsai in letting us go to Lop-nor, and so giving us an opportunity to carry out in this part of Eastern Turkestan the instructions we had received at Nanking.

The letters quoted above show clearly how much we had to thank General Bektieieff for the happy fulfilment of our plans and wishes.

HOW GEORG AND EFFE FLED WITH BIG HORSE

Not till we reached the village of Shinnega, on the way down the new river, did I find a quiet moment in which to pump Georg and Effe about their experiences on Big Horse's headlong flight to Kucha with the whole of our convoy of lorries.

They had raced along the same road which we had followed on March 7, 8 and 9. Our capable Swedish mechanics and the two Mongols, Serat and Jomcha, had of course no choice but to obey orders. To have made notes of the course of events would have been dangerous and would have aroused suspicions; besides, there was neither time nor opportunity to do so. The description I received, therefore, was not entirely clear and explicit. For example, they were not always sure on what day a certain event had occurred; nor was it so easy to remember the names of all the generals and other Tungan officers for whom they had driven and with whom they had talked. But they could describe the main features of that marvellous trip clearly enough to give us a general impression of what had happened. They had been spectators of a historic event, when the hands of the clock of war were approaching twelve.

In the fearful *débâcle* which had been the end of Ma Chung-yin's arrogant, ambitious invasion of Sinkiang, Georg and Effe's tactics were to keep his spirits up, make him forget his present reverses, and paint his future in the brightest colours, not caring how thick they laid it on. The relationship between Big Horse and his Swedish drivers soon became friendly and confidential.

It would have been absolutely priceless to be able to listen to the conversations between Big Horse and Effe on the occasions when they drove together.

We heard from Chinese, Tungans and Turkis alike that Ma

Chung-yin's plans were gigantic. His ambition did not go so far as to seek equality with Genghis Khan, but he was not content with anything below a level with Tamerlane. Timur the Lame had dominated the whole of Western Asia, and at the time of his death he had just begun a campaign against the Emperor of China, Yung Lo. He had spies and agents all over Eastern Turkestan and as far as Suchow by way of Tun-hwang. His successor in our time, Ma Chung-yin, was first to conquer the whole of Sinkiang and Kansu, and then unite with his kingdom the whole of Russian Turkestan as far as the Caspian Sea and the frontier of Iran. He was himself a Mohammedan, and his aim was to bring the whole of the Turki world in Central Asia under his sceptre. He would become Sultan in Turan, just as Riza Shah in Teheran was King of Iran.

Ma Chung-yin's enemies—Chinese, Russians, Turkis, Torguts and Tungan deserters—thought that in fleeing to Kucha with our cars he was entering a rat-trap from which there was no escape, and was irretrievably lost. Behind him he had the northern army advancing by way of Kara-shahr and Korla. Before him he had the Ili army, which had marched over the Tien-shan to Aksu and Bai. Hodja Nias Hadji's forces, which certainly were inefficient as soldiers, were also being assembled to fight on this front. To retreat northward across the mountains was impossible. The only line of retreat imaginable was to the southward.

People who were acquainted with Ma Chung-yin's past, and knew that hitherto he had always come safely out of apparently hopeless situations, thought he would not let himself be captured now any more than then. He would disappear and conceal himself under a disguise, and bide his time till the next opportunity arose. So long as he was alive and at liberty there would never be peace in Central Asia.

Well, the new world-conqueror was now sitting in one of our driver's cabins, beside that lively, cheery lad Karl Efraim Hill, a missionary's son from Feng-chen and of pure Swedish blood. It must have been a gorgeous sight to see these two young fellows, the general of twenty-three[1] and the driver of twenty, side by side on the road to Kucha.

We knew Effe well enough to be sure that the general had not been bored in his company. None of us had ever seen Effe serious or gloomy. The only night he had not sung was that time at Korla when we had pistols held to our hearts and were on the point of being shot. Ordinarily he was full of life and gaiety and kept the expedition, both masters and men, in the best of spirits.

When I asked Effe how he had entertained his distinguished passenger, he replied simply and modestly:

"I didn't leave him in peace a moment. I sang him funny Chinese songs, and he laughed till he choked."

"What did you talk about?"

"Oh, I told him stories and adventures I'd had, and soon he began to tell me about his campaigns, and the tight corners he'd been in, in Kansu and Sinkiang."

"What was he like? Was he stand-offish, or condescending and jolly?"

"He was charming. We were like a couple of schoolboys. When we parted, he declared that he had never had such fun in his life. And I was really sorry to say good-bye to him."

"Weren't you afraid he'd have you shot, to put out of the way two dangerous witnesses to his weakness?"

"Yes, I thought nearly all the time that it was our last drive. But when he was at his most charming, and promising us anything we liked to ask as soon as he'd captured the whole of Sinkiang, I felt that such a decent, generous fellow couldn't possibly mean to do us any harm, least of all when it was we who had helped him to get away from the northern army. But when I think of the whole business, I feel that only God's infinite mercy brought us out of it alive."

"Did he ask you anything about our expedition?"

"Yes, I had to tell him all about its organisation, its orders and aims. He thought it a wise and necessary thing to make motor-

[1] This was Ma's official age five years earlier.

roads through the Gobi to Sinkiang and in the province. He wanted to know how many there were of us and what each of us had to do. He knew our chief had travelled a lot in Sinkiang and Tibet, and was sorry not to have met him. One thing he couldn't understand was how the chief, a man of nearly seventy, could stand such a hárd journey as ours."

We have already witnessed the departure of Georg, Effe, Serat and Jomcha from our yard at midday on March 13. They drove to the little Chinese house, where Hummel and Yew had seen Big Horse just for a moment a few hours before, and he had politely stepped aside in the narrow alley to let them pass by. He himself had then been going to join the troop of followers who were to ride with him out of the town.

The convoy stopped outside the gate of the house, where multitudes of soldiers, both wounded and unwounded, pressed round the cars and tried to clamber on board. The wounded general of cavalry Ma, whom Hummel had tended, was dressing for the journey and was carried out on a stretcher, which was placed in "Edsel". He had a lot of baggage with him, and as many wounded as could be got into the cars were taken.

Old General Ma Lü-chang took his seat beside Georg in the driver's cabin and nervously bade him drive off at once, although the three other lorries were not ready. Georg put on speed and drove away from the oasis. When he came out on to the barren plain he turned round and looked for the others. As they were not in sight, he stopped to wait, and jumped down to see to the engine. But his neighbour cried, "Drive on!" and Georg drove straight on as far as Chadir. There he was ordered to stop and wait. It was not long before they saw clouds of dust to the eastward, and the others came along and drove up alongside "Edsel".

The foremost of the three was Effe. A tall, slim young officer sprang nimbly out of the driver's cabin. He was good-looking, but his features were at the same time hard and keen. He wore a field-grey uniform, a peaked cap and riding-boots. Georg knew at once who he was, although he had never seen him before. No one but Big Horse could look like that. It was clear at once that he was in an excellent humour, and Georg realised that he had had his first lesson from Effe. As Georg was driving ahead and had not seen the general on the road, he guessed that Effe had picked him up at some house by the roadside.

Big Horse walked about talking in a humorous, jesting manner to the officers who had been waiting for him and now saluted the commander-in-chief, standing stiffly to attention. He chaffed some and laughed at others' replies, while others again had to receive orders about the retreat to Kucha, movements of troops, rationing, and the order in which the convoy of lorries was to proceed.

Then he went up to Georg, held out his hand to him smiling, and greeted him as a comrade, without a trace of embarrassment.

"I am sincerely sorry", he said; "I deeply regret that I have been obliged to take the expedition's cars, but circumstances have compelled me to do so. I hope I shall not cause your chief too much inconvenience during the time I have to keep them."

Georg Söderbom, who had grown up, and become adroit enough, in the diplomatic school of East Asiatic life, put on his broadest smile, bowed, and assured Ma in the most flowery language that it was to the four drivers an imperishable honour to serve so great and mighty a commander.

Georg told me later, when describing this first interview:

"When I saw that Big Horse's disposition was friendly, I took the opportunity to make a good impression on him and win his confidence and friendship. The wounded general of cavalry Ma had driven in my car, and I asked how he felt and whether the jolting on the bad road had been painful to his leg. Both Big Horse and the wounded man himself declared that he felt pretty fit and that we could drive as fast as we liked. Some of the officers who had driven in Serat's and Jomcha's lorries looked surly and eyed me threateningly. But I joked with them, and told them how seasick Chang and his crowd had been when I drove them to Kucha on the 6th of March. Then the officers laughed, and the atmosphere became jolly and cheerful."

But now Big Horse called "Get on!" and jumped up to his seat beside Effe, while all the others took their places with lightning speed. The convoy rolled on westward. The sun blazed like a conflagration behind the willows of a village avenue; the twilight came on and then the dark, and the fleeing general gave Effe good advice as to how and where he should drive, and made various observations on the state of the road. "The road must really be mended here", he would say. Sometimes he shouted through the window to retreating soldiers, and asked where they had last spent the night or if they had found anything to eat. But there were no long conversations. He hurried farther and farther westward. Perhaps he hoped to find at Kucha loyal adherents and arms enough to enable him to make a stand and resist his pursuers, while his subordinate commanders collected and marshalled new legions on the road to Aksu and Kashgar. He talked quite openly in this strain to Effe, who received the impression that he was quite unconcerned at his defeat and convinced that his retreat from Dzungaria and the Turfan basin was of no importance so long as he still held Eastern Turkestan.

"The northern army could never have driven me from Urumchi, Dawancheng and Turfan if it hadn't got Russian help. It wasn't easy for my troops to stand their ground against aeroplanes which rained bombs, and armoured cars, and stronger artillery. But my army will pull itself together at Kucha, and if the other side are too strong there too, I shall go off to Aksu and Kashgar and win over supporters all through Nan-lu, at Yarkand and Khotan and as far as Charkhlik. It'll take time, but I shall conquer the whole of Sinkiang."

At midnight the convoy had reached Yering-kuo. There it stopped, and Big Horse ordered food and drink to be produced. They ate mutton, bread and rice, and drank tea. Then Ma lay down to sleep on a blanket in the rest-house.

At 2 A.M. on March 14 Ma sprang up and sounded the alarm.

The drivers were not asleep, but were sitting by their lorries smoking while they waited. The tanks had been filled, and the lorries were ready to start at once.

In the neighbourhood of Yangi-hissar they had an adventure which might have had a bad end. Serat had told us about it already, but now we were able to hear the details from Effe. They had just driven through the bazaar of the little town and were not far west of the spot where on March 8, with our heavily loaded cars, we had stuck fast on the wet road so many times. Now they had no weight to carry to speak of, and got over the wet places with ease. It was early in the morning. They were at the moment driving on a dry stretch of road. Georg was a good way ahead in "Edsel". Effe, with Ma Chung-yin, came first of the three others, with Serat hard on his heels. Effe flung up such impenetrable clouds of dust that Serat could only see a few yards. Airmen from the northern army were droning over their heads. Serat became alarmed, and thought the best thing he could do was to drive on at full speed. But the dust prevented him from seeing that Effe had stopped abruptly. He drove right into him at full speed and smashed his own radiator and one splashboard.

General Ma and Effe jumped out to see what had happened. It was seen at once that Serat's lorry was so badly damaged as to need thorough repair. The general was annoyed, but uttered no reproaches; he only said that Serat must try to get to Yangi-hissar and have the damage repaired. He did not give any orders as to what Serat was to do after his lorry was repaired. Serat felt lonely and miserable when the others had abandoned him. But Effe thought:

"Good. Now *he's* got a chance of bolting at any rate!"

It was still early when they reached Bugur, where Georg was waiting for the others with his general of cavalry. When Effe arrived, Big Horse jumped off again and ordered food and tea. He said to Georg:

"I'm sorry one of Dr. Hedin's cars has had a smash, but it will soon be repaired."

Then he ordered the local magistrates to send twenty horses to Serat to tow the wrecked car into Yangi-hissar.

The Chinese driver Wang, who had driven Ma's only armoured car, taken at the siege of Urumchi, was also riding on Georg's lorry. We had met Wang at Korla. Ma now called to Wang and ordered him to go back to Serat on horseback and stop and help him with the repairs to the lorry.

So the wrecked car was towed into the village, and the repairs began. They soldered together the radiator as well as they could, and took the lorry for a trial trip. But progress was slow. Serat was anxious not to mend it properly, and thought of every possible dodge to spin out time. He hoped the advance guard of the northern army would arrive and save him before he received orders to go on to Kucha.

Ma, in the meantime, could not wait at Bugur, but gave orders to drive on. It was still early in the morning of the 14th. Now one lorry, then another stuck in the clay on the road. Ma never grew impatient. He took everything quietly.

At four o'clock in the afternoon the convoy drove into Kucha and stopped at the Tungan headquarters. The commandant at Kucha, Wang Sse-ling, received orders from Ma to see that the drivers were made as comfortable as possible. They were offered excellent food and tea, and allotted sleeping places on the roof. In the same billet, but indoors, were quartered Big Horse, an elderly general, and the agreeable Chang Sin-ming, commander of the training corps, who had been so kind to us at Turfan. Strict orders were given that no one might go near the lorries, and sentries were posted round them.

Georg, Effe and Jomcha had complete freedom in Kucha. Of course they could not get far without the cars; but they could have escaped on horseback if they had been willing to smash up the cars. Ma Chung-yin seemed to have confidence in them.

The very first evening they walked to that part of the oasis which is called Dushambe-bazar, where the Swedish Missionary Association has one of its posts. Miss Engwall, seventy years old, has been living there quite alone for the last seventeen years. She spoke very kindly of the members of our former expedition, who "had been so nice". When the Citroën expedition passed through Kucha in 1931, she saw motor-cars for the first time in her life. She begged Georg that when we passed through Kucha on the way to Kashgar she might be allowed to come too, for she thought she was too old to go on living in solitude any longer. She had not had a single letter for two years. It gave her indescribable pleasure to meet two young Swedes, and they missionaries' sons into the bargain.

Unfortunately we were never able to fulfil her wish to drive with us to the mission at Kashgar, which would have been a great pleasure to us. I was sorry, too, not to be able to meet Miss Engwall. To live alone for seventeen years in a small town in Central Asia may be tolerable, if one is sustained by the lofty ideals for which one is fighting. But to live there with war raging, ceaselessly menaced with looting and violence, is no small thing, least of all for a woman. Yet no one dared touch her. The most savage Tungan rabble passed by her house as if she had had an invisible guard. One of the drivers had heard that the leader of a robber band had come to her house to steal her horse. She had given him so sound a box on the ears that the man forgot the horse he had meant to take for sheer astonishment.

When we had called on the mayor of Bugur, Jemaleddin Hadji, and bombarded him with questions about the military situation, he said:

"When your driver was at Kucha, why did he not ask the foreign woman missionary at Dushambe-bazar? She knows everything!"

On March 15 the drivers did not know what was going to happen to them, and Georg attempted in vain to speak fair words to the general about permission to return to Korla. Instead, he was ordered to drive Big Horse to the mayor's *yamen*. The whole courtyard there was packed with fugitives from Ili, soldiers who had deserted and now handed over their arms to Ma Chung-yin, and also civilian inhabitants with women and children, a crowd of a thousand or so come to surrender itself to the tender mercies of the lord of Kucha—that oasis which was now actually the last scrap of territory still possessed by Ma and obedient to his commands. So swiftly had the sun gone down on his dreams of empire. Even on February 12, when we left Hami to drive to Korla, little more than six weeks before, he had dominated the whole of Tien-shan-nan-lu as far as Kashgar, and had still hoped to take Urumchi, to which he had laid siege.

Now he had lost everything except Kucha. The Russian advanced troops were approaching Yangi-hissar to the east, and to the west he had enemies at Bai. Kucha was the last scrap of Ma's overthrown dominion which was still ruled by his broken sceptre.

But his courage, his unquenchable optimism, his personal bravery and his iron will—these things he still had, and he laughed at his enemies' desperate efforts to lay him by the heels.

With a self-confidence worthy of a Tamerlane he ascended to a beflagged tribune on one side of the large courtyard of the *yamen* and delivered, in a voice that never trembled, a speech which thrilled the thousand deserters from the Ili army to the marrow. He was surrounded on all sides by tightly packed crowds of starving ragamuffins, listening to his glowing words and his seductive promises. Georg and Effe, who also stood by, told me that Big Horse spoke splendidly, and with as much certainty and conviction as if his brow were already crowned with the victor's laurel, and he had been about to conquer the last remaining fragment of Eastern Turkestan. In the course of his speech he said:

"Welcome, brethren, friends, soldiers! Welcome to my army! Together we will beat the northern army and all our enemies who still dare to attempt to stop our victorious progress. Under the leaders of the northern army you have nothing to expect but starvation, suffering and thraldom. Perhaps you have heard of Ka Sse-ling [the 'Little Commandant'] of Kansu? I am Ka Sse-ling! It is I who shall unite all the peoples and races in these lands into one great dominion. With your support and your help I shall work for the happiness and prosperity of the whole people. I promise to give you freedom, well-being, enough and to spare of everything. Together we will organise this country and make it great, strong and powerful."

For the Ili troops, who had toiled over the snow-covered passes of the Celestial Mountains in cold, storm and privation, it must have been alluring and kindling to listen to those words, and to stand face to face with so great and mighty a leader. There was not one man in that crowd of soldiers who did not know who Ma Chung-yin was—"the little commandant" from Kansu. It was against him they had been mobilised. But their commander the governor of Ili, Chang Pei-yuan, had been abandoned by his own troops and finally had committed suicide. The fragments of his army had now made their way to Kucha.

And yet it was only a few days later that the bazaars of Kucha resounded with cries akin to the "*Hannibal ante portas*" of the Romans, and the northern army's advanced troops stood outside the eastern gate! And the brave, eloquent orator of the mayor's courtyard had to give way before superior forces and continue his flight westward.

In the meantime the speech was finished, and Georg was leading Big Horse back to his stable. As he did so, he talked seriously to the young general.

"What will happen to us? What will happen to the expedition when the Urumchi troops come and take us and our cars, and perhaps shoot us? Wouldn't it be better for us to try to reach Aksu under your protection?"

Big Horse smiled and thought the drivers need not worry.

Late in the afternoon of the 16th Georg had a conversation with Ma Ho-san and asked him to intercede with Big Horse on their behalf and help them to regain their freedom. In the evening our friend Hwang Wen-ching, the commandant at Kara-shahr, came to Georg's quarters and said:

"General Ma Chung-yin wants to know if you are willing to drive him and his staff to Aksu."

Georg, who had ascertained that a journey by way of Bai, where there was a strongly held front, and on to Aksu in all probability meant death to the drivers and the loss of the lorries, replied:

"No, we can't!"

Hwang then asked:

"Will you drive the general to Aksu in *one* car?"

"If I'm going to drive one car to Aksu, I must go on from there to Kashgar. And if I get there, I shall surrender both myself and the car to the protection of the British Consul-General."

"Why?"

"I'm a Swedish subject and a neutral, and the war is no business of mine. If I don't get General Ma's permission to return to Dr. Hedin and the expedition, I shall not hold it up, but will surrender myself to the British Consulate-General and send off telegrams and letters telling the whole world that the expedition has been cut off from its car-park and is in grave danger."

"No", Hwang replied, "that must not happen. Nothing shall be done which could disturb the good relations between us. You give us the car we need, and the other two can go back. For that matter, you've got a fourth at Yangi-hissar."

Georg declared to me later that the general began to moderate his demands when he and those round him thought over what Georg had been saying all the time—that the expedition, and Georg and Effe in particular, would see that General Ma got a good reputation all over the world and gained sympathies—if he treated the drivers generously. When Ma had reflected for a time, he said to his officers:

"It's wiser to let them go than to break off the good relations we have established with the expedition."

Then he said to Georg:

"You can leave Kucha to-morrow. I don't need your help any longer. Here's my portrait. I give it you in memory of our friendship."

On the morning of the 17th Georg bought 300 gallons of paraffin and paid for it with 130 silver dollars. Big Horse insisted that he himself should pay the sum—in his now worthless notes—and Georg took the amount, but without swindling the merchant. Big Horse asked for and kept one of our large thirty-gallon drums of petrol.

Just before the start the drivers received a visit from a senior officer, who handed over to them two black and white lambskin furs as presents for Dr. Hummel and me, as well as a fur for each of the three drivers. Big Horse again sent me his kind regards, and begged my pardon for having taken our cars; he hoped I understood that he was compelled to do so, as it was a matter of life and death for him to get away in time. Lastly, they were given a passport entitling them to travel through Ma Chung-yin's dominions and bearing his stamp, and also two letters, one to General Hai Han lü-chang and the other to the commander of the 3rd Brigade, "San-lü lü-chang" (*lüchang* = general). Both letters contained orders to help the drivers and not to detain them in any way or make use of their cars.

In the afternoon they said good-bye to Miss Engwall and drove out of Kucha with light hearts. On the road outside the oasis they met thousands of refugees—men with or without rifles; women, many of them carrying rifles; children riding on donkeys; wounded borne on stretchers; carts carrying luggage, riders, pedestrians—a confused swarm of people, all making their way westward, all in fear of being overtaken by the northern army's advance-guard.

At the village of Erh-pa-tai, fifteen miles west of Bugur, the back axle of Effe's car broke, and they were obliged to camp. There was not a single Turki in the village. They took up their quarters in an abandoned farm and cooked their supper.

On the morning of the 18th Georg had to drive to Yangi-hissar, because the tools needed for the repairs were on Serat's lorry. He was attacked on the way by a mob of Tungan soldiers, who jumped up on to the lorry and were about to rob him of what little he had with him. He produced Ma's passport, and they went away.

Arriving at Yangi-hissar about midday, he called on the commander of the 3rd Brigade and was very amiably received. He soon found Serat, who had been robbed by soldiers and was pale and nervous. The fact that he had a big Swedish flag on his lorry, as the three others had on theirs, had availed him nothing. Georg asked the commander of the 3rd Brigade to give orders that no one should molest Serat, and the general promised at once to protect him.

Then Georg returned with the tools. At Bugur he applied to the mayor and got a blacksmith to help him. He took the Chinese driver Wang with him from Yangi-hissar. At Erh-pa-tai they found that Effe and Jomcha had barricaded the door of their yard so firmly that they had difficulty in getting in. They worked on the back axle the whole night and next day, and exchanged it for a spare axle.

On the evening of the 20th the three drove on eastward. At Bugur they met the commander of the 3rd Brigade, who was furiously angry because the mayor, our friend Jemaleddin Hadji, had cleared out and locked the doors of his *yamen*. The soldiers forced the doors open. They ordered food, wine and tea to be produced, and invited the drivers to a feast. The officers and men of the 3rd Brigade had really neither time nor inclination for little jollifications of this kind, but pretended to enjoy them "in order that Ma Chung-yin should not lose prestige".

Georg tried to prolong the festivity in order that the 3rd Brigade might weary of it and continue its march. At last he got fresh stamps on Ma's passport and was able to drive on. All the bridges were burned, and it was a fearfully hard job getting the lorries over the canals in the darkness of the night.

They reached Yangi-hissar and found the town occupied.

The drivers were amazed, and Georg lost his head for the first time. He jumped off his lorry and began shouting in Chinese:

"We belong to Ma Chung-yin's army!"

Most fortunately, they cannot have understood what he meant. And when at the same moment he heard them talking Mongolian to one another, he saw that they belonged to the northern army and cried:

"We've got Mongolian passports from Peking. Ma Chung-yin captured us, but we've escaped!"

He was taken to a Torgut officer and showed his Mongolian pass. With that all ties with Big Horse were broken, and he disappeared from the scene as far as the expedition was concerned. Ma's newly stamped passport was a danger rather than a help, and was well hidden until it was destroyed. The officer gave orders that the cars should be driven into a farm-yard. On the way there they met Serat, who came running towards them, shouting like a madman:

"They're only our Mongolian troops!"

It appeared later that when the three lorries drove into the town, the Torguts had thought that Big Horse was making an attack. But soon the real position was made clear. The drivers were taken to the Torgut general's adjutant. He offered them food and tea, saying:

"You know him. You and we belong to the same family and are friends. I suppose you have no Tungans hidden in your lorries? Can we have your passports?"

The passports were shown and all suspicions disappeared.

On the 21st the Torgut leaders invited the drivers to a big party, which calmed their nerves. They also received fresh passports in Mongolian. The Torgut adjutant explained that he had to start for Chadir to meet the Russian commanders there, and said that all the bridges were burnt. Georg thereupon offered to accompany him with one car to look at the road, and at the same time ask the Russian commanders if the drivers might proceed to Korla.

The Torgut adjutant allowed, or rather ordered Georg to drive to Chadir at once with all four cars. The repairing of Serat's lorry was accelerated. But this took time, and March 22 was consumed as well. On the 21st a new Torgut colonel came and asked Georg to wait, because an officer of high rank was to arrive shortly. The Torgut told him that the expedition was having a quiet time in Korla.

On the evening of the 21st a Russian Ford lorry drove into Yangi-hissar. In the driver's cabin sat General Bektieieff.

Soon afterwards the drivers were summoned to the Russian headquarters and subjected to the most thorough examination about all their experiences with Big Horse. At last the officer in charge of the examination said to them :

"How in the name of all reason can you possibly have managed to wriggle out of the robber chief's hands alive?"

"We flattered Big Horse by saying pleasant things to him."

Now Colonel Proshkurakoff reappeared and delivered himself as follows:

"You must stay with us for four or five days. Two of your cars will go to Korla and two will come to Kucha with us. You are to carry forage for us."

The safe arrival of Serat and Jomcha at Korla has already been described. On March 22 Georg and Effe loaded their lorries with hay and maize and drove to Bugur, which in the meantime had been taken by the Torguts. The Tungans and their brigadiers had continued their retreat to Kucha. At Bugur the two Swedes were billeted in a place inhabited by Russian soldiers. They quarrelled with the Russians because they neglected the cars, and moved to other quarters. In the morning they drove General Bektieieff to Erh-pa-tai. Then they drove to Tu-to-pa and spent the night in a field.

On the 24th they went on to Tokhone, 90 li from Kucha. The whole of the wireless installation and General Bektieieff's baggage was carried on the two cars. Georg had lost his passport and complained to the general, who ordered a thorough inquiry. It was duly recovered. In the evening the drivers got a decent billet.

Georg had been indiscreet enough to nail up Big Horse's portrait in his driver's cabin. Proshkurakoff asked if he might borrow it for mass reproduction. It was to be distributed throughout the northern army so that all should recognise the fleeing Horse and catch him if they met him. Georg never got the portrait back.

They entered Kucha on the morning of the 25th in the company of the Torgut troops. When it became known that they had returned hundreds of Turkis in white turbans gathered to welcome them. They were all delighted to see Georg and Effe alive again. Everyone wanted to shake hands with them.

"How did you get away alive?" they asked.

It was as though Georg and Effe had won the war and put to flight that plaguy Big Horse. They were billeted in the same house where he had stayed, and where Bekticieff also now took up his quarters.

Not till the evening of March 27 did they get permission to leave Kucha; then they drove to Bugur and stayed the night there. Next day they reached the outskirts of the Korla oasis and on the 29th, as has been seen, drove into our yard safe and sound.

BIG HORSE'S FLIGHT TO RUSSIAN TURKESTAN

MARCH 31 was our last day inside our prison walls at Korla. We hauled down the dear Swedish flag over our gate without an atom of regret, and received with interest the new *okhrana* which had been ordered by General Bektieieff to accompany us like a shadow on the road to Lop-nor and thence to the capital of Sinkiang. Only one man, a young Solon[1] from Semirjetchensk, spoke Turki. The three others were Russians. One of them, Gagarin, originally a carpenter at Archangel, told me that his regiment of five hundred mounted men had started from Turfan, ridden over the Kuruk-tagh to Ying-pan, crossed the new river Kum-daria on the road to Tikenlik and from there ridden to Korla, all in sixteen days. There were still a few Tungans in Tikenlik, but all the Turkis had fled. This information confirmed the rumours we had heard before about the routes taken by the Russian troops.

I asked Colonel Salomakhin if he had any news of Ma Chung-yin. He replied that the twelfth hour of the war had struck and that Big Horse was shut up in the little town of Bai, between Kucha and Aksu, with his last men, perhaps eight hundred. The young general had no longer any hope of saving himself.

But early in the summer I heard quite different versions of his fate. Some thought he had slipped out of the trap around Bai, and that he would drift down the Tarim to Lop-nor with a handful of faithful adherents in ferry-boats; thence he would make his way across the desert to Tun-hwang to recapture the part of Kansu he had abandoned to Ma Pu-fang a year before. It was feared that in such an event he might become dangerous to us, and might appropriate our cars yet again.

The Soviet Russian Consul-General at Urumchi, G. A. Apresoff, told us that he had received a letter from his colleague at

---

[1] An Asiatic tribesman.

Kashgar saying that Ma had fought his way through to that place with the fragments of his army and finally, with 120 men, had fled by way of Irkeshtam into Russian territory. He and his men had been arrested and disarmed there and taken to Tashkent. The Consul-General did not know whether he would go on to Moscow.

Another report said that he had gone from Kashgar to Khotan and there, after sanguinary street fighting, had made himself master of the oasis, reorganised his army, and incorporated Keriya, Cherchen and Charkhlik in his new domain. It was expected that he would return to Korla by way of Charkhlik to stir up the Tungans, take the northern army in the rear, and finally get the whole of Sinkiang into his power.

When I was at Nanking nearly a year later, in February, 1935, it was said that Ma Chung-yin had arrived at Peking. All the papers announced this surprising piece of news. When I returned from Nanking to Peking in March, the press stated that Ma had gone to Nanking to talk to Chiang Kai-shek. In April the German Consul at Novo Sibirsk, Grosskopf, reported that Ma had been taken by the Russians to Alma Ata (Vernij), where it was presumed that he was kept in captivity. Yet another rumour declared that he had died in Russia. Indeed, there were people who thought it likely that Big Horse had gone to India to secure English help in a new campaign against Eastern Turkestan. Then he was to manage the affairs of the country to the advantage of British interests.

There was nothing of which Big Horse was not thought capable. When the fear was expressed that he would march through the desert to Tun-hwang, and I objected that this was impossible because of the stifling summer heat and lack of water, the reply was:

"Yes, it would be impossible for anyone else. But Ma could do it. He has done things like that before. No difficult ground, not even icebergs or sand deserts, no climate—neither piercing cold nor fiery heat—can stop his advance. He goes at every obstacle and always gets through. If he is beaten at one place, he turns up at another."

"Some say he's dead, don't they?"

"No, he won't die; he'll go on with the war, and as long as he is sailing about the desert seas like the Flying Dutchman, there'll be no peace in this part of Asia."

Legends and sayings had already begun to spin their web about Big Horse and his doings, of late so bloody, now so silent and secret. A mysterious glamour had from early years clung to his name, his actions, his personality. Even as a boy he had been called Ka Sse-ling (the "Little Commandant"). Everyone talked, but those who had seen him could easily be counted. All had something to tell of his phenomenally swift forced marches through the deserts, but no one knew where he was. He hissed through the wilderness and steppes like a meteor, and fire and blood gushed out where he had trodden. Big Horse sped by and vanished like lightning. He was like the wind; no one knew whence he came or whither he went, but his voice was heard. Many had listened to tales of his bloody deeds; some doubted his existence, others feared his coming like death, and waited to see the rider on the eerie pale horse come galloping over the earth where he was least expected.

So had Ka Sse-ling (the "Little Commandant") or Ta Ma ("Big Horse") acquired a strange power over men's senses through his reckless bravery, his pitiless cruelty and his baffling swiftness. We ourselves were greeted with a message of welcome from him, and the hospitality we received within his domains was given at his orders. But only some of our men saw him. When we reached Turfan he had just left the town, where he had been celebrating the Chinese New Year. When we were the prisoners of his garrison at Korla, he himself came to the town and apologised for not being able to visit us. If we had not had concrete proof of his existence by his taking our lorries, we should have been tempted to doubt if there was such a person.

The very first day we set foot in his realm, we had a feeling that we were walking on a quicksand. Then we travelled five hundred miles through that realm and saw it shrinking behind us like a snow-field that is devoured by the spring sun. And he himself came rushing by like a cyclone, a whirlwind sweeping up the deathly pale dust from the earth, speeding away to westward like a spectre of the mists and vanishing on the horizon.

Even after all links between Ma Chung-yin and ourselves had been severed by the drivers' return, his ghost walked again and again in our encampments.

The last evening in Korla we heard his name mentioned in a rather significant connection. When I said good-night to our host, Abdul Kerim, and thanked him for the hospitality he had shown us by letting the whole of his house to us as a prison, he led me to a remote corner and, having made sure that there were no guards in the neighbourhood, whispered:

"I dared not tell you before, but as you are leaving Korla to-morrow I can tell you that I was sent for to headquarters a fortnight ago, the same day the Russian troops entered Korla, and thoroughly examined about you and your expedition. It lasted four hours, and all my answers were taken down. I was asked:

" 'Had Dr. Hedin or any other member of his expedition any intercourse with General Ma Chung-yin?'

" 'Did Ma visit the quarters of the expedition when he was in Korla on March 13?'

" 'Did Dr. Hedin or any of his staff visit General Ma?'

" 'Did any of Ma's staff visit the expedition?'

" 'With whom does the expedition associate in Korla, and who comes to your house to meet it?'

" 'Did the expedition give its cars up to Ma Chung-yin willingly, or only after forcible pressure?'

"These questions, and a lot of others I have forgotten, were put to me by the Russian officers, and I replied by telling the truth—that you had had no communication whatever with Ma Chung-yin."

They could not, then, get rid of the suspicion that we, who had helped Big Horse with our cars, had some secret relations with him, and that it was in our interest to hasten his flight. The circumstance that the same cars which had helped him to flee were later used by his enemies to accelerate his capture improved our position in some degree. My repeated assurances that the government at Nanking, in its instructions, had absolutely forbidden us to concern ourselves with the internal politics of Sinkiang were presumably regarded as diplomatic evasions. The suspicions remained, and found expression several months later in our prolonged and enervating detention at Urumchi.

Quite recently, at the beginning of September, 1935, I received a budget of news about the situation in Eastern Turkestan, which may well be given here as a conclusion to this condensed narrative of war in Asia.

In August, 1934, the Chinese were masters in Eastern Turkestan. This reconquest differed from Tso Tsung-tang's, fifty-six years earlier, in that Tso's was undertaken by the Imperial Government in Peking and was carried out without Russian help.

The defeated Tungan army had in August, 1934, retired to the Khotan oasis, and dominated the country as far as the Yarkand-daria. There was, therefore, a not inconsiderable area which had not yet been recovered by the Chinese.

The Tungans thus controlled two of the caravan routes to Ladak and India.

A Tungan force from Turfan arrived at Kashgar as early as May, 1933. At first they got on well with the Turkis, but soon quarrels arose between them and the Turkis, and the Kirghizes joined the latter. At last the Tungans had to shut themselves up in Han-cheng or Yangi-shahr, the "new city" close to Kashgar. This was besieged for six months by the combined Turkis and Kirghizes. But the town was never taken, not even after Hodja Nias Hadji had come with an army from the north to try to relieve it. The Hodja had come to those parts to receive a consignment of weapons, bombs and ammunition which he had bought from the Soviet. But he was defeated in January, 1934, and had to flee to Kashgar with the remains of his army.

On February 6, 1934, the day on which we made our entrance into Hami, two thousand Tungans pushed forward to Kashgar. The Turkis, who had heard rumours of their approach, had already abandoned the siege of Han-cheng and retired. From that day the Tungans were masters of Kashgar for six months. The garrison of Han-cheng was thus freed, and the town gates, so long shut, were reopened. There were Chinese and Turkis too in Han-cheng, which was turned into a hell upon earth; the missionaries of the Swedish Missionary Association had all their work cut out to look after the wounded and impoverished people.

The main force of the defeated Tungan army, whose flight through Korla we had witnessed, arrived at Kashgar on April 7, 1934, under the command of Big Horse and his staff, who had been conveyed to Kucha by our drivers on March 13 and 14. So Big Horse had not been encircled at Bai as Colonel Saloma-khin believed, but had got through to Kashgar and covered the 375 miles quickly enough without our cars.

With him arrived several Chinese who had formerly filled high offices in the province, among them the commander of Kucheng-tse Li Hai-jo, our friend from Turfan. The Tungans remained at Kashgar till the beginning of August, 1934. Half the army was stationed at Kashgar under the command of General Ma Chung-yin himself; the other lay at Maralbashi under the command of the general of cavalry Ma Ho-san, the same man whom Dr. Hummel had treated at Turfan and Korla for a wound in the right thigh from a bomb splinter. Ma Ho-san went to the Swedish mission-aries' clinic and handed them the letter which Hummel had written asking them to look after the general. It was a piece of luck for this general that he fell into the hands of such clever Swedes, and a piece of luck for us that Hummel saved his leg, for, as I have said before, this cure undoubtedly helped to save our drivers and lorries.

During his stay in Kashgar General Ma Chung-yin visited the

Swedish missionary station, was courteous in his bearing, and talked pleasantly with everyone. He played tennis with enjoyment and was in the best of humours. He paid repeated visits to the British and Russian consulates-general, presumably hoping to be able to buy arms and ammunition from one country or the other with the money he had stolen from the merchants. These attempts were evidently unsuccessful.

After Big Horse had disappeared from the theatre of war, the chief command was taken over by General Ma Ho-san. In August, 1934, the Tungans affixed to the houses in Kashgar proclamations announcing that an agreement had been reached between the Chinese at Urumchi and the Tungans at Kashgar, according to which the last-named town was to be ceded to the Chinese, while the Tungans were recognised as possessors of the Khotan oasis. The Tungans then marched away from Kashgar.

The first new-comers were Turkis under the command of Mahmet Sze-chang. Then Chinese forces arrived under the command of General Liu Pin. He had flown to Maralbashi and been conveyed from that place in a Russian car. He became, and still is, the strong man in Kashgar. I met him at Urumchi the day before he left the town by aeroplane.

The Chinese employed Turkis to fill high posts on a larger scale than before. Hodja Nias Hadji became civilian deputy-governor of Sinkiang, and several governors and mayors were Turkis. But the Russian influence behind the Chinese was noticeable.

According to the very latest news I received from Eastern Turkestan (July 12, 1935), a fresh rebellion had broken out in Han-cheng, and General Liu Pin had nearly been killed.

The Tungans, under their leader General Ma Ho-san, are still firmly established in Khotan and right along to the Yarkand-daria, which is their western frontier. They hold, therefore, the towns of Posgam, Karghalik, Guma, Khotan, Chira, Keriya, Cherchen and Charkhlik. So long as they stay there, the prospects of peace and security in Eastern Turkestan cannot be great.

The last news of Big Horse was that he had continued his flight into Soviet Russian territory. At the beginning of 1936 he was reported to be in Moscow. He can hardly run any risk of being handed over to the Sinkiang authorities against whom he took the field. But what destiny awaits him, interned in Russia? If the Russians have an interest in the maintenance of peace in Sinkiang, the hospitality he enjoys under the shelter of the Red Flag may last a considerable time.

The most puzzling step, indeed, that Big Horse has taken in his stormy career was his flight to Russia, which he hated because of the help it had given to the government of Sinkiang. His military position must have been very weak for him to take so momentous a decision. One would have expected that he of all men would have founded a new dominion with Khotan as capital, a line of communication with Kansu, and why not another to Tibet? But what would have happened if he had taken this step, and whether he will bob up again one fine day in the heart of the deserts—it is no use prophesying in a country where anything may happen, in a time in which all things are possible![1]

It does not look as if the Russians intended to occupy Sinkiang. The administration and military organisation of over a million square miles of occupied territory would be too expensive. The main thing for Soviet Russia is to control the province economically and commercially, and this aim is already secured. When we were in Sinkiang all trade was going to and from Russia, while trade with China proper had quite come to an end and the exchange of goods with India was diminishing.

[1] The *Journal of the Royal Central Asian Society*, vol. xxii, January 1935, published a well-written article entitled "The Rebellion in Chinese Turkestan". This contains the following passage (Part I, p. 102): "When the Chinese north-eastern army reached Kashgar, Ma Chung-yin was advised by the Soviet Consul-General there to go to Russia. He was therefore escorted to the frontier at Ulughchat (which used to be close to Irkeshtam, but has been 'advanced') by M. Constantinoff, the Secretary, and several members of the trade agency of the Bolshevik Consulate. It was reported that he had died on his arrival in Moscow."

On Easter Day, April 1, the convoy stood ready to start for the promised land of the Lop desert, in which we had already vainly endeavoured to take refuge on March 11 to escape the tempests of war.

Colonel Salomakhin himself had come to say good-bye and to receive a huge bundle of letters and some telegrams to our homes in Sweden and China. The bundle of letters was addressed to the postmaster at Urumchi, Mr. Harald Kierkegaard, who had done us so many services. All the letters reached their destinations, but nothing was ever heard of the telegrams, and this caused great anxiety to those at home, who did not hear the first reports of our adventures and our captivity till several months later.

The colonel also wished to introduce to us Captain Deviashin, the new commandant of the Korla garrison, a man of honest appearance and military bearing. He was to be responsible for the lorry we were leaving behind, and the baggage which was super-fluous on the journey we were about to undertake. Deviashin received the key of our store-room, and the colonel ordered him always to keep two sentries at Abdul Kerim's house by day and by night.

And so we started on one of the most delightful journeys I have ever undertaken in the heart of Asia. For now I was returning, after thirty-four years, to my old domain around the ruins of Lou-lan, and to the wandering lake. We were going to another world, aloof and serene, through which the desert breezes murmur. We had had enough of the war in Sinkiang. Now for a time we were to bring balm to our souls in a region where the very earth is full of memories of thousands of years ago, and whose greatest charm it is that no cruelties and no sufferings disturb its peace, and that no men tread its classic soil.

THE END